DATA MODELING

MASTER CLASS

Steve Hoberman's Best Practices Approach to Developing a Competency in Data Modeling

Steve Hoberman
Steve Hoberman & Associates, LLC

me@stevehoberman.com
www.stevehoberman.com
www.TechnicsPub.com
www.DataModelingZone.com

Published by:

Technics Publications, LLC

966 Woodmere Drive

Westfield, NJ 07090 U.S.A.

me@stevehoberman.com

www.technicspub.com

Cover design by Mark Brye

The publisher offers discounts on this book when ordered in quantity for special sales. For more information, please contact:

Technics Publications Corporate Sales Division

966 Woodmere Drive

Westfield, NJ 07090 U.S.A.

me@stevehoberman.com

ISBN, print ed.   978-1-9355044-1-2

First Printing First Edition 2008

First Printing Second Edition 2011

First Printing Third Edition 2011

First Printing Fourth Edition 2012

Printed in the United States of America

Library of Congress Control Number: 2012943404

About the Data Modeling Master Class

The Master Class is a complete course on requirements elicitation and data modeling, containing three days of practical techniques for producing conceptual, logical, and physical relational and dimensional data models. After learning the styles and steps in capturing and modeling requirements, you will apply a **best practices approach** to building and validating data models through the Data Model Scorecard®. You will know not just how to build a data model, but also how to build a data model *well*. Two case studies and many exercises reinforce the material and will enable you to apply these techniques in your current projects.

By the end of the course, you will know how to...

1. Explain data modeling building blocks and identify these constructs by following a question-driven approach to ensure model precision
2. Demonstrate reading a data model of any size and complexity with the same confidence as reading a book
3. Validate any data model with key "settings" (scope, abstraction, timeframe, function, and format) as well as through the Data Model Scorecard®
4. Apply requirements elicitation techniques including interviewing and prototyping
5. Build relational and dimensional conceptual and logical data models, and know the tradeoffs on the physical side (including with NoSQL), through two case studies
6. Practice finding structural soundness issues and standards violations
7. Recognize situations where abstraction would be most valuable and situations where abstraction would be most dangerous, and where industry data models can prove an important head start
8. Use a series of templates for capturing and validating requirements, and for data profiling
9. Evaluate definitions for clarity, completeness, and correctness
10. Leverage the Grain Matrix, Data Vault, and enterprise data model for a successful enterprise architecture

About Steve

Steve Hoberman balances the formality and precision of data modeling with the realities of building software systems with severe time, budget, and people constraints. In his consulting and teaching, he focuses on templates, tools, and guidelines to reap the benefits of data modeling with minimal investment. He taught his first data modeling class in 1992 and has educated more than 10,000 people about data modeling and business intelligence techniques since then, spanning every continent except Africa and Antarctica. Steve is the recipient of the 2012 Data Administration Management Association (DAMA) International Professional Achievement Award, and is the author of five books on data modeling, including the bestseller *Data Modeling Made Simple*.

- **Abstraction**. Part of the logical data modeling process and is usually performed after normalizing. Abstraction brings flexibility to your logical data models by redefining and combining some of the data elements, entities, and relationships within the model into more generic terms.
- **Accumulating measure**. Monitor progress of a business process. Frequently the amount of days required to complete a certain business process step are tracked, such as Remaining Days Count or Settlement Days Count.
- **Aggregate**. A table which contains the resolution of a one-to-one relationship.
- **Alternate key**. The one or more data elements that uniquely identify a value in an entity and that is not chosen to be *the* unique identifier.
- **Behavioral dimension**. A dimension that is created based upon measurements. Measurement ranges are grouped together in the dimension, such as by sales amounts or performance. Ideal when the users recognize the same set of bands, and they are stable.
- **Bridge table**. A table which resolves a many-to-many relationship from the dimension to the meter. In other words, a given meter instance may need to refer to more than one dimension instance. Bridge tables can be shown as the typical resolution of a many-to-many on a logical, but may need a different physical structure depending on reporting tools.
- **Candidate key**. The one or many data elements that uniquely identify a value in an entity. Candidate keys are either primary or alternate keys.
- **Cardinality**. The symbols on both ends of a relationship that define the number of instances of each entity that can participate in the relationship. It is through cardinality that the data rules are captured and enforced. The domain of values to choose from to represent cardinality on a relationship is limited to three values: zero, one, or many. *Many* (some people read it as *more*) means any number greater than one.
- **Conformed dimension**. Built with the organization in mind, instead of just a particular application, to support drill across queries and enterprise consistency. Conformed dimensions do not need to be identical with each other, they just need to be from the same superset. Conformed dimensions allow the navigator the ability to ask questions that cross multiple marts.
- **Data element**. A property of importance to the business whose values contribute to identifying, describing, or measuring instances of an entity.
- **Data model**. A set of symbols and text which describes an information landscape.
- **Data Model Scorecard®**. A set of 10 categories for validating the quality of a data model.
- **Degenerate dimension**. A dimension whose data element(s) have been moved to the fact table. A degenerate dimension is most common when the original dimension contained only a single data element such as a transaction identifier.

- **Denormalization**. The process of selectively violating normalization rules and reintroducing redundancy into the model. This extra redundancy can reduce data retrieval time and produce a more user-friendly model.
- **Dependent entity**. Also known as a weak entity, a dependent entity is an object of interest to the business that depends on one or many other entities for its existence. The entities that a dependent entity depends on can be independent entities or other dependent entities. A dependent entity is depicted as a rectangle with rounded edges.
- **Dimension**. Subjects whose only purpose is to add meaning to the measures. Dimensions are either hierarchies or lookups.
- **Domain**. The complete set of all possible values that a data element can be assigned.
- **Drill across**. Navigation from one dimensional model to another dimensional model.
- **Drill down**. When the context for the measure goes from higher level to lower level. For example, needing to see the measures at a month level and then at a day level.
- **Drill up**. When the context for the measure goes from lower level to higher level. For example, needing to see the measures at a day level and then at a month level.
- **Elicitation**. To draw forth or bring out. "Eliciting requirements" is a more collaborative term than "gathering requirements".
- **Enterprise Data Model (EDM)**. A subject-oriented and integrated data model representing all of the data produced and consumed across an entire organization. Subject-oriented means that the concepts on a data model fit together as the CEO sees the company, as opposed to how individual functional or department heads see their view of the company. Integration means that all of the data and rules in an organization are depicted once and fit together seamlessly.
- **Entity**. Something of interest to the business. An entity is a collection of information about something that the business deems important and worthy of capture. An entity is a who, what, when, where, why, or how.
- **Family Tree**. A spreadsheet which documents the lineage for each data element in the data model.
- **Fact**. *See measure.*
- **Factless fact**. A fact table that does not contain any facts. Factless facts count events by summing relationship occurrences between the dimensions.
- **Fold Up But Easily Separate (FUBES)**. A denormalization technique where tables are combined yet there is still the ability to access individual instances from each of the entities.
- **Foreign key**. A data element that provides a link to another entity.
- **Grain**. A meter's lowest level of detail. It should be capable of answering all of the business questions within the scope of the dimensional model.
- **Grain Matrix**. A spreadsheet, which captures the levels of reporting for each fact or measurement. It is the spreadsheet view of an initial design, which could result in a star schema.
- **Hierarchy**. An arrangement of items (objects, names, values, categories, etc.) in which the items are represented as being "above," "below," or "at the same level as" one another.

- **Independent entity**. Also known as a kernel entity, an independent entity is an object of interest to the business that does not depend on any other entity for its identification. Each occurrence of an independent entity can be identified without referring to any other entity on the model. An independent entity is depicted as a rectangle.
- **Inversion Entry (IE)**. A non-unique index (also known as a secondary key).
- **Junk dimension**. A dimension containing all the possible combinations of a small and somewhat related set of indicators and codes.
- **Logical Data Model (LDM)**. A representation of a detailed business solution.
- **Measure**. A data element that a set of business users need to 'see', and which can also be mathematically manipulated. Gross Sales Amount is an example of a measure.
- **Metadata**. Text that describes what the audience needs to see.
- **Meter**. An entity containing a related set of measures. It is not a person, place, event, or thing, as we would expect on the relational model. Instead, it is a bucket of common measures. Common measures as a group address a business concern, such as Profitability, Employee Satisfaction, and Sales. The logical meter becomes one or more physical fact tables.
- **Model**. A set of symbols and text used to make a complex concept easier to grasp.
- **Network**. A many-to-many relationship between entities (or between entity instances).
- **Normalization**. The process of building the relational data model. It is a formal process of asking business questions where in the resulting data model "Every data element depends upon the key, the whole key, and nothing but the key."
- **Physical Data Model (PDM)**. A representation of a detailed technology solution.
- **Primary key**. The one or more data elements that uniquely identify a value in an entity and that is chosen to be *the* unique identifier.
- **Relationship**. The line connecting two entities. On a relational data model the line represents a business rule and on a dimensional data model the line represents a navigation path.
- **Snapshot measure**. Monitor the impact of events created from a business process, such as Account Balance Amount, Ozone Layer Thickness, and Average Survey Question Score. It is (at least theoretically) possible to produce snapshot measures by summing transaction measures. For example, to determine the Account Balance Amount we can sum the results of all individual account transactions such as deposits and withdrawals.
- **Slowly Changing Dimension (SCD)**. A reference subject area where there is a need to maintain history. That is, when values of a reference subject area get updated, there are three ways to manage this change. Type I means no history, Type 2 is all history, and Type 3 is some history.
- **Snowflake**. A physical dimensional modeling structure where each set of tables is implemented separately, very similar in structure to the logical dimensional model.
- **Star schema**. A physical dimensional modeling structure where each set of tables that make up a dimension is flattened into a single table.

- **Conceptual Data Model (CDM)**. A representation of the business at a very high level. It is a very broad view containing only the basic and critical concepts for a given scope.
- **Subtyping**. Grouping together the common properties of entities while retaining what is unique within each entity.
- **Summarization**. A table which contains information at a higher level of granularity than exists in the business.
- **Surrogate key**. A unique identifier of a table. The surrogate key is usually a system-generated counter.
- **Transaction measure**. Monitor events created from business processes, such as Order Quantity, Customer Count, and Gross Sales Amount. An important property of transaction measures is that they are fully additive across all dimensions.
- **View**. A virtual table. It is a "view" into one or many tables or other views that contain or reference the actual data elements. A view runs the SQL to retrieve data at the point when a data element in the view is requested.
- **Wayfinding**. Encompasses all of the ways in which people and animals orient themselves in physical space and navigate from place to place. Urban planner Kevin A. Lynch coined the term in his 1960 book Image of the City, where he defined wayfinding as "a consistent use and organization of definite sensory cues from the external environment".

Questions to ask when building a data model

For entities

- <u>Who</u> did it? <u>Who</u> else was involved?
- <u>What</u> was it done to?
- <u>When</u> did it happen?
- <u>Where</u> did it happen?
- <u>Why</u> did it happen?
- <u>How</u> did it happen?

For data elements

- What is important to know about:
  - <u>Who</u> did it? <u>Who</u> else was involved?
  - <u>What</u> was it done to?
  - <u>When</u> did it happen?
  - <u>Where</u> did it happen?
  - <u>Why</u> did it happen?
  - <u>How</u> did it happen?

For relationships

- Participation
  - Can a Customer own more than one Account?
  - Can an Account be owned by more than one Customer?
- Optionality
  - Can a Customer exist without an Account?
  - Can an Account exist without a Customer?
- Identification
  - Do I need to know the Customer to bring back their Account(s)?
  - Do I need to know the Account to bring back its Owner(s)?

For keys

- Which mandatory, unique, and stable data element(s) identify each entity?

For subtypes

- To identify subtypes
  - Are there examples of this entity that would be valuable to show on the model, either for communication purposes or to enforce certain rules?
  - Does this entity go through a lifecycle?
- To identify supertypes
  - Do these entities have relationships or data elements in common?
  - Are these entities different phases of the same lifecycle?
- To identify subtyping type
  - Can an entity be more than one of these entities at the same time?
  - Can there ever be another subtype?

For slowly changing dimensions

- Which data elements within this entity can change?
- For those that can change, do you only need the original, or only the current, or everything, or somewhere in between?

For definitions

- How is this term defined?

For domains

- What is the length and format of this data element?
- What are the valid values this data element can contain?

TABLE OF CONTENTS

Module 0

Getting Started

Data model explanation

Modeling a book

Title	Book description	AUTHOR(S)	PUBLISHER	ISBN	IMAGE
Data Modeling Made Simple	"Read today's..."	STEVE HOBERMAN	TECHNICS PUBLICATIONS, LLC	9 780977	APPLE

Data model explanation

Modeling a book

BACKGROUND

When a publisher announces that a new title is coming out, organizations who sell books such as Amazon® require knowing certain information about the book, such as the book's title. Often this information is required in a spreadsheet format.

FIRST DATA MODEL OF THE COURSE

Study the front and back cover and decide what types of information are important to capture. Write the type of information in the first spreadsheet row, and then the actual value under it.

WHY THIS EXERCISE?

- **Process.** The steps you went through in building this "model" are the same steps we go through in building any model. It is all about organizing information. Data modelers are fantastic organizers. We take the chaotic real world and show it in a precise form, such as a spreadsheet.
- **Creativity.** There are numerous modeling notations (including spreadsheets), some being more intuitive, precise, and extensible than others.
- **Just like the real world!** There is never enough time or information provided to make the model perfect. No matter whether we are given a day or year to complete a data model, we always wish for more time. Similar with information – "If only we can interview one more person…if only there was a requirements document." The 80/20 rule (or 90/10) rule prevails in data modeling. "Is the model good enough?"
- **Coming to consensus.** As William Kent said in **Data and Reality** (1978), *So, once again, if we are going to have a database about books, before we can know what one representative stands for, we had better have a consensus among all users as to what "one book" is.*

EDITION	REFERENCES				
2nd EDITION	WWW.				

Data model explanation

Definition

Wayfinding encompasses all of the ways in which people and animals orient themselves in physical space and navigate from place to place

Models are a set of symbols and text used to make a complex concept easier to grasp

Author	write	Book

A message to mapmakers: highways are not painted red, rivers don't have county lines running down the middle, and you can't see contour lines on a mountain.

William Kent, Data and Reality

Data model explanation

Definition

WAYFINDING

Wayfinding encompasses all of the ways in which people and animals orient themselves in physical space and navigate from place to place. Urban planner Kevin A. Lynch coined the term in his 1960 book Image of the City, where he defined wayfinding as "a consistent use and organization of definite sensory cues from the external environment". Historically, wayfinding refers to the techniques used by travelers over land and sea to find relatively unmarked and often mislabeled routes. These include but are not limited to dead reckoning, map and compass, astronomical positioning and, more recently, global positioning. *Wikipedia*

The ability to transform "cognitive maps" gained from personal experience into symbolic visual representations provided humans with a powerful cooperative advantage. Maps enabled us to share wayfinding experiences and geographic knowledge, thereby extending our communal ability to explore wider and wider regions without becoming afraid or getting lost. *Peter Morville, Ambient Findability*

MODEL DEFINITION

A model is a set of symbols and text used to make a complex concept easier to grasp. The world around us is full of obstacles that can overwhelm our senses and make it very challenging to focus only on the relevant information needed to make intelligent decisions. A map helps a visitor navigate a city. An organization chart helps an employee understand reporting relationships. A blueprint helps an architect communicate building plans. The map, organization chart, and blueprint are all types of models that represent a filtered simplified view of something complex.

DATA MODEL DEFINITION

A data model uses symbols and text to help developers and analysts better understand a set of data elements and their business rules. An increase in understanding the data leads to an improved communication level within the organization and therefore a more flexible and stable application environment.

> *Modeling is a tool for coping with problems of largeness.*
> Tom DeMarco

Data model explanation

Favorite modeling quotes and some poetry

> **The soul never thinks without a picture.**
> Aristotle

> **Dad, it's like a story!**
> Sadie Hoberman

> **Where is the wisdom? Lost in the knowledge.**
> **Where is the knowledge? Lost in the information.**
> T.S. Eliot

> **Where is the information? Lost in the data.**
> **Where is the data? Lost in the database.**
> Joe Celko

A piece of craftsmanship built and not bought
born amid a storm of conflicting ideas and unplanned
        thoughts
with ultimate almost utopic aim but noble to be fought
to bring perfect balance to the future,
learned from what past taught
hoping the art will long last, but prepared if not!

Leonardo Netto
Data Architecture, Telus

Data model explanation

Favorite modeling quotes and some poetry

MOTIVATING WORDS

There are so many great quotes that capture the value of pictures and in simplifying the complex world around us using pictures.

Data model explanation

Data model purpose

We build data models to confirm and document our understanding of other perspectives.

To describe something new

To describe something that exists

Knowledge transfer

Risk mitigation

Understand the business

Forward engineer

Reverse engineer

Data model explanation

Data model purpose

BACKGROUND

Traditionally, data models have been built during the analysis and design phases of a project to ensure that the requirements for a new application are fully understood and correctly captured before the actual database is created (i.e. forward engineering). There are, however, other uses for modeling than simply building databases. Among the uses are the following:

- **Risk mitigation**. A data model can capture the concepts and interactions that are impacted by a development project or program. What is the impact of adding or modifying structures for an application already in production? One example of impact analysis would be to use data modeling to determine what impact modifying its structures would have on the purchased software.

- **Reverse engineer**. We can derive a data model from an existing application by examining the application's database and building a data model of its structures. The technical term for the process of building data models from existing applications is 'reverse engineering'. The trend in many industries is to buy more packaged software and to build less internally; therefore our roles as modelers are expanding and changing. Instead of modeling a new application, the data modeler may capture the information in existing systems, such as packaged software.

- **Understand the business**. As a prerequisite to a large development effort, it usually is necessary to understand how the business works before you can understand how the applications that support the business will work. Before building an order entry system, for example, you need to understand the order entry business process.

- **Knowledge transfer**. When new team members need to come up to speed or developers need to understand requirements, a data model is an effective explanatory medium.

Data model explanation

A data model is precise

99

The Customer Identifier
is the identifier for the customer

N/A

-1

Employee is someone
who breathes oxygen

Data model explanation

A data model is precise

BACKGROUND

The data modeling symbols representing rules can be read only one way. You might argue with others about whether the rule is accurate, but that is a different argument. In other words, it is not possible for you to view a symbol on a model and say, "I see A here" and for someone else to view the same symbol and respond, "I see B here."

POOR DEFINITIONS WEAKEN PRECISION

If the definitions behind the terms on a data model are nonexistent or poor, multiple interpretations become a strong possibility. Imagine a business rule on our model that states that an employee must have at least one benefits package. If the definition of *employee* is lacking, we may wonder, for example, whether this business rule includes job applicants and retired employees.

DUMMY VALUES WEAKEN PRECISION

The second situation occurs when we introduce data that are outside the normal set of data values that we would expect in a particular data grouping. For example, if a rule on a model specified that a book must have a subtitle, allowing dummy values such as "other" or "99" or "not applicable" could be used when no subtitle exists.

Data model explanation

Data modeler characteristics

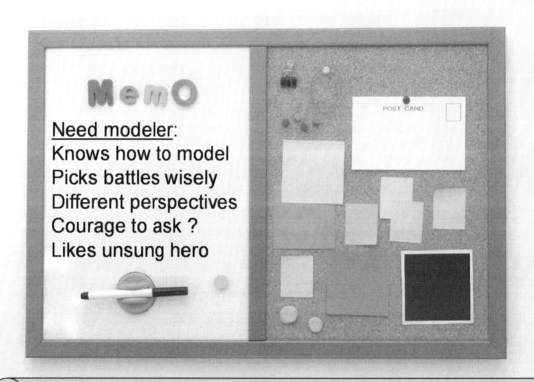

The Lone Ranger Fantasy

When the clients don't show their appreciation, pretend that they're stunned by your performance – but never forget that it's your fantasy, not theirs.

Gerald Weinberg, The Secrets of Consulting

Data model explanation

Data modeler characteristics

BACKGROUND

Besides knowing how to build models, there are several other essential skills the modeler must have.

PICKS BATTLES WISELY

There are going to be discussions and arguments that the modeler will need to decide whether they are worth the battle. Sometimes for example, forcing a project team to rename all of their non-compliant data element names a week before production can isolate the modeler and the modeling team. Even though it is the right thing to do, is it the right thing to do in a particular situation? Pick your battles wisely!

DIFFERENT PERSPECTIVES

There are several different perspectives the modeler must have during the modeling process. Having both a project and program view can sometimes be conflicting and it will be important for the modeler to understand where to make the tradeoffs. The same holds true for an ivory tower versus real world view. What might be right in a textbook may not be practical for a particular application.

COURAGE TO ASK QUESTIONS

Even if the modeler risks exposing a lack of understanding on her part or on the parts of IT or the business, the modeler has the courage to ask questions. Asking questions is the primary method of eliciting requirements.

I used to work with a data modeler who would start every interview off by saying "Pretend you're being questioned by a six-year old." There is also that famous quote from the book *Zen and the Art of Systems Analysis*, "Five Why's will make you Wise."

OK WITH UNSUNG HERO ROLE

If the modeler does everything right, she should get no credit whatsoever. This is a little bit of an exaggeration, but what is meant is that if the model meets the requirements and is fairly flexible, there should be no surprises and the modeling activity can become a non-event (which is a really good thing!).

Data model settings

Overview

Which setting is right for your model? As with photographing the sunset, it depends on the purpose. Match the goals of your model with the appropriate model settings. I believe there is always more than one solution to a problem – yet there is also always one best solution. *It is one thing to be correct. It is quite another thing to be right.*

Data model settings

Overview

CAMERA HAS SETTINGS

A camera has many settings available to take the perfect picture. Imagine facing an awesome sunset with your camera. With the same exact sunset, you can capture a very different image based on the camera's settings such as the focus, timer, and zoom.

MODEL HAS SETTINGS

There are four settings on a camera that translate directly over to the model: zoom, focus, timer, and filter. A model is characterized by one setting value from each setting. Which setting is right for your model? As with photographing the sunset, it depends on the purpose.

YOU CAN USE THIS TOOL TO...

Ensure you are choosing the right settings for the data model, assess existing or proposed data models to make sure they have the right settings, and confirm the model's purpose and audience.

SETTINGS OVERVIEW

The zoom setting on the camera allows the photographer to capture a broad area with minimal detail, or a detailed area without much context. Similarly, the scope setting for the model varies how much you see in the picture as well. The focus setting on the camera can make certain objects appear sharp or blurry. Similarly, the abstraction setting for the model can use generic concepts such as Party and Event to "blur" the distinction between concepts. The timer allows for a real time snapshot or a snapshot for some time in the future. Similarly, the time setting for the model can capture a current view or a "to be" view sometime in the future. The filter setting can taint the appearance of the entire picture to produce a certain effect. Similarly, the function setting for the model taints the model with either a business or application view.

AND THEN TAKE THE PICTURE!

Eventually we take the picture. That is, we solve the problem. There are three steps in solving the problem: first we identify the need for the picture (that is, what we want to solve). Then we take the picture (solve the business solution in the eyes of the picture taker). Then the picture is captured with the necessary technical settings.

Data model settings
Scope

Zoom = scope setting

Project	Sales reporting Auto claims processing New features in existing app
Program	Data warehouse SAP implementation Enterprise architecture
Industry	Healthcare Manufacturing Finance

Data model settings
Scope

SCOPE

We can model a relatively small amount of information for a business process, such as order processing. Typically the scope for projects fall into either entire projects, programs or the industry.

PROJECT

The most common type of modeling assignment has project-level scope. We are asked to model an operational or business intelligence area with the final goal being to have a successful application at the end of the development process.

PROGRAM

A program is a large centrally-organized initiative that contains multiple projects. For example, a data warehouse or operational data store are program-level initiatives that each contain many projects. Becoming more common is the enterprise scope. We are modeling an entire organization and at times even information outside the organization such as competitor or regulator information. These can be very complex and require long-term modeling assignments.

INDUSTRY

There is much work underway in many industries to share a common data model. Industries such as health care and telecommunications have consortiums where data modeling common structures are being developed. Having such a common structure makes it quicker to build applications and easier to share information across organizations.

Data model settings

Abstraction

Focus =
abstraction setting

In the business clouds oOnly generic business terms	Party Event Document
In the database clouds oOnly generic database terms	Object Table Entity
On the ground oMinimal generic terms oMostly concrete business terms	Customer Product Employee

Data model settings

Abstraction

ABSTRACTION

Similar to how the focus on a camera allows you to make the picture sharp or fuzzy, the abstraction setting for a model allows you to represent "sharp" (concrete) or "fuzzy" (generic) concepts. Abstraction brings flexibility to your data models by redefining and combining some of the data elements, entities, and relationships within the model into more generic terms. Abstraction is the removal of details in such a way as to broaden applicability to a wide class of situations while preserving the important properties and essential nature from concepts or subjects.

IN THE BUSINESS CLOUDS

At this level of abstraction, only generic *business* terms are used across the model. The business clouds model hides much of the real complexity within generic concepts such as Person, Transaction, and Document. In fact, both a candy company and insurance company can look very similar to each other using business cloud entities.

IN THE DATABASE CLOUDS

At this level of abstraction, only generic *database* terms are used across the model. The database clouds model is the easiest level to create, as the modeler is "hiding" all of the business complexity within database concepts such as Entity, Object, and Attribute.

ON THE GROUND

This model uses a minimal amount of business and database cloud entities, with a majority of the entities representing concrete business terms such as Student, Course, and Instructor. This model takes the most time to create of the three varieties. It also can add the most value towards understanding the business and resolving data issues.

Data model settings

Time

Today	"A price is the same across all restaurants."
oCurrent view	
Tomorrow	"A price can vary based on restaurant."
oEnd of year, 5 years out, 10 years out oCoincides with big change oIdealistic view	

Data model settings
Time

TIME

Similar to how the timer on a camera allows you to photograph a future scene, the time setting for a model allows you to represent a future "to be" view on a model. A model can represent how a business works today or how a business might work sometime in the future.

TODAY

A model with the today setting captures how the business works today. If there are archaic business rules, they will appear on this model even if the business is planning on modifying them in the near future. In addition, if an organization is in the process of buying another company, selling a company, or changing lines of business, a today view would not show any of this. It would only capture how the business works today.

TOMORROW

A model with the tomorrow setting can represent any time period in the future. Whether end of the year, five years out, or 10 years out, a tomorrow setting represents an ideal view of the organization. When a model needs to support an organization's vision or strategic view, a tomorrow setting is preferred. I worked on a university model that represented an end of year view, as that would be when a large application migration would be completed. Note that most organizations who need a tomorrow view, first have to build a today view to create a starting point.

Data model settings
Function

Filter =
function setting

Business Business terminology and rules	The business calls it 'classification' and 'classification value'
Application Application terminology and rules	SAP/R3 calls it 'characteristic' and 'characteristic value'

Data model settings
Function

FUNCTION	Similar to how a filter on a camera can change the appearance of a scene, the function setting for a model allows you to represent either a business or functional view on the model. Are we modeling the application's view of the world or the business' view of the world? Sometimes they can be the same (or very close to the same).
BUSINESS	This view uses business terminology and rules. The model represents an application independent view. It does not matter whether the organization is using SAP or Siebel, the business will be represented in business concepts.
APPLICATION	This view uses application terminology and rules. It is a view of the business through the eyes of an application. If the application uses the term 'Object' for the term 'Product', it will appear as Object on the model and be defined according to how the application defines the term, not how the business defines it. The application filter is used when reverse engineering databases.

Data model settings

Click

Conceptual ("Big Picture")
 	
Aerial business solution
    Important terms, along
    with rules and meanings
"This is what I want to take a
    picture of."
	"Don't they look cute!"
	
	"This would be great for our album."
	
	"I always want to remember this."

Logical (Composition) Detailed business solution Independent of technology "I don't care how the camera works!"	
Physical (Exposure) Detailed technical solution Compromised for technology "These are the ideal settings to capture the image."	Make — SONY Model — DSLR-A350 ISO Speed Ratings — 100 Exposure Time — 1/125 sec F-Stop — f/14 Focal Length in 35mm Film — 52 Focal Length — 35.00 mm Flash — Fired, compulsory

Data model settings

Click

CLICK

Eventually we take the picture. That is, we solve the problem. There are three steps in solving the problem: first we identify the need for the picture (that is, what we want to solve). Then we take the picture (solve the business solution in the eyes of the picture taker). Then the picture is captured with the necessary technical settings.

CONCEPTUAL ("BIG PICTURE")

I.E. keep logical "timeless".

Somebody gets the idea for a photo. It may start off with the familiar phrases "Isn't she cute!", "This would be great for our album.", "I always want to remember this." This idea or need for the photo is similar to the conceptual data model, in that the conceptual captures the "big picture" in the form of a set of terms along with their rules and meanings – it is often a great starting point.

LOGICAL (COMPOSITION)

KEEP LOGICAL FREE OF HISTORY SCENARIO

E.G. A MANAGER HAS ONE OFFICE AT ANY GIVEN TIME BUT PHYSICAL MULTIPLE OFFICES OVER A PERIOD SEVERAL (EXPOSURE) YEARS.

ONLY PDB MUST DEPICT HISTORY SCENARIO.

Now that we know what the "photo requester" wants, we need to consider composition. Composition is the placement or arrangement of visual elements in the photograph. We need to make sure we capture all of the details requested, which is similar to the logical data model (LDM), the detailed business solution. "I don't care how the camera works, I just want to push the button!"

In addition to composition, we need to consider exposure, the amount of light which falls upon the camera's image sensor. There are several technical settings to consider, such as shutter speed, depth of field, and film speed. These are the technical details behind the photograph, similar to the physical data model (PDM) which represents the detailed technology solution.

Data model settings
Some fun!

Scenario	Scope	Abstraction	Time	Function	Format
Capture the details for the current book ordering process to be used as an evaluation tool to select a vendor package. Need to include orders across all sales channels.	__Project __Program __Industry	__Bus Clouds __DB Clouds __Ground	__Today __Tomorrow	__Bus __App	__CDM __LDM __PDM
Study the technical design of a proposed vendor package to determine which fields are needed for sales reporting.	__Project __Program ✗Industry	✗Bus Clouds __DB Clouds __Ground	__Today ✗Tomorrow	__Bus ✗App	__CDM __LDM ✗PDM
Capture all of the business requirements for a brand new sales reporting system focusing only on consumer-direct (that is, sales made directly to individuals).	✗Project __Program __Industry	__Bus Clouds __DB Clouds ✗Ground	__Today ✗Tomorrow	✗Bus __App	__CDM ✗LDM __PDM
Explain this brand new sales reporting system to the business sponsor who does not have a technical background.	✗Project __Program __Industry	__Bus Clouds __DB Clouds __Ground	__Today ✗Tomorrow	✗Bus __App	✗CDM __LDM __PDM
Explain an existing data dictionary tool to agile developers who will need to extract definitions for the sales reporting system.	__Project ✗Program __Industry	__Bus Clouds ✗DB Clouds __Ground	✗Today __Tomorrow	__Bus ✗App	__CDM __LDM ✗PDM

Data model settings

Some fun!

BACKGROUND   Check off what you think is the <u>most appropriate</u> settings for each of these scenarios.

TIP   Always consider the audience and why the model is being built.

Data model components

Entity, entity instance, and data element

Answer these questions for entities:
- **<u>Who</u>** did it? **<u>Who</u>** else was involved?
- **<u>What</u>** was it done to?
- **<u>When</u>** did it happen?
- **<u>Where</u>** did it happen?
- **<u>Why</u>** did it happen?
- **<u>How</u>** did it happen?

Answer these questions for data elements:
- **What is important to know about:**
  - **<u>Who</u>** did it? **<u>Who</u>** else was involved?
  - **<u>What</u>** was it done to?
  - **<u>When</u>** did it happen?
  - **<u>Where</u>** did it happen?
  - **<u>Why</u>** did it happen?
  - **<u>How</u>** did it happen?

Data model components

Entity, entity instance, and data element

ENTITY

An entity is something of interest to the business. *Entity* is a noun. An entity is a collection of information about something that the business deems important and worthy of capture. An entity is a who, what, when, where, why, or how. Each of these categories has slightly different behavior and dependencies. Here are some examples of each of these:

Who?   Party and role, person, organization, employee, cust
vendor,
student, Hotmail account owner

What?   product, service, raw material, finished good, course, song, photograph

When?   time, date, year, calendar, fiscal period, minute

Where?   location, mailing address, distribution point, website URl
server where documents are stored, IP address

Why?   transaction, order, return, complaint, compliment, inquiry

How?   document, invoice, contract, agreement, account, speeding t

ENTITY INSTANCE

Entity instances are the occurrences, representatives, or values of a particular entity. The entity *customer* can have instances Bob, Joe, Jane, and so forth. The entity *account* can have instances for Bob's checking account, Bob's savings account, Joe's brokerage account, and so on.

DATA ELEMENT

A data element is a property of importance to the business whose values contribute to identifying, describing, or measuring instances of an entity. The data element *claim number* uniquely identifies each claim. The data element *student last name* describes the last name of each student. The data element *gross sales amount* measures total sales.

Data model components

Relationship

> A rule is an instruction about how to behave in a specific situation. A static rule is represented on a model via a relationship.

- Static Rules
  - Structure
    - Each product can appear on one or many order lines.
    - Each order line must contain one and only one product.
    - Each student must have a unique student number.
  - RI
    - An order line cannot exist without a valid product.
    - A claim cannot exist without a valid policy.
    - A student cannot exist without a valid student number.
- Action Rules
  - Freshman students can register for at most 18 credits a semester.
  - A policy must have at least three claims against it to be considered high-risk.
  - Take 10% off an order if the order contains more than five products.

Data model components

Relationship

BACKGROUND

In its most general sense, a rule is an instruction about how to behave in a specific situation. The following are examples of rules that we have set or rules that have been set for us:

- Your room must be cleaned before you can go outside and play.
- If you get three strikes, you are out and it is the next batter's turn.
- The speed limit is 55 mph.

When we build an application, setting rules means defining constraints on what the application (and therefore the user) can and cannot do. Rules are visually captured on our data models through relationships.

STATIC VS ACTION RULES

At the highest level, a rule can be either a static rule or an action rule. Static rules are instructions on how data relate to one another. Action rules are instructions on *what* to do when data elements contain certain values. There are both structural and referential integrity (RI) static rules. Structural rules (also known as cardinality rules) define the quantity of each entity instance that can participate in a relationship. For example:

- Each product can appear on one or many order lines.
- Each order line must contain one and only one product.
- Each student must have a unique student number.

RI rules focus on ensuring valid values:

- An order line cannot exist without a valid product.
- A claim cannot exist without a valid policy.
- A student cannot exist without a valid student number.

Action rules are instructions on *what* to do when elements contain certain values, which usually take the form of 'if-then' statements:

- Freshman students can register for at most 18 credits a semester.
- A policy must have at least three claims against it to be considered high-risk.
- Take 10% off an order if the order contains more than five products.

In our data models, we can represent and enforce static rules, yet (with the exception of views) only represent the data to support action rules.

Data model components

Cardinality

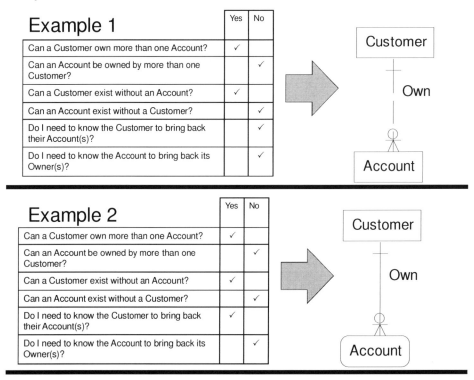

Example 1

	Yes	No
Can a Customer own more than one Account?	✓	
Can an Account be owned by more than one Customer?		✓
Can a Customer exist without an Account?	✓	
Can an Account exist without a Customer?		✓
Do I need to know the Customer to bring back their Account(s)?		✓
Do I need to know the Account to bring back its Owner(s)?		✓

Example 2

	Yes	No
Can a Customer own more than one Account?	✓	
Can an Account be owned by more than one Customer?		✓
Can a Customer exist without an Account?	✓	
Can an Account exist without a Customer?		✓
Do I need to know the Customer to bring back their Account(s)?	✓	
Do I need to know the Account to bring back its Owner(s)?		✓

It comes down to how entity instances on the many side are identified:

Example 1

Account Num	Customer Id
34	123
37	123
42	156
16	167

Example 2

Account Num	Customer Id
34	123
37	123
34	156
34	167

Account ← Strong   Weak → Account

Data model components

Cardinality

BACKGROUND

Cardinality represents the symbols on both ends of a relationship that define the number of instances of each entity that can participate in the relationship. It is through cardinality that the data rules are captured and enforced. The domain of values to choose from to represent cardinality on a relationship is limited to three values: zero, one, or many. *Many* (some people read it as *more*) means any number greater than one. We can't specify an exact number (other than through documentation), as in "A car has four tires." We can only say, "A car has many tires."

Each side of a relationship can have a combination of zero, one, or many. Through the specification of one or many, the structural portion of the cardinality represents the quantity of each entity instance in the relationship. The RI portion of the cardinality focuses on ensuring valid values through the specification of zero or one.

6 QUESTIONS

To be precise, every relationship requires asking 6 questions on participation, optionality, and identification. If for example, a requirement takes the form of "A Customer has Accounts", we need to ask the following questions:

- Participation
  - Can a Customer own more than one Account?
  - Can an Account be owned by more than one Customer?
- Optionality
  - Can a Customer exist without an Account?
  - Can an Account exist without a Customer?
- Identification
  - Do I need to know the Customer to bring back their Account(s)?
  - Do I need to know the Account to bring back its Owner(s)?

STRONG VS WEAK ENTITIES

A strong entity has instances which can be identified by one or more data elements belonging to that entity. A weak entity has instances which can only be identified with at least one data element from another entity.

Data model components

Cardinality

Example 3

	Yes	No
Can a Customer own more than one Account?		✓
Can an Account be owned by more than one Customer?		✓
Can a Customer exist without an Account?	✓	
Can an Account exist without a Customer?		✓
Do I need to know the Customer to bring back their Account(s)?		✓
Do I need to know the Account to bring back its Owner(s)?		✓

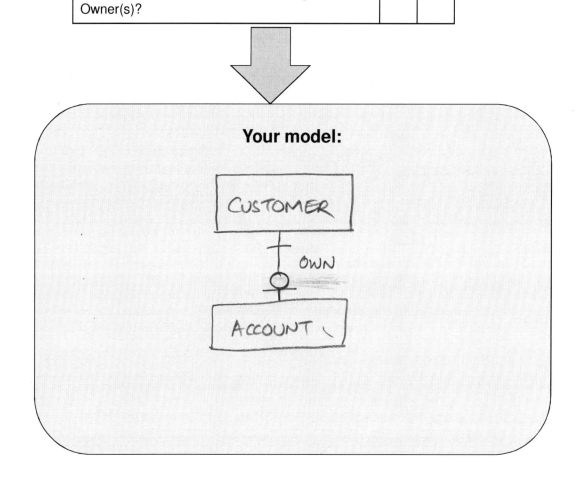

Your model:

Data model components

Cardinality

Part A: Check the cells where the model supports the business rules:

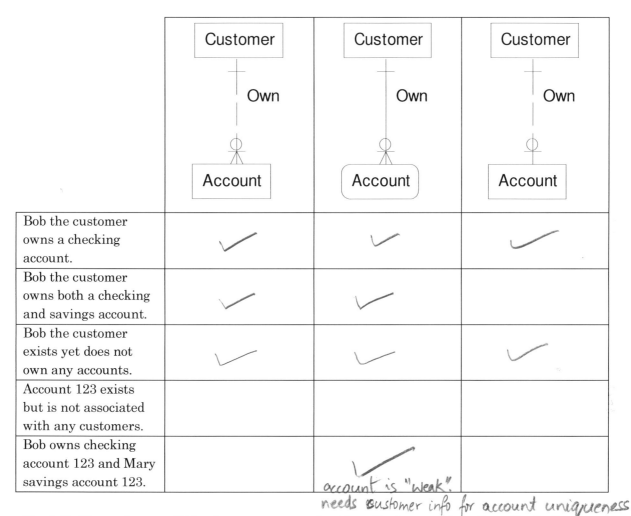

	Customer — Own — Account	Customer — Own — Account	Customer — Own — Account
Bob the customer owns a checking account.	✓	✓	✓
Bob the customer owns both a checking and savings account.	✓	✓	
Bob the customer exists yet does not own any accounts.	✓	✓	✓
Account 123 exists but is not associated with any customers.			
Bob owns checking account 123 and Mary savings account 123.		✓	

account is "weak".
needs customer info for account uniqueness

Part B: Draw two entities in your organization that are related and ask the six questions to create the relationship with correct cardinality:

Data model components

A Key helps you find entity instances

Candidate key	• Set of mandatory, unique, and stable data element(s) that identify an entity • Could be PK or AK
This question gives you the candidate keys	• Which mandatory, unique, and stable data element(s) identify each entity? • Natural key = Business key • Surrogate key = IT key, often a counter
Secondary key	• Non-unique index • Used to improve retrieval time (physical) • IE = Inversion Entry

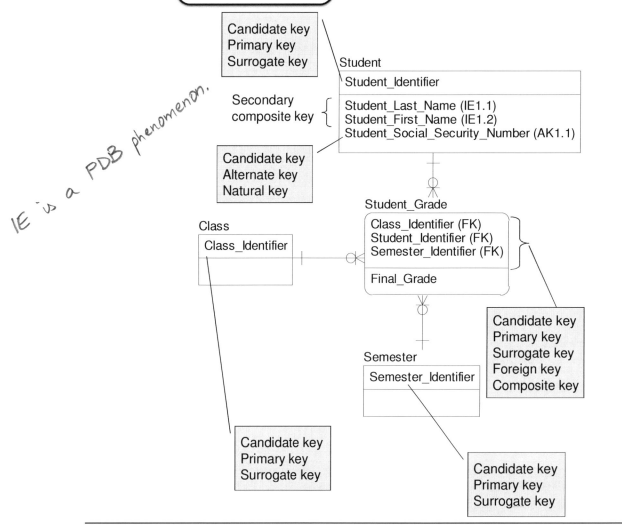

IE is a PDB phenomenon.

Candidate key
Primary key
Surrogate key

Student

Student_Identifier

Secondary composite key
Student_Last_Name (IE1.1)
Student_First_Name (IE1.2)
Student_Social_Security_Number (AK1.1)

Candidate key
Alternate key
Natural key

Student_Grade

Class_Identifier (FK)
Student_Identifier (FK)
Semester_Identifier (FK)

Final_Grade

Class

Class_Identifier

Candidate key
Primary key
Surrogate key
Foreign key
Composite key

Semester

Semester_Identifier

Candidate key
Primary key
Surrogate key

Candidate key
Primary key
Surrogate key

Data model components

A Key helps you find entity instances

BACKGROUND

A data element becomes a key or non-key upon assignment to an entity. A key data element partly or fully identifies an entity instance, and/or partly or fully references a unique instance from another entity. By *partly*, I mean that a data element is part of a key, in which case there is more than one data element that makes up the entire key. The term *composite key* is used when there is more than one data element that makes up the key. Non-key data elements include all those that are not a key or part of a key.

A candidate key represents the one or many data elements that uniquely identify a value in an entity. Candidate keys are either primary or alternate keys. A primary key represents the one or more data elements that uniquely identify a value in an entity and that is chosen to be *the* unique identifier, as opposed to an alternate key that also uniquely identifies entity occurrences but is not chosen as the unique key. Both primary and alternate keys must be unique, minimal, and stable (that is, the values can't change over time).

FOREIGN KEY

A foreign key is a data element that provides a link to another entity. When a relationship is created between two entities, the entity on the "many" side of the relationship inherits the primary key from the entity on the "one" side of the relationship. The foreign key allows for navigation between structures.

Sample values for Student Grade

Class Identifier	Student Identifier	Semester Identifier	Final Grade
123	44	39	C
45	44	39	B
123	32	39	B
123	44	40	A

Data model components
Surrogate key explanation

> A substitute for a <u>natural key, used by IT</u> to facilitate integration and introduce database efficiencies. It is usually a <u>meaningless integer counter.</u>

BACKGROUND

Surrogate keys must not be exposed to the Business.

A surrogate key is a unique identifier of a table. A surrogate key is an integer whose meaning is unrelated to its face value. (In other words, you can't look at a month identifier of 1 and assume that it represents January.) The surrogate key is usually a system-generated counter. Surrogate keys should not be visible to the business. They remain behind the scenes to help maintain uniqueness, allow for more efficient navigation across structures, and facilitate integration across applications. Context is also important: one application's surrogate key could be another application's natural key.

DEFINE AN ALTERNATE KEY WHEN USING A SURROGATE

- **Reduces the chances of bad data getting in.** You cannot load the same natural key twice.
- **Helps with processing records (distinguish inserts from updates).** We can easily check by seeing if the alternate key already exists. If it does, do an update. If it does not, do an insert.
- **Forces the modeler to understand what *really* makes a record unique.** It is very easy to slap on a counter and continue on our way. What requires more analysis and therefore increases our understanding of the entity, is to identify the business data elements that make the record unique. If no business AKs exist, use system AKs.

VIRTUAL KEY

Constrain transactions to INSERT only.

There might be times however, when it is not possible to assign an alternate key when using a surrogate key. If there is truly no way to uniquely identify an entity instance, then we can't use the term *surrogate key*. This is because a surrogate key is a substitute for the actual key, and if we don't have an actual key then we don't have a surrogate key. We use the term *virtual key* in this situation.

Data model components

Subtyping explanation

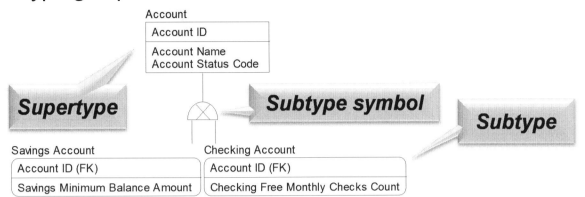

BACKGROUND

SUBTYPING ✓
CDB — ✓
LDB — ✓
PDB — ✗

Subtyping is grouping together the common properties of entities while retaining what is unique within each entity. The subtyping relationship exists between the supertype and each of its subtypes. There is no relationship implied by the subtyping symbol between the subtypes, except insofar as these subtypes share the same set of properties.

SYMBOLS

A subtype relationship connects an entity that defines the category and two or more additional entities that define each of the elements of the category. The parent entity of the category is considered the supertype and each child entity is considered a subtype. There is a relationship defined between the supertype and subtypes that groups these subtypes together under the supertype. The subtype entities inherit all of the properties from the supertype entity, meaning any data elements or relationships at the supertype level also belong to the subtype entity.

A SUBTYPING SYMBOL CANNOT EXIST IN A RELATIONAL DB

It is important to note that the subtyping symbol cannot exist in a relational database. It is purely a conceptual or logical construct. There are a number of options we will discuss when converting subtyping to a physical relational database design. However, an object oriented design could have subtyping both in the logical and physical models.

Subtyping

Different notations

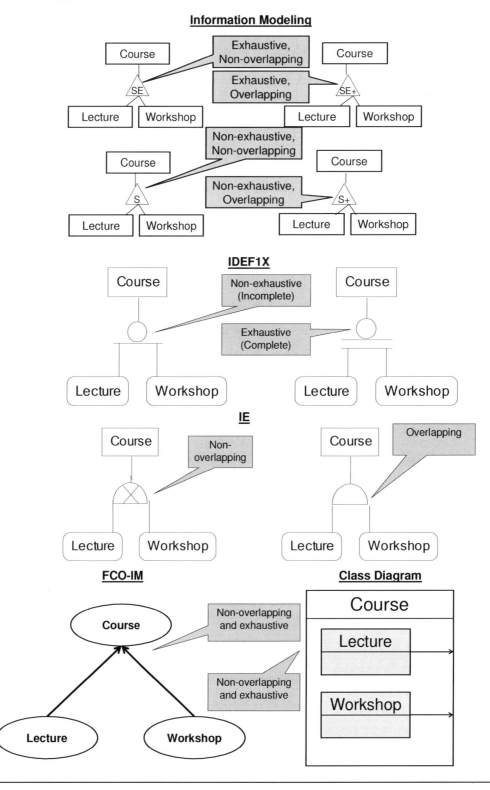

Subtyping

Different notations

INFORMATION MODELING

Bell Communications Research (Bellcore) was a pioneer in Information Modeling in the early 1990s during my time in their data modeling team. It is a notation that is the most comprehensive of the ones we will study, because it can represent all 4 possible types of subtypes. These 4 types represent different combinations of Exhaustive and Overlapping. Exhaustive means that one of the shown relationships must exist for a given supertype instance. Non-exhaustive means that there could be more subtypes that are not shown. Think of exhaustive as complete, and non-exhaustive as incomplete. Overlapping means that the same supertype instance can have properties from two or more of the subtypes. Non-overlapping means that a supertype can be at most one of the subtypes.

- SE (Exhaustive, Non-overlapping). There are no other options for course besides lecture or workshop. And a course can either be a lecture or workshop, not both.
- SE+ (Exhaustive, Overlapping). There are no other options for course besides lecture or workshop. And a course can be a lecture or workshop or have properties of both.
- S (Non-exhaustive, Non-overlapping). There can be other options for course besides lecture or workshop, such as a tutorial or boot camp. And a course can either be a lecture or workshop or something else.
- S+ (Non-exhaustive, Overlapping). There can be other options for course besides lecture or workshop, such as a tutorial or boot camp. And a course can either be a lecture or workshop or something else, or have properties of more than one of these.

IDEF1X

Integration DEFinition for Information Modeling (IDEF1X) shows subtyping as only Exhaustive or Non-exhaustive, it does not represent the overlapping concept.

IE

Information Engineering (IE) shows subtyping as only Non-overlapping or Overlapping, it does not represent the exhaustive concept.

FCO-IM

Sjir Nijssen developed the Natural Language Information Analysis Method (NIAM) in the 1970s and shortly thereafter Object Role Modeling (ORM) was developed based upon NIAM. ORM is a conceptual modeling approach that views the world in terms of objects and the roles they play. In 1992, Fully Communication Oriented Information Modeling (FCO-IM) was developed also based upon NIAM. NIAM, ORM, and FCO-IM are fact-oriented modeling techniques.

CLASS DIAGRAM

The Unified Modeling Language (UML) Class Diagram can only show non-overlapping and exhaustive subtypes.

Subtyping

Questions to ask

- To identify subtypes
  - Are there examples of this entity that would be valuable to show on the model, either for communication purposes or to enforce certain rules?
  - Does this entity go through a lifecycle?
- To identify supertypes
  - Do these entities have relationships or data elements in common?
  - Are these entities different phases of the same lifecycle?
- To identify subtyping type
  - Can an entity be more than one of these entities at the same time?
  - Can there ever be another subtype?

An example with relationships

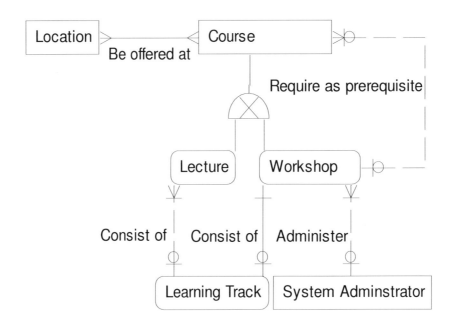

Subtyping

Questions to ask

QUESTIONS

There are six questions that are important to ask to identify subtypes and supertypes along with the right type of relationship between them. Asking for examples of an entity or whether the entity goes through a lifecycle can identify subtypes. Looking for commonality across existing entities or whether entities are just different phases of the same lifecycle can identify supertypes. The last two questions can help identify the type of subtype relationship. "Can an entity be more than one of these at the same time?" tells us whether the relationship is overlapping or not. "Can there ever be another subtype?" tells us whether the relationship is complete or not.

AN EXAMPLE WITH RELATIONSHIPS

The example on the facing page shows several important types of relationships that can exist when supertypes and subtypes appear on a design.

In some cases the subtype can have business relationships to the supertype. Here a Course can be a Lecture or a Workshop. In addition, a Workshop usually requires prerequisites before taking it. Prerequisites can be both lectures and other workshops. In this example Lectures do not require prerequisites.

The supertype is related to the Location entity, inferring that both Lectures and Workshop can be offered at many Locations, and a Location can host many Lectures and Workshops.

Also note that a Learning Track must contain many Lectures but only a single Workshop, probably as the final course in the track.

A System Administrator can support many Workshops, and a Workshop can be supported by one System Administrator.

Subtyping

Pros and cons of subtyping

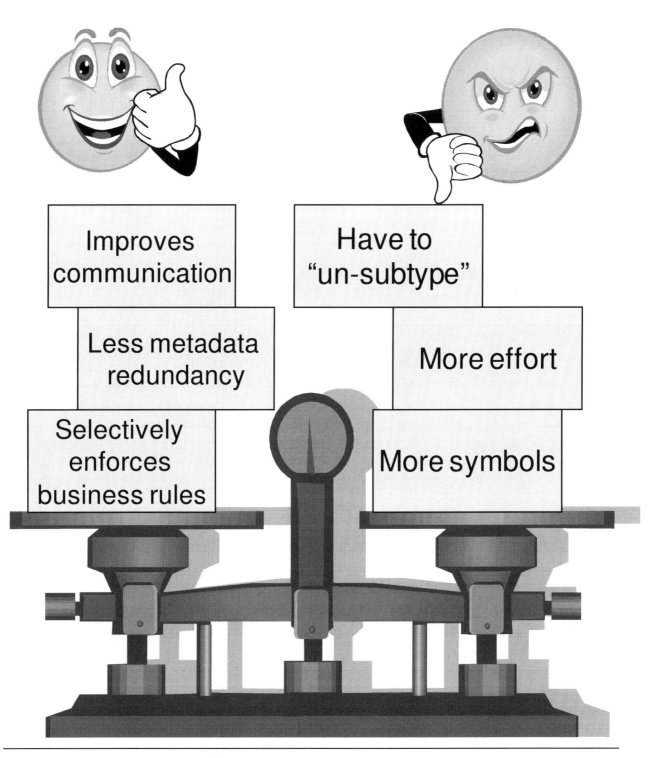

Subtyping

Pros and cons of subtyping

PROS

- **Selectively enforce business rules.** When we abstract, we lose relationships and therefore can lose the rules behind those relationships. Subtyping lets us selectively represent business rules. If there is a relationship to enforce for only a particular subtype, we can do it and leave the relationship off the supertype.
- **Less metadata redundancy.** When we subtype, we move those data elements and relationships that are common across entities to a single supertype. This reduces redundancy, because we are not repeating those common properties. However, it does not automatically reduce <u>data</u> redundancy. This means that without an effort to clean up redundant data, there will still be redundant information.
- **Improves communication.** You can show or hide supertypes and subtypes depending on the business expertise of the audience. For instance, you would show the business user manager only the higher level supertype Contract, whereas the functional analyst might see all the different subtypes of Contracts. Also subtyping helps you play the politician. When groups have different terms for the same general concept, you can allow each term (at least initially) to exist on the model underneath a common supertype. One group might call it Off Invoice, the other might call it Bill Back but they are all promotion allowances.

CONS

- **More entities and relationships on the model than pure abstraction.** Although you reduce redundancy when you subtype, more boxes and lines are on the model. When showing all supertypes and subtypes on the design, it can make the model cluttered and therefore more overwhelming to the audience. However, if you properly arrange the model, it will be less overwhelming.
- **More effort to create the design.** You will need to not only determine the common ground between subtypes, but also determine which data elements and relationships should still exist at the subtype level. Therefore, this is even more work than just applying the three abstraction questions of commonality, value, and effort.
- **Have to "un-subtype" anyway when you get to the physical.** This is true but I believe your resulting physical design will be a better design if you first realized it was important to subtype on the logical. You would have already reduced redundancy and possibly optimize certain relationships if you subtype first on the logical.

Data model components

Modeling a publisher log file

#	ISBN	Title	Subtitle	Author(s)	Library of Congress #	Format	Publication Date
1.	9780977140022	Data Quality Assessment		Arkady Maydanchik	2007902970	Print	May 14th, 2007
2.	9780977140060	Data Modeling Made Simple	A Practical Guide for Business and IT Professionals	Steve Hoberman	2008910373	Print	June 2009
3.	9780977140077	Data Modeling for the Business	A Handbook for Aligning the Business with IT using High-Level Data Models	Steve Hoberman Donna Burbank Chris Bradley	2008912011	Print	April 2009
4.	9780977140084	DAMA Guide to the Data Management Body of Knowledge		DAMA International		CD-ROM	April 2009
5.	9781935504047	Building the Unstructured Data Warehouse	Architecture, Analysis, and Design	Bill Inmon Krish Krishnan	2010938989	Print	1/1/11
6.	9781935504351	Building the Unstructured Data Warehouse	Architecture, Analysis, and Design	Bill Inmon Krish Krishnan		Kindle	1/1/11
7.	9781935504375	Data Modeling for the Business	A Handbook for Aligning the Business with IT using High-Level Data Models	Steve Hoberman Donna Burbank Chris Bradley		Kindle	April 2009
8.	9781935504429	Data Quality Assessment		Arkady Maydanchik		Kindle	May 14th, 2007

Data model components

Modeling a publisher log file

BACKGROUND

A publisher log file is a spreadsheet containing very basic information about a title, and is used for ISBN assignment. This log file helps prevent the same ISBN from being assigned to more than one title, and also tells the publisher when it is time to order more ISBNs. The facing page contains a subset of my log file.

Be the data archeologist and build a data model for my log file, based upon this sample data. Use primary, foreign, and alternate keys, as well as subtyping. Ask the six questions between Title and Author.

Your model:

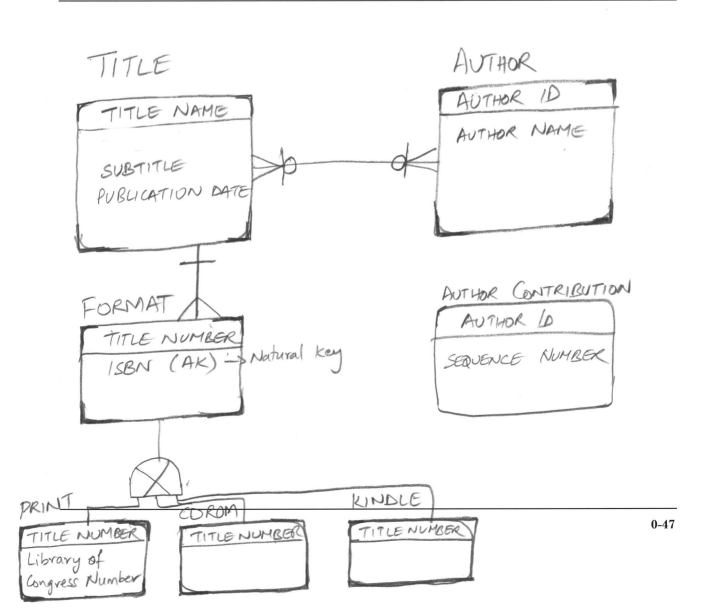

Data model components

Hierarchy

Hierarchy example (most general)

- An Order may contain one or many Order Lines.
- An Order Line must belong to one Order.

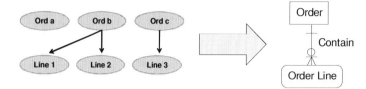

Build the data model capturing this hierarchy
(HINT: Subsumptive = Subtype)

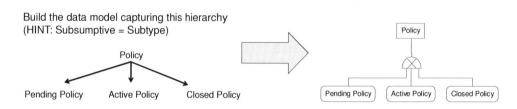

Build the data model capturing this sales structure

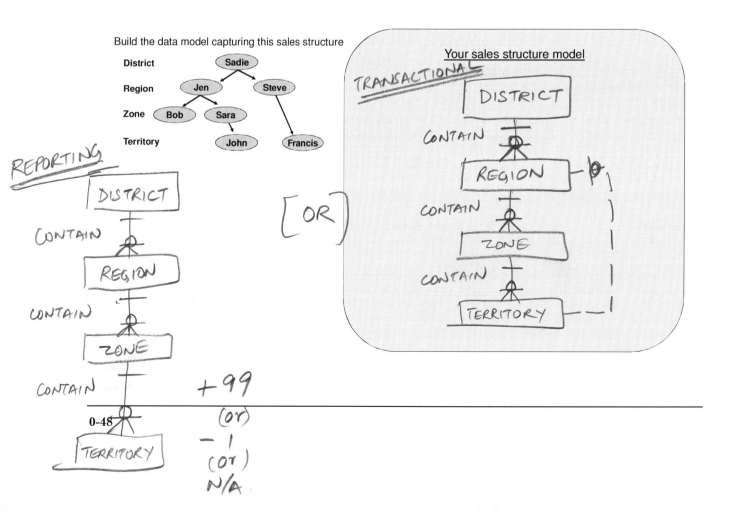

Data model components

Hierarchy

BACKGROUND

A hierarchy is an arrangement of items (objects, names, values, categories, etc.) in which the items are represented as being "above," "below," or "at the same level as" one another. Abstractly, a hierarchy is simply an ordered set or an acyclic graph. A hierarchy can link entities either directly or indirectly, and either vertically or horizontally. The only direct links in a hierarchy, in so far as they are hierarchical, are to one's immediate superior or to one of one's subordinates. Wikipedia

Defining a hierarchy within the context of data modeling, it is a relationship between entities (or entity instances) where one entity (the child), can be related to at most one of the other entity (the parent). Unbalanced hierarchies have a varying number of levels, and ragged hierarchies contain nodes that skip levels.

TERMINOLOGY

Degree of branching refers to the number of direct subordinates or children an object has (equivalent to the number of vertices a node has). Hierarchies can be categorized based on the "maximum degree", the highest degree present in the system as a whole. Categorization in this way yields two broad classes: linear and branching.

In a **linear** hierarchy, the maximum degree is 1. In other words, all of the objects can be visualized in a lineup, and each object (excluding the top and bottom ones) has exactly one direct subordinate and one direct superior. In a **branching** hierarchy, one or more objects have a degree of 2 or more (and therefore the maximum degree is 2 or higher). Wikipedia

MOST COMMON TYPES

The most general type of hierarchy is the one-to-many relationship on a data model. Other common types include subsumptive hierarchy (aka taxonomic or IS-A) and compositional hierarchy. Subsumptive is represented most commonly through subtyping on a data model. Compositional hierarchies are the most used structures for dimensions.

Data model components

Network

- A many-to-many relationship between entities (or between entity instances)

  - A Project must be assigned to many Employees.
  - An Employee must work for many Projects.

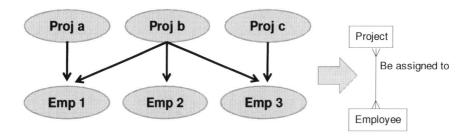

Build the data model that captures all of the materials required to make a finished product

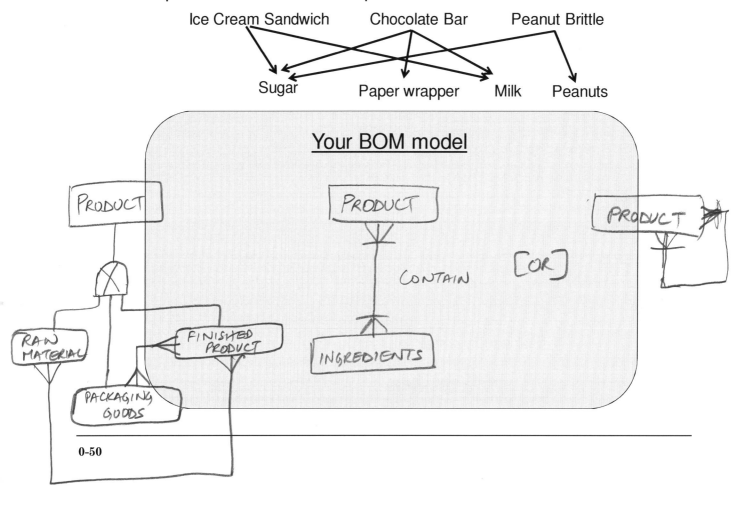

Data model components

Network

BACKGROUND

A network is a many-to-many relationship between entities (or between entity instances).

RECURSIVE EMOTION

Data modelers have a love-hate relationship with recursion. On the one hand, recursion makes modeling a complex structure a relatively painless procedure. On the other hand, some consider using recursion to be taking the easy way out of a difficult modeling situation. There are many rules that can be obscured by recursion. *Bill of materials*, for example, contains many complex rules that could lead the modeler to subtype *product* into *raw material, ingredient,* and so on, and show all the rules between these entities. Those in favor of recursion argue that you may not be aware of all the rules and that recursion protects you from having an incomplete model. The recursion adds in a level of flexibility that ensures that any rules not previously considered are also handled by the model. It is therefore wise to consider recursion on a situation-by-situation basis.

Data model components

Relationship labels

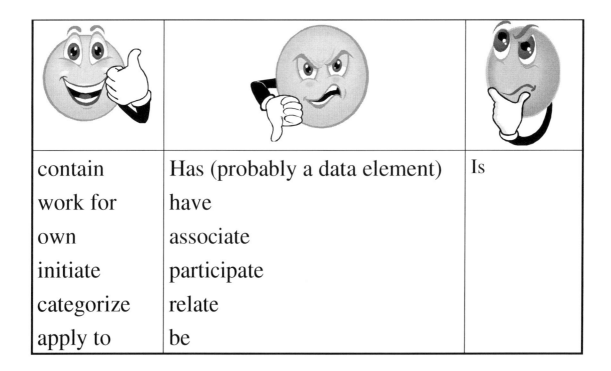

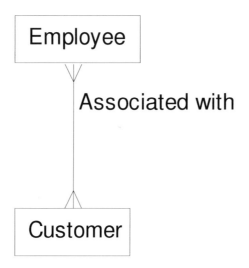		
contain	Has (probably a data element)	Is
work for	have	
own	associate	
initiate	participate	
categorize	relate	
apply to	be	

What do you think the 'reason' is in this relationship?

Employee

Associated with

Customer

Data model components

Relationship labels

BACKGROUND

Labels are the verbs that appear on the relationship lines. Labels allow us to describe a rule directly on the model. Labels should be as descriptive as possible. The label "has" usually indicates a data element, such as Product Has Product Weight. Customer has Customer Last Name. Account has Account Open Date.

THE VALUE OF LABELS FROM WILLIAM KENT, DATA AND REALITY

"A relationship is an association among several things, with that association having a particular significance. For brevity, I will refer to the significance of an association as its 'reason'. There is an association between you and your car, for the reason that you own it. There's an association between a teacher and a class, because he teaches it. There's an association between a part and a warehouse, because the part is stored there."

GOOD LABELS

Here are some examples of good label names:
- contain
- work for
- own
- initiate
- categorize
- apply to

BAD LABELS

Always avoid the following words as label names, as they provide no additional information to the reader (you can use these words in combination with other words to make a meaningful label name; just avoid using these words by themselves):
- has (probably this is referring to a data element)
- have
- associate
- participate
- relate
- be
- is (ok to use though when reading from subtype to supertype)

Data model components

Fun reading a data model

Read the story in the model below and write the statements. Remember these pointers:

- Use the word 'Each' and start at the one side of the relationship (or the supertype), and work clockwise around the relationship
- Zero means "may", without the zero means "must"
- Use meaningful business labels (business reason)
- Dashed and solid lines read the same way when there are no data elements

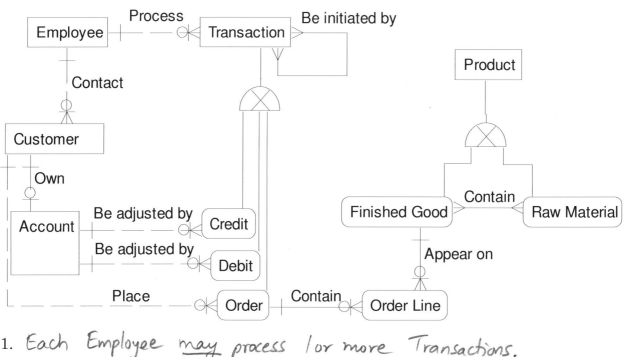

1. Each Employee _may_ process 1 or more Transactions.
2. Each Transaction _must_ be processed by 1 Employee.
3. Each Employee _may_ Contact 1 or more Customers.
4. Each Customer _must_ be contacted by 1 Employee.
5. Each Customer _may_ own 1 Account.

Data model components

Fun reading a data model

6. Each Account <u>must</u> be owned by 1 Customer.

7. Each Customer <u>may</u> place 1 or more Orders.

8. Each Order <u>must</u> be placed by 1 Customer.

9. Each Account <u>may</u> be adjusted by 1 or more Credits.

10. Each Credit <u>must</u> be an adjustment for 1 Account.

11. Each Account <u>may</u> be adjusted by 1 or more Debits.

12. Each Debit <u>must</u> be an adjustment for 1 Account.

13. Each Transaction <u>must</u> be initiated by 1 or more Transactions.

14. Each Transaction is either Credit, Debit or Order.

15. Each Credit, Debit & Order is a Transaction.

16.

17.

18.

19.

20.

21.

22.

23.

24.

25.

Data model components

The corner office

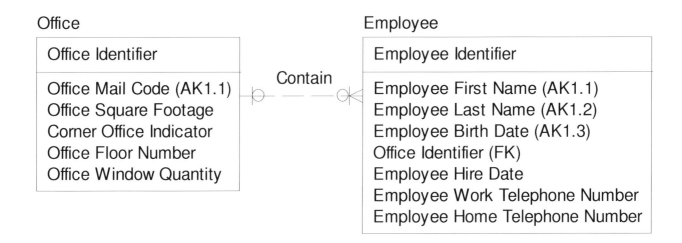

Here is the model with Office First Occupied Date included:

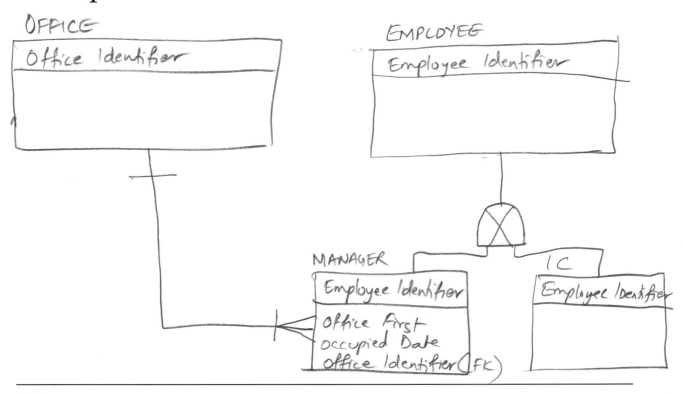

Data model components

The corner office

BACKGROUND

You are working on a logical data model, a subset appearing on the opposite page. The relationship states:

- Each Office can contain many Employees.
- Each Employee may reside in one Office.

You need to add the data element **Office First Occupied Date** to this model.

Office First Occupied Date is the official date as recorded in the Human Resources database as to when a person first took residence in an office. It must be a business day (that is, not a weekend day or holiday).

The business expert in this area provides you with the following three rules:
- Office First Occupied Date is a mandatory field for each employee that has an office.
- Only managers have an office and all managers have an office.
- A manager resides in one and only one office.

CHALLENGE

Modify this model to accommodate this new data element and these three business rules.

Data Model Scorecard® Overview

Importance of data model quality

> Model these 2 business rules:
> 1. A Student can take many Classes.
> 2. An Instructor can teach many Classes.

How would you model these rules?

Leverage

1. Bob the Student is the same person as Bob the Instructor.
2. A Class can be team taught.
3. A Student can be an Applicant who has not taken any classes yet.

Data quality

1. How many people are on campus this semester?
2. How many Students teach Classes?
3. How many Instructors are not teaching Classes this semester?

"Big Picture"

Our data warehouse has a single view of 'Class'. We need to integrate systems that have something called 'Course' with other systems that call something 'Class' with other systems that call something 'Session'.

Data Model Scorecard® Overview

Importance of data model quality

LEVERAGE

Using given resources in such a way that the potential positive or negative outcome is magnified. Wikipedia.

All of the development including interface, extract, screen designs, and functionality are built upon the database design. The database design is built from the data model. Therefore the data model can make or break an entire application. Once an application is built upon a good data model, it becomes easier to support and expand, leading to a long and stable application life. A poor data model is the exact opposite, possibly taking a shorter time to develop but shifting the time and cost to support which will outweigh the cost of development in a short time and eventually lead to the demise of the application.

The key reason for giving special attention to data organization is leverage in the sense that a small change to a data model may have a major impact on the system as a whole. Data Modeling Essentials

DATA QUALITY

My favorite definition for data quality is from the book **Data Quality Assessment**: *Fit for use.* I also like this definition of data quality from a university: *The degree of excellence of data.*

Although the data model can't represent all business rules, it can enforce quite a bit through referential integrity (RI). What it does enforce in terms of data rules can dramatically improve data quality and catch many data errors before they are loaded into the application. Also clear and concise definitions can help people make better decisions, and raise possible issues before development begins. Naming standards help people understand the content of an entity or data element by its name. For example, following the guidelines of one Subject, zero, one, or more Modifiers, and one Class word, help make data elements more easily understood.

"BIG PICTURE"

The data modeler wears both project and program hats. Although a model might be built to support a particular application, the terminology and structures on the model should have a level of consistency across the enterprise. This helps create a single version of the truth or "Big Picture" for an organization. This can make the delivery of large scale projects such as data warehouses possible, as Bill Inmon's definition of a data warehouse includes "subject-oriented" and "integrated".

Data Model Scorecard® Overview

Traditional data model review methods

Data Model Review of HAL
9:00-9:30: Review HAL reqs
9:30-10:00: Quick recap of
Bob's last 3 models which
were not reviewed
10:00-10:30: Come up with
model review approach for
this model
10:30-11:30: Review model
11:30-12:00: Agree to start
from scratch again next time

I'm surprised we were able to review HAL's LDM in less than 10 minutes. Here's another model I would like reviewed that I know you haven't seen yet and they are moving this into production next week...

This is a review of HAL's LDM. Shouldn't there be someone else here besides the DBAs and developers?

I really don't like this Account structure. Surely, you are a senior modeler and could do better here. What a BAD structure!

Data Model Scorecard® Overview

Traditional data model review methods

APPROACH

A majority of model reviews tend to be organized and performed with minimal structure and formality. There is usually missing a set of activities that are reusable across model reviews, and checklists are also missing which are used for verification during the review process. In addition, many models escape from being reviewed. Those models that are reviewed usually are reviewed inconsistently with other models because the same process is never followed twice.

AUDIENCE

Due to missing a standard review process and checklist, many organizations fail to include the right people in the review. For example, I have been in logical data model reviews where there were only technical people present (DBAs and developers) and no one from the business or functional side.

TIMING

Reviews need to happen as early as possible and usually more than one review needs to occur for each model. I have been in too many situations where I received a comment such as this from the project manager: "Can you take a quick look at our data model? We are going into production next week and were told we need your blessing before we go live." Also, during a model review, action items to change the model can come up that require another review to ensure the changes happened correctly and to review the model again in its entirety after the changes have been made. It is important to timebox a review so that it does not reach the point of diminishing returns. Also, if too many people are in the room it will be counterproductive, and if too few people are in the room it will not be considered a complete review.

JUDGMENT & EMOTION

A model should not be considered "good" or "bad". Judgment needs to be removed from the model and so does emotion. I was once in a model review where the modeler left the room in tears. At another time I was having one of my models reviewed and someone in the room actually stood up on the table and looked down at me explaining with a fair amount of emotion what she did not like about my model. It is best for team rapport and model quality to be objective when reviewing a model.

Data Model Scorecard® Overview

Scorecard characteristics

Acknowledges strengths and makes recommendations

Data Model Scorecard™ review of HAL application

...

25. "There is a perfect balance of abstraction on the model because..."

...

125. "A surrogate key requires an alternate key. On this entity you might consider the alternate key to be..."

Objective and externally-defined

Easy to apply and customize

Let's see, the next category on the Scorecard is Standards. Are all my entity names singular?

Supports all types of models

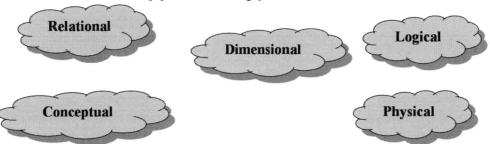

Data Model Scorecard® Overview

Scorecard characteristics

BACKGROUND

Aim, wind, and gravity influence an arrow's trajectory, much the same way as deadlines, skills, and experience influence a data model's trajectory, strongly impacting whether a model will reach its target of accuracy, longevity, practicality, and consistency. The archer's score can be quickly calculated and we can easily see the success or failure of her work. This is where the analogy ends however, because there is no standard way of measuring the strengths and weaknesses of our models, leaving much up to interpretation, perception, and the test of time. After years of reviewing hundreds of data models, I have formalized a set of data model quality criteria into what I call the Data Model Scorecard®. The Scorecard contains 10 clear and distinct criteria for validating a data model. The scorecard has four main characteristics that make it an invaluable tool.

ACKNOWLEDGE STRENGTHS AND RECOMMEND AREAS FOR IMPROVEMENT

It is important to just not focus on what could be better, but to also focus on the strengths of a model. The Scorecard highlights strengths, giving specific examples of what was done using best design practices. It also makes recommendations on areas for improvement, along with detailed recommendations that can be made directly to the model.

OBJECTIVE AND EXTERNALLY-DEFINED

I have participated in model reviews where modelers take the review personally and comments take the form of "I don't like what you did here..." or "You are still not getting this structure right..." We need to step back from the 'I' and 'You', and critique the model with an external and objective perspective. Team rapport remains intact as you as the reviewer are not criticizing their model, but rather this objective and external scale believes there are areas for improvement. The Scorecard uses a points system and several metrics for measuring model quality.

EASY TO APPLY AND CUSTOMIZE

The scorecard was designed for even those new to modeling to critique their own models and models of their colleagues. It should be incorporated into a methodology as a final checkpoint before the model is considered complete.

SUPPORTS ALL TYPES OF MODELS

The Scorecard is designed to be used for all model levels of detail: conceptual, logical, and physical. It also supports both relational and dimensional modeling.

Data Model Scorecard® Overview

Scorecard template

#	Category	Total score	Model score	%	Comments
1	How well does the model capture the requirements?	15			
2	How complete is the model?	15			
3	How well do the characteristics of the model support the type of model?	10			
4	How structurally sound is the model?	15			
5	How well does the model leverage generic structures?	10			
6	How well does the model follow naming standards?	5			
7	How well has the model been arranged for readability?	5			
8	How good are the definitions?	10			
9	How consistent is the model with the enterprise?	5			
10	How well does the metadata match the data?	10			
	TOTAL SCORE	100			

Scorecard example (plus a 50 page document!)

#	Category	Total score	Model score	%	Comments
1.	How well does the model capture the requirements?	15	14	93%	Revisit some AKs
2.	How complete is the model?	15	15	100%	Legacy system mapping
3.	How well do the characteristics of the model support the type of model?	10	10	100%	Lots of processing data elements
4.	How structurally sound is the model?	15	10	67%	Null AKs
5.	How well does the model leverage generic structures?	10	10	100%	Perfect use of abstraction
6.	How well does the model follow naming standards?	5	4	80%	Great standard for table naming
7.	How well has the model been arranged for readability?	5	4	80%	Incorporate a conceptual data model
8.	How good are the definitions?	10	9	90%	Very comprehensive definitions
9.	How consistent is the model with the enterprise?	5	5	100%	Great rapport with business
10.	How well does the metadata match the data?	10	10	100%	Handles changing natural account numbers
	TOTAL SCORE	100	91		

Data Model Scorecard® Overview

Scorecard template

BACKGROUND

Each of the 10 categories has a total score that relates to the value your organization places on the question. Remember, just as in any assessment, the total must be 100. The model score column contains the results of how a particular model scored. For example, if a model received 10 on "How well does the model capture the requirements?" then that is what would go in this column. The % column stores the model score in category divided by the total score in category. For example, receiving 10 out of 15 would lead to 66%. The comments column contains any pertinent information to explain the score in more details or to capture the action items on what is required to fix the model. The last row contains the total score, and this can be tallied up or averaged for each of the columns to arrive at an overall score.

EXAMPLE

The model that was reviewed in this example received a score of 91. Category 4 was a strong area for improvement and categories 6 and 7 also contain areas for improvement. There was a 50 page document that accompanied this Scorecard. This document explained the results in detail. Both strengths and areas for improvement were explained in detail through a complete set or representative set of examples. For example, Category 2 lost some points because this model was missing some alternate keys. In the accompanying document, those entities missing alternate keys were listed as well as those entities with suspect alternate keys.

YOU CAN USE THE DATA MODEL SCORECARD® – READ LEGAL STUFF

Steve Hoberman & Associates, LLC hereby grants to companies a non-exclusive royalty free limited use license to use the Data Model Scorecard® solely for internal data model improvement purposes. The name 'Steve Hoberman & Associates, LLC' and the website 'www.stevehoberman.com' must appear on every document referencing the Data Model Scorecard®. Companies have no right to sublicense the Data Model Scorecard® and no right to use the Data Model Scorecard® for any purposes outside of company's business.

Data Model Scorecard® Overview

1. How well does the model capture the requirements?

correctness

EXPLANATION

This is the "correctness" category. That is, we need to understand the content of what is being modeled. This can be the most difficult of all 10 categories to grade, the reason being that we really need to understand how the business works and what the business wants from their application. If we are modeling a *sales data mart*, for example, we need to understand both how the invoicing process works in our company, as well as what reports and queries will be needed to answer key sales questions from the business.

PURPOSE

We need to ensure our model represents the data requirements, as the costs can be devastating if there is even a slight difference between what was required and what was delivered. Besides not delivering what was expected is the potential that the IT/business relationship will suffer. The model needs to meet business expectations.

CHALLENGE

What makes this category even more challenging is the possibility that perhaps the business requirements are not well-defined, or differ from verbal requirements, or keep changing usually with the scope expanding instead of contracting.

Data Model Scorecard® Overview

2. How complete is the model?

EXPLANATION

This category checks for data model components that are not in the requirements or requirements that are not represented on the model. If the scope of the model is greater than the requirements, we have a situation known as "scope creep." This means that we are planning on delivering more than what was originally required. If the model scope is less than the requirements, we will be leaving information out of the resulting application, usually leading to an enhancement or "phase 2" shortly after the application is in production. For completeness, we need to make sure the scope of the project and model match, as well as ensuring all the necessary metadata on the model is populated.

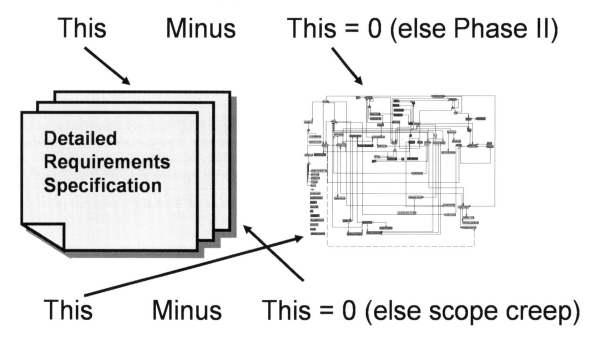

Data Model Scorecard® Overview

3. How well do the characteristics of the model support the type of model?

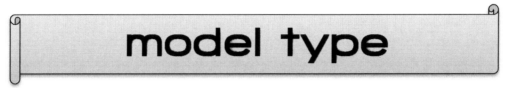

EXPLANATION

This question ensures that the model type (conceptual, logical, or physical – and then either relational or dimensional or NoSQL) of the model satisfies the criteria for this level of detail. In general terms, the conceptual data model should contain a well-defined scope, the logical data model should be application-independent and represent a business solution, and the physical data model should be tuned for performance, security, and consider development tool constraints (e.g. cube technology, database limitations, etc.). The physical data model should represent a technical solution. A dimensional model is built when there is a need to play with numbers and a relational is built for everything else except for when the technology is not relational in which case NoSQL is chosen.

	Relational	Dimensional	NoSQL
Conceptual			
Logical		?	
Physical			

Data Model Scorecard® Overview

4. How structurally sound is the model?

EXPLANATION

This is the "Data Modeling 101" category. This category validates the design practices employed to build the model. We don't need to necessarily understand the content of the model to score this category. Just the structure. Many of the potential problems from this category are quickly and automatically flagged by our modeling and database tools. Examples include prohibiting having two data elements with the same exact name in the same entity, a null data element in a primary key, and certain reserved words in data element and entity names. This category ensures that the model follows good design principles independent of content.

Some violations are difficult to detect. For example, what is the structural soundness issue on this model?

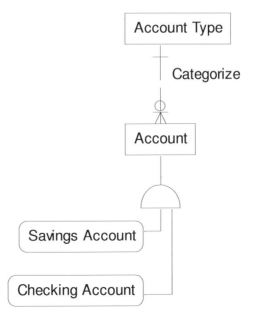

Data Model Scorecard® Overview

5. How well does the model leverage generic structures?

abstraction

EXPLANATION This category gauges the use of generic data element, entity, and relationship structures. One of the most powerful tools a data modeler has at their disposal is abstraction, the ability to increase the types of information a design can accommodate using generic concepts. Going from Customer Location to a more generic Location for example, allows the design to more easily handle other types of locations, such as warehouses and distribution centers. This category ensures the correct level of abstraction is applied on the model.

PURPOSE To have the right level of flexibility.

CHALLENGE You need to know how to phrase "what if" scenarios, and find people in the business who can answer these questions.

Data Model Scorecard® Overview

6. How well does the model follow naming standards?

standards

EXPLANATION
Correct and consistent naming standards are extremely helpful for knowledge transfer and integration. New team members who are familiar with similar naming conventions on other projects will avoid the time to learn a new set of naming standards. This category focuses on naming standard structure, abbreviations, and syntax.

STRUCTURE
Structure includes the components of a name. A popular standard for data element structure is one Prime, zero, one, or many Modifiers, and one Class Word. A prime is a concept that is basic and critical to the business. A modifier qualifies this prime and a class word is the high-level domain for a data element. Examples of class words are Quantity, Amount, Code, and Date.

TERM
Term includes proper spelling and abbreviation. An abbreviations list can be used to name each logical and physical term. Organizations should have a process in place for efficiently creating new abbreviations if a term cannot be found on a list. The process should be carefully managed to prevent different abbreviations being created for the same or similar term, and for creating the same abbreviation for completely different terms.

SYNTAX
Syntax includes whether the term should be plural or singular, whether hyphens, spaces, or Camelback (i.e. initial upper case with no spaces in between words such as customerLastName) should be used, and case (i.e. upper case, initial upper case, or lower case).

Data Model Scorecard® Overview

7. How well has the model been arranged for readability?

Proper layout ensures your model is easy to read so that the other scorecard categories can be accurately measured

EXPLANATION

This question checks to make sure the model is visually easy to follow. Readability needs to be considered at a model, entity, data element, and relationship level.

PURPOSE

Ensures your model is easy to read so that the other scorecard categories can be accurately measured.

Data Model Scorecard® Overview

8. How good are the definitions?

definitions

Ensures entity and data element definitions are
<u>clear</u>, <u>complete</u>, and <u>correct</u>

EXPLANATION   This category includes checking all definition to make sure they are clear, complete, and correct. Clarity means that a reader can understand the meaning of a term by reading the definition only once. Completeness ensures the definition is at the appropriate level of detail, and that it includes all the necessary components such as derivations and examples. Correctness focuses on having a definition that totally matches what the term means, and is consistent with the rest of the business.

PURPOSE   Ensures no doubt exists about the contents of data elements and the relationships between entities. Doubts and misinterpretations lead to model ambiguity.

CHALLENGE   You will need to find business people from outside your department or project to validate the definitions.

Data Model Scorecard® Overview

9. How consistent is the model with the enterprise?

Does this model complement the "Big Picture"?

EXPLANATION

Does this model complement the "big picture"? The structures that appear in a data model should be consistent in terminology and usage to structures that appear in related data models, and with the enterprise model if one exists. This way there will be consistency across projects.

PURPOSE

Ensures the information is represented in a broad and consistent context, so that one set of terminology and rules can be spoken in the organization.

CHALLENGE

Not all organizations have an enterprise data model. If no enterprise model exists, I look for widely accepted existing models for comparison, ERP models if they are accessible and intelligible, or universal models which are models that are built for a particular industry or function.

Data Model Scorecard® Overview

10. How well does the metadata match the data?

Determines how well the structure matches reality
What's really "under the hood"?

EXPLANATION This category determines how well the data elements and their rules match reality. Does the data element Customer Last Name really contain the customer's last name, for example?

PURPOSE Ensures the model and the actual data that will be stored within the resulting tables are consistent with each other, so to reduce surprises later on in software development.

CHALLENGE This might be very difficult to do early in a project's life cycle because data can be difficult to access from the source system before development has begun. However, the earlier the better so you can avoid future surprises which can be much more costly.

Data Model Scorecard® Overview

Introducing the Scorecard into your organization

Let me first spend 5 minutes on the subject area view of this model.

Ok, we did that. Now let's focus in on this part of the model. I created a separate view for this.

Ok, thanks for applying the Scorecard categories to this model. Let's meet again next week to review the updated model.

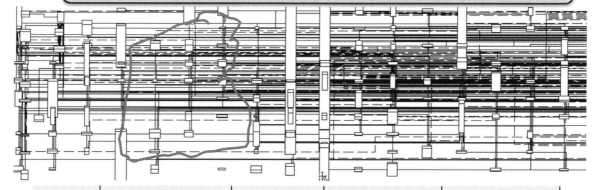

#	Category	Total score	Model score	%
1	Correctness	15	0.74	5
2	Completeness	15	15	100
3	Structure	15	11.8	79
4	Abstraction	10	9.51	95
5	Standards	5	4.26	85
6	Readability	5	4.67	93
7	Definitions	10	8.85	89
8	Detail	10	10	100
9	Consistency	5	4.43	89
10	Data	10	8.85	89
	TOTAL SCORE	**100**	**78.11**	

Data Model Scorecard® Overview

Introducing the Scorecard into your organization

REVIEW PROCESS

I am a believer in spending a two-hour model review doing a "deep dive" as opposed to a "broad brush" approach. The comments are usually much richer and as long as time permits, the modeler can schedule several reviews, each being a two-hour deep dive, to accomplish the model review.

FEEDBACK FROM GMAC

GMAC has applied the Scorecard and reports the following positive feedback:

- Sets expectations for the modeler.
- Reduce model iterations.
- Sharing resources across LOBs and countries is possible if using the same criteria.
- Provides meaningful metrics.
- Provides a measuring stick for existing applications. That is, provides a starting score for systems we know have designs that need work.

Data Model Scorecard® Overview

Scorecard challenges

- ☑ Resources
- ☑ Objectivity
- ☑ Emotion
- ☑ Iteration
- ☑ Need to set ideal amount of time:

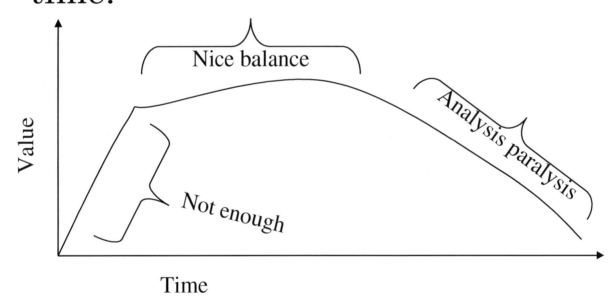

Data Model Scorecard® Overview

Scorecard challenges

RESOURCES

One of the challenges with reviewing the model with other modelers however, is that in today's lean and mean organizations, there aren't many people just doing modeling. Years ago, I worked in a group that had 9 data modelers full time. Later, I worked on a team that had 6 data modelers full time. Today where I work there aren't any full time data modelers! In situations like this, it is best to borrow some time from a modeler or a related project or perhaps your organization has a person who reviews models for best practice guidelines, at least part time.

OBJECTIVITY

Not everyone grades the same way. An easy grader may give four of out five, a hard grader two out of five. By reviewing models in groups, or averaging scores, a more objective final score can be achieved.

EMOTION

It is critical that emotion be filtered out of the Scorecard work. It is very easy to get attached to the model and translate areas for improvement on the model with weaknesses of the data modeler. We should not connect the model with the modeler when applying the Scorecard.

ITERATION

It is important to have a follow up review of the model after initial review. This is so you can ensure recommendations to the model have been correctly applied and to have a second look at the model with the opportunity of identifying other areas for improvement that might have been missed during the first application of the Scorecard.

TIME

Whenever anyone asks me how long it will take to build a data model, my response is always "How much time do I have?" Modeling will take as much time as is allocated. If I am building a model for a Sales data mart for example, and I am given two weeks for the modeling I will finish the effort in two weeks. If I am given two months, I will finish the effort in two months. The same is true for the Scorecard; it will take as much time as allocated. Make sure you set enough time to provide valuable suggestions to the modeler but not too much time where analysis paralysis sets in.

Modules 1 and 2

Category Question:	How well does the model capture the requirements?
This module is your guide to:	Ensuring the model captures the requirements

Category Question:	How complete is the model?
This module is your guide to:	Validating model scope

Category overview

1. How well does the model capture the requirements?

Confirms the model meets the requirements

Not easy to validate!

o Need to understand content!
o Sketchy requirements
o Conflicting requirements
o Changing requirements
o Often can't use a model!

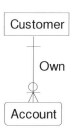

1. Each Customer can own many Accounts.

2. Each Account must be owned by one and only one Customer. This means you can't have joint accounts. Is this true Sally the Steward?

EXPLANATION

This is the "correctness" category. This category confirms that the model meets the requirements. All of the functionality detailed in a requirements document should be supported in the model. All reports required of a data mart should be producible from the data model. If there are no written requirements (or inadequate written requirements), there needs to be a business user or sponsor who can confirm that the model meets the requirements.

CHALLENGE

This can be the most difficult of all 10 categories to grade, the reason being that we really need to understand how the business works and what the business wants from their application. What makes this category even more challenging is the possibility that perhaps the business requirements are not well-defined, or differ from verbal requirements, or keep changing usually with the scope expanding instead of contracting.

Category overview

2. How complete is the model?

Confirms all requirements are in the model, and nothing extra

This   Minus   This = 0 (else Phase II)

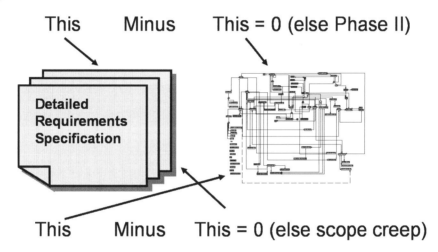

This   Minus   This = 0 (else scope creep)

EXPLANATION

This category checks for data model components that are not in the requirements or requirements that are not represented on the model. If the scope of the model is greater than the requirements, we have a situation known as "scope creep." If the model scope is less than the requirements, we will be leaving information out of the resulting application, usually leading to an enhancement or "Phase 2" shortly after the application is in production. For completeness, we need to make sure the scope of the project and model match, as well as ensuring all the necessary metadata on the model is populated. Regarding metadata, there are certain types that tend to get overlooked when modeling, such as definitions and alternate keys. These types of metadata along with ones that are mandatory parts of our model such as data element name and format information need to be checked for completeness in this category.

CHALLENGE

It can be difficult to grade this category without written signed off requirements and without a metadata checklist which contains the types of metadata that are required and those that are optional.

Category overview

Metadata Bingo

B	I	N	G	O
Entity definition	Data element format	Model name	Data element name	Entity name alias
Model purpose	Entity name	Entity lineage	Modeling tool	Model description
Data governance	Data element definition	★	Model version	Data element purpose
Scorecard score	History requirements	Modeler	Data element lineage	Sample values
Default value	Nullability	Key identification	Volumetrics	Data element name alias

BACKGROUND

Metadata Bingo is a game where the people on your project team complete "cards" identifying which types of metadata are most important to capture at different levels of detail. You can mix up the metadata above to create different cards, and replace the metadata or add more as you see fit. The "player" puts an "x" on any cell that they feel is essential for the modeler to capture. We then consolidate these cards, and tally the scores to see which types of metadata "win" and will be captured. By knowing up front as a team which types of metadata we will capture, we will meet expectations in this area during our data modeling.

METADATA DESCRIPTIONS

- **Entity definition**. A complete description of what the entity means.
- **Data element format**. The format domain and length of the data element, such as Character(16), Integer, Decimal(15,2), Varchar(256), etc.
- **Model name**. This is the full unabbreviated name of the data model.

Category overview

Metadata Bingo

METADATA DESCRIPTIONS (CONTINUED)

- **Data element name.** This includes both the logical and physical names.
- **Entity name alias.** Another name for an entity, often a department- or functional-specific name.
- **Model purpose.** The reason why the model is being built. Can also include the audience.
- **Entity name.** This includes both the logical and physical names.
- **Entity lineage.** The source information for the entity.
- **Modeling tool.** The software tool that was used to build the model.
- **Model description.** The description for a data model might include a number of important pieces of information, including an overview to the subject areas included in the model or the type of design (operational or BI).
- **Data governance.** The steward name is the name of the person or department who is responsible for the actual data within an entity.
- **Data element definition.** A complete description of what the data element means.
- **Model version.** This includes a record of any changes made to the model over time.
- **Data element purpose.** The business reason why we have this data element.
- **Scorecard score.** The most recent Data Model Scorecard® score of the model.
- **History requirements.** The amount of event history along with type of profile history such as full (audit), only most recent, or no history needed (equivalent to SCD Types 1, 2, and 3).
- **Modeler.** The person who built or maintains the model.
- **Data element lineage.** The source information along with transformations required to populate the data element.
- **Sample values.** Showing some actual values is extremely useful for codes.
- **Default value.** If the data element is left blank what value will be stored in it? Will it stay blank or will it default to a "Yes", a "No", or "Blue", or some other value.
- **Nullability.** Whether the data element can be left empty.
- **Key identification.** Capture whether a data element is a primary, foreign, or alternate key (could also include surrogate and natural key).
- **Volumetrics.** The initial data space required for a data element, along with the rate of change over time.
- **Data element name alias.** Another name for the data element, which could be a department or functional name.

Requirements lifecycle

How the pieces fit together

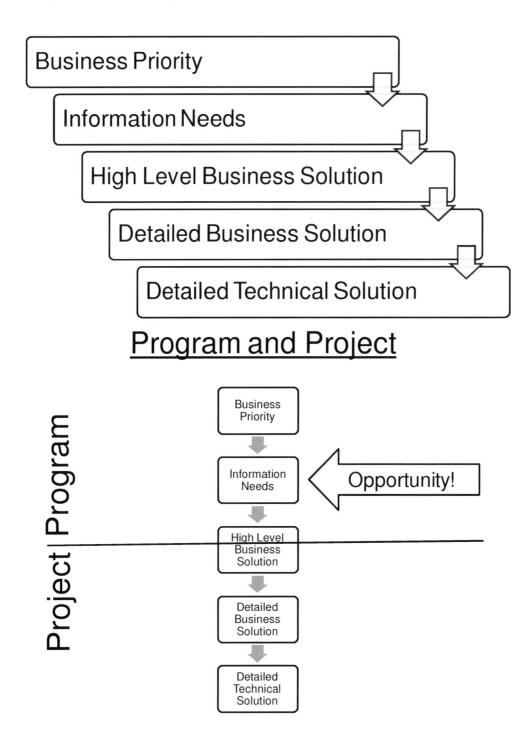

Requirements lifecycle

How the pieces fit together

EXPLANATION

Results from requirements elicitation techniques are captured in software development deliverables. For example, the interface analysis work is typically captured in a source/target mapping document. There are many complexities involved with producing deliverables, including not all deliverables are relevant for all situations and there are dependencies between deliverables. This is where a framework is needed.

A framework is a logical structure for classifying and organizing information. There are a number of different frameworks such as the Zachman Framework and TOGAF. Common themes across frameworks are acknowledging levels of detail and separation of data from process. The framework I use is shown on the facing page.

There are different levels of detail starting with business priorities. A business priority can be based upon goals, strategies, drivers, or directions the business would like to take. It is a great idea to connect projects with a business priority to ensure each small piece contributes to some larger whole (also good for job security ☺).

Business priorities require knowing information, like how well we've done, what we are planning on doing next, and how we stack up against the competition. This information is made precise through templates such as the Interview Template and Grain Matrix.

The high level business solution captures how to meet the information needs on one piece of paper. I have found it valuable over the years to have both enterprise and project high level conceptual data models (CDMs).

The detailed business solution equates to the logical data model (LDM) and captures all of the data elements and business rules independent of technology. The detailed technical solution adds the technology and is frequently called the physical data model (PDM).

PROGRAM VS PROJECT

A program is a large cross-department and often enterprise effort for the purpose of accomplishing something big such as enterprise analytics, cross-platform integration, Customer Relationship Management (CRM), etc. It has a begin date and if lucky no end date. A program contains multiple projects. A project is a tactical timeboxed effort for the purpose of delivering part of its corresponding program.

Technics Publications Case Study

Overview

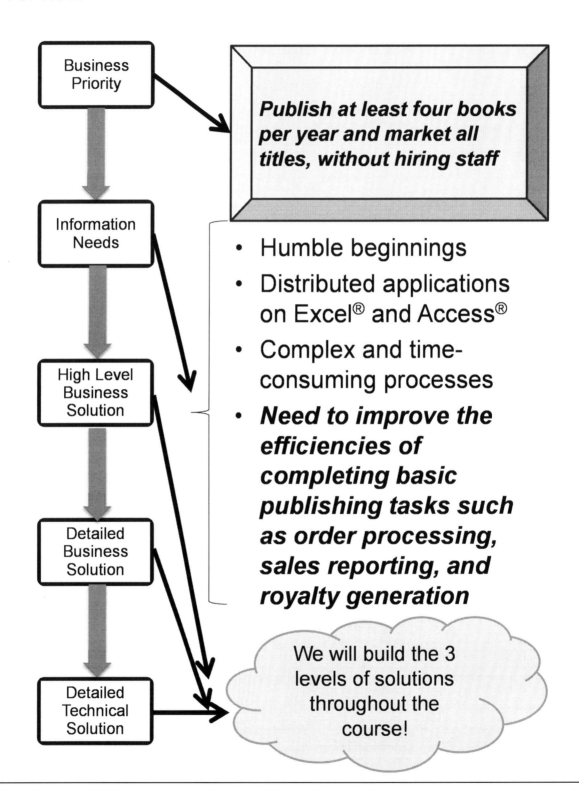

Business Priority

Publish at least four books per year and market all titles, without hiring staff

Information Needs

High Level Business Solution

Detailed Business Solution

Detailed Technical Solution

- Humble beginnings
- Distributed applications on Excel® and Access®
- Complex and time-consuming processes
- *Need to improve the efficiencies of completing basic publishing tasks such as order processing, sales reporting, and royalty generation*

We will build the 3 levels of solutions throughout the course!

Technics Publications Case Study

Overview

ABOUT TECHNICS PUBLICATIONS

Steve Hoberman's first title, **Data Modeler's Workbench**, was published by John Wiley & Sons in 2001. For his second title, **Data Modeling Made Simple**, Steve decided to publish it himself. This book was released in 2005. Although an extremely painful process, he documented every activity along the journey. Well-documented processes are repeatable, and since his first book he has published over 25 titles including the **DAMA Data Management Body of Knowledge**, **Building the Unstructured Data Warehouse** by Bill Inmon, and **Secrets of Analytical Leaders** by Wayne Eckerson. Steve is currently the CEO of Technics Publications (www.technicspub.com), a publishing empire dedicated to **making the world a better place by releasing the most practical, easy-to-read, and innovative business intelligence and data management titles**.

BUSINESS PRIORITIES

Steve wants to continue to grow Technics Publications, without hiring any staff. That is, release at least four titles per year without needing any employees.

INFORMATION NEEDS

Technics Publications grew from very humble beginnings, with a majority of his operational processes such as book order entry and royalty generation, still being run on Microsoft® Excel® and Microsoft Access®. Managing many day-to-day operations is quite time consuming, for example, copying and pasting each order from Amazon® into an Order Excel worksheet. Managing more complex and less periodic operations, such as calculating author royalties, is even more complex and time-consuming. Steve's number one priority is to improve the efficiencies of completing basic publishing tasks such as order processing, sales reporting, and royalty generation.

DELIVERABLES

We will work directly with Steve the CEO (and sometimes his authors and distributors), to elicit requirements and build the designs necessary to take his company to the next level. Each module from this point forward will contain deliverables which as a whole will address Steve's information needs and satisfy his business priority of improving the efficiencies of completing basic publishing tasks.

Techniques for eliciting requirements

About elicitation

> **Elicitation is:**
> • **To draw forth or bring out (something latent or potential)**
> • **To call forth or draw out (as information or a response)**
>
> Merriam-Webster Online Dictionary

- More work than simply *gathering* requirements
- Emphasis is on actively engaging stakeholders

> **A factor present in every successful project and absent in every unsuccessful project is sufficient attention to requirements.**
>
> Suzanne & James Robertson (Robertson 2004)

> **Start where you are. Use what you have. Do what you can.**
>
> Arthur Ashe

Techniques for eliciting requirements

About elicitation

FROM MERRIAM-WEBSTER ONLINE DICTIONARY

The definition of elicitation is:
to draw forth or bring out (something latent or potential)
to call forth or draw out (as information or a response).

ELICITATION TECHNIQUES FROM BABOK 2.0

There are a number of different techniques that can be used, depending on the resources available and level of detail required from the outcome. The main techniques are:

- Interviews [Interviewer]
- Document and Interface Analysis [Data Archeologist]
- Job Shadowing [Observer]
- Workshops [Facilitator]
- Prototyping [Detective]

I put in square brackets after each of these elicitation techniques, the role we play during eliciting using this technique.

Note that much of the information in the next few pages that go into each of these techniques are based upon BABOK 2.0 supplemented with my own experiences.

Techniques for eliciting requirements

Interviews

Preparation
- Define the interview's focus or goal
- Identify potential interviewees
- Design the interview

Session
- Opening: State purpose of interview
- During: Maintain focus on interview goals
- Closing: Summarize session – also anything overlooked?

Wrap up
- Interviewer organizes the information and sends the notes to the interviewee for review

I keep six honest serving men, They taught me all I knew; Their names are what and why and when and how and where and who.

Rudyard Kipling

Closed questions	**Open questions**
Useful to check accuracy of the communication	Encourage elaboration on subject
Allow specific facts to be gathered	Draw out ideas and feelings
Easy to answer and seldom intimidating	Do not lead the answer

Techniques for eliciting requirements

Interviews

EXPLANATION

An interview is a systematic approach designed to elicit information from a person or group of people in an informal or formal setting by talking to an interviewee, asking relevant questions and documenting the responses. Success factors include interviewee experience, interviewer preparation, willingness to participate, and rapport. For the purpose of eliciting requirements, interviews are of two basic types:

- **Structured Interview** where the interviewer has a pre-defined set of questions and is looking for answers.
- **Unstructured Interview** where, without any pre-defined questions, the interviewer and the interviewee discuss topics of interest in an open-ended way.

PROS

- Encourages participation and establishes rapport
- Observation of non-verbal behavior
- Interactions enable follow-up questions

CONS

- Can require considerable business user time
- "Lost in translation"

DESIGNING THE INTERVIEW

Designing the interview requires crafting questions considering:

- Interview time limitations (and whether it is a one-shot interview)
- Personality of the interviewee
- Interviewee technical expertise (e.g. Can they read a data model?)
- Balancing closed questions (brief answers) with open questions (wider range of responses)

BALANCING OPEN WITH CLOSED QUESTIONS

Tony Alessandra, in The Art of Asking Questions, has some great pointers on when to ask open vs closed questions:

Closed questions:

- Allow specific facts to be gathered
- Are easy to answer and seldom intimidating
- Useful to check the accuracy of the communication

Open questions:

- Do not lead the answer
- Draw out ideas and feelings
- Encourage elaboration on objectives and problems

Techniques for eliciting requirements

Interviews: Write the opening question

Bob has worked 15 years on the support for the order entry operational system which is the major source of data for book sales. He always makes time for a good conversation.

Your opening interview question:

Can you describe the Order Entry system & how Reporting is done today?

Mary is the key business user. She thinks she knows exactly what she wants from the Book Sales application.

Your opening interview question:

What key data do you need on these reports?

Steve is the CEO of the publishing company. He is extremely busy and Mary will provide sales reports to him.

Your opening interview question:

Techniques for eliciting requirements
Interviews: Write the opening question

INSTRUCTIONS You have the opportunity to interview several people for the Book Sales application. Write the opening question you would ask for each of these individuals.

Jim works in IT in producing reports from the order entry operational system for the business. He will no longer provide this function after the Book Sales application is in production. He can be confrontational at times.

Your opening interview question:

Joan was the key business user for the Royalty Reporting application. This project was a dismal failure and Joan stopped talking to the IT department as a result.

Your opening interview question:

Techniques for eliciting requirements

Document and Interface Analysis

Amazon.com Advantage Unit Sales and Inventory Report

Download the Reports Guide (PDF) here.

Read more about Unit Sales & Inventory Reports - including definitions, Frequently Asked Questions, and Instructions on how to download your Sales reports - here.

Report Last updated: July 21, 2012

Page 1

Displaying 1 to 26 of 26 Items

Title	ASIN	ISBN/UPC/EAN	Price	Discount	Cost	Status	Unit Sales 05/2012	Unit Sales 06/2012	Unit Sales 07/2012	Sellable Inventory	Unsellable Inventory	Customer Owned	Total Inventory Units	Unit Sales Amount - Current MTD
The DAMA Guide to the Data Management Body of Knowledge (DAMA-DMBOK)	9771140083	9780977140084	$54.95	55	$24.73	Active	17	29	13	13	0	0	13	$321.49
Data Quality Assessment	9771140024	9780977140022	$54.95	55	$24.73	Active	12	10	7	8	0	0	8	$173.11
fruITion: Creating the Ultimate Corporate Strategy for Information Technology	9771140032	9780977140039	$18.95	55	$8.53	Active	7	2	2	69	0	0	69	$17.06
Data Modeling Theory and Practice	9771140016	9780977140015	$58.95	55	$26.53	Active	2	0	0	1	0	0	1	$0.00
The DAMA Dictionary of Data Management, 2nd Edition: Over 2,000 Terms Defined for IT and Business Professionals	1935504118	9781935504115	$49.95	55	$22.48	Active	1	2	4	135	0	0	135	$89.92
The Hidden Corporation: A Data Management Security Novel	1935504185	9781935504184	$18.95	55	$8.53	Active	0	0	0	0	0	0	0	$0.00
recrEAtion: Realizing the Extraordinary Contribution of Your Enterprise Architects	1935504088	9781935504085	$18.95	55	$8.53	Active	0	0	0	0	0	0	0	$0.00

Techniques for eliciting requirements
Document and Interface Analysis

EXPLANATION

Sometimes (and especially in the absence of business professional to talk to), we rely heavily on any documentation. Documentation can take the form of requirements documents, interface layouts, existing file structures, existing reports...anything that is written about current or proposed systems.

ROLE

We play the role of data archeologist. Just like an archeologist finds a piece of clay and needs to determine if it is from a pot or cup, we as data archeologists find a column in a spreadsheet, a tag in an XML file, or field in a database, and try to determine what it is and whether it is useful or not.

EXAMPLE

The example on the facing page is an existing Amazon unit sales report. Reports such as these can be used to capture requirements for new applications. As data archeologists, we need to figure out quite a bit of information on this report (luckily for this one, Amazon has great definitions for each of these elements).

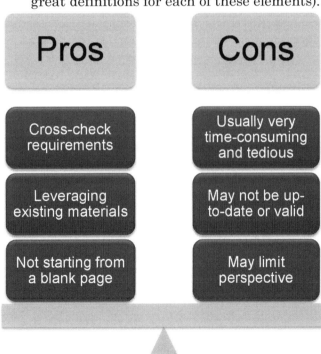

Pros	Cons
Cross-check requirements	Usually very time-consuming and tedious
Leveraging existing materials	May not be up-to-date or valid
Not starting from a blank page	May limit perspective

Techniques for eliciting requirements

Job Shadowing

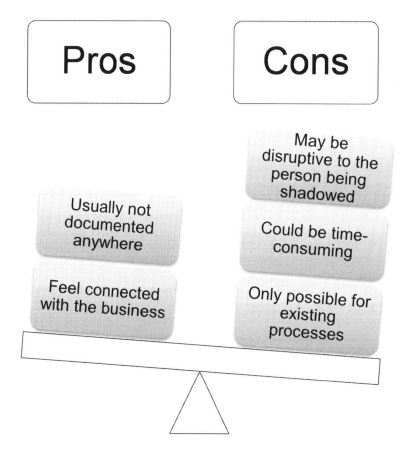

Pros

Cons

Usually not documented anywhere

Feel connected with the business

May be disruptive to the person being shadowed

Could be time-consuming

Only possible for existing processes

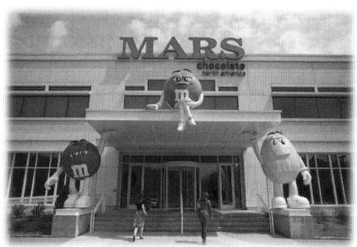

Techniques for eliciting requirements

Job Shadowing

EXPLANATION

Job Shadowing is a means of eliciting requirements by conducting an assessment of the business professional's work environment. This technique is appropriate when documenting details about current processes or if the project is intended to enhance or change a current process. Some people have their work routine down to such a habit that they have difficulty explaining what they do or why. The observer may need to watch them perform their work in order to understand the flow of work. In certain projects, it is important to understand the current processes to better assess the process modifications that may be needed.

VARIATIONS

In the passive approach, the observer observes the user working through the business routine but does not ask questions. The observer records what is observed, but otherwise stays out of the way. The observer waits until the entire process has been completed before asking any questions. In the active approach, while the observer observes the current process and takes notes they may dialog with the user. When the observer has questions as to why something is being done as it is, they ask questions right away, even if it breaks the routine of the user. Sometimes the observer might participate in the actual work to get a hands-on feel for how the business process works today.

ROLE

We play the role of an observer. Sometimes the best way to understand what the business professional needs is to watch him/her work and see the pain points (opportunities) first hand. In John Giles' book, **The Nimble Elephant**, he uses the Aussie phrase "ride the truck", meaning sit right beside the business users and watch what they do.

Techniques for eliciting requirements

Workshops

Handwritten notes in left margin:
Look into:
a idef φ " methodology
Reference Book :
How work Gets Done

- Structured way to capture requirements
- Human dynamics plays a big part
- Facilitator
- Example
  - Formal workshop to capture title requirements

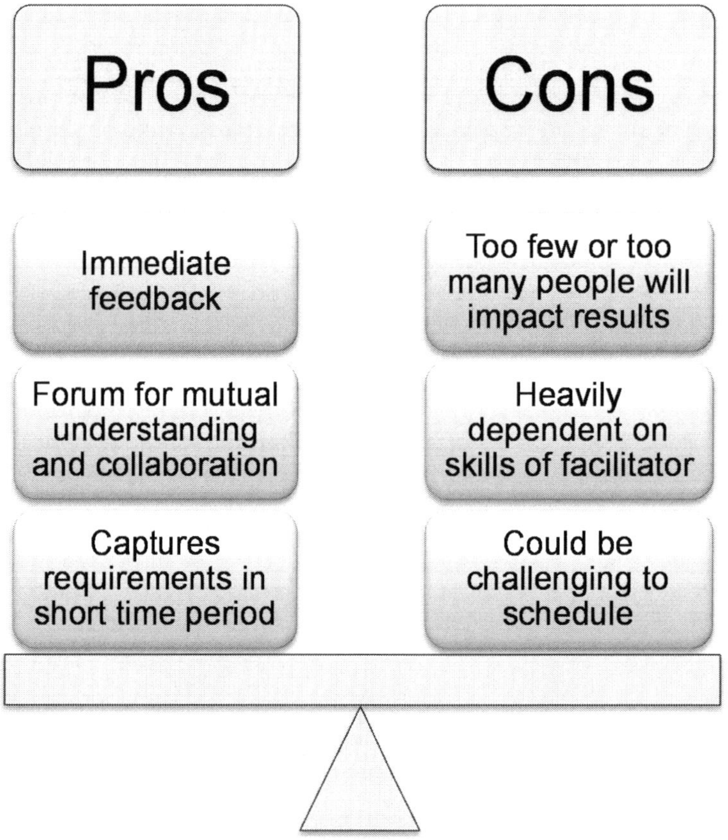

Pros	Cons
Immediate feedback	Too few or too many people will impact results
Forum for mutual understanding and collaboration	Heavily dependent on skills of facilitator
Captures requirements in short time period	Could be challenging to schedule

Techniques for eliciting requirements

Workshops

EXPLANATION

A requirements workshop is a structured way to capture requirements. A workshop may be used to scope, discover, define, prioritize and reach closure on requirements for the target system. Well-run workshops are considered one of the most effective ways to deliver high quality requirements quickly. They can promote trust, mutual understanding, and strong communications among the project stakeholders and project team and produce deliverables that structure and guide future analysis.

ROLE

We play the role of a facilitator. We need to make sure the workshop is as productive as possible, and that there is active and balanced participation from the participants.

Techniques for eliciting requirements
Prototyping

TITLE SALES CUSTOM DATE RANGE PLUS DETAILS

User selects date range

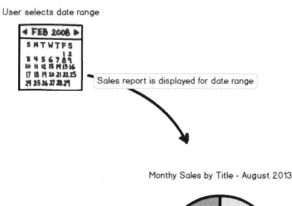

Sales report is displayed for date range

Monthy Sales by Title - August 2013

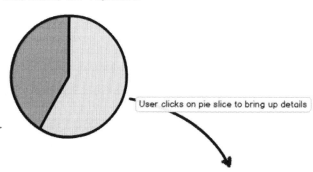

User clicks on pie slice to bring up details

Date	Title	ISBN	Quantity	Sales
8/1/2013	Secrets of Analytical Leaders	9781935504597	3	$135
8/3/2013	Secrets of Analytical Leaders	9781935504597	1	$35
8/7/2013	Secrets of Analytical Leaders	9781935504597	10	$400
8/10/2013	Secrets of Analytical Leaders	9781935504597	2	$60
8/25/2013	Secrets of Analytical Leaders	9781935504597	30	$1000
8/1/2013	Secrets of Analytical Leaders	9781935504597	3	$135
8/1/2013	UML Database Modeling Workbook	9781935504511	7	$210
8/23/2013	UML Database Modeling Workbook	9781935504511	1	$30
8/27/2013	UML Database Modeling Workbook	9781935504511	9	$250
8/30/2013	UML Database Modeling Workbook	9781935504511	4	$120

New Search | Print | Return

Techniques for eliciting requirements

Prototyping

EXPLANATION

Prototyping is a concrete means of identifying, describing and validating relational and dimensional requirements. There are some very easy to use tools available to create prototypes, such as Excel® and Balsamiq®. Balsamiq is a very user-friendly way to create screen mock-ups (see www.balsamiq.com for more details).

VARIATIONS

A horizontal prototype models a shallow and possibly wide view of the system's functionality. It typically does not have any business logic running behind the visualization. A vertical prototype models a deep and usually narrow slice of the entire system's functionality.

ROLE

We play the role of a detective. Just like a detective can sketch a headshot of someone and ask a witness if "this is the guy", we do this with application requirements.

EXAMPLE

The facing page contains an example of prototyping. This prototype was built using Balsamiq Mockups.

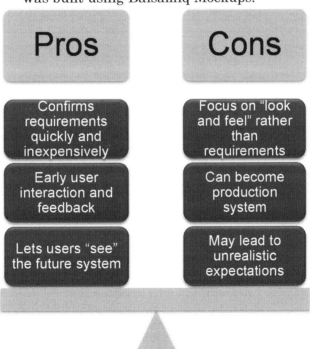

Applying the Data Model Scorecard®
Capturing interactions

There is a requirement to build a business application that reports trends on consumer interactions. An interaction is a contact between an employee and a consumer for a specific product. An interaction can take place through a variety of medium such as through phone, email, and mail. Interactions fit into one of three categories: complaints, compliments and questions. Here are examples of some of the interactions:

"I love your product." (compliment)
"I hate your product." (complaint)
"I found a strange object in your product." (complaint)
"Where can I buy your product?" (question)
"I found your product difficult to assemble." (complaint)

A consumer can have many interactions on many products. For example, Bob can call Monday because he didn't like Product XYZ, he can call Tuesday and say that he now liked Product XYZ, and can call Wednesday and say that he loves Product ABC. Consumer Interaction in this example would contain three records, and at a high level look something like this:

Consumer	Product	Employee	Interaction	Date received
Bob	XYZ	Mary	Didn't like product	Monday 4/1/2011
Bob	XYZ	Jane	Liked product	Tuesday 4/2/2011
Bob	ABC	Mary	Loved product	Wednesday 4/3/2011

The requirement is to produce a report for each product that shows for the previous 12 months, the number of complaints, compliments and questions. This report has to allow the users to "drill down" to get to the interaction level of detail and see the actual interaction such as "Loved product". See bar chart on facing page.

How good is the data model on the facing page?

Applying the Data Model Scorecard®
Capturing interactions

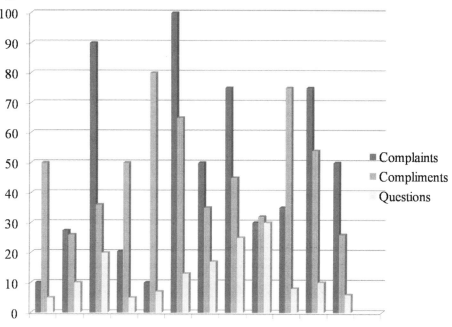

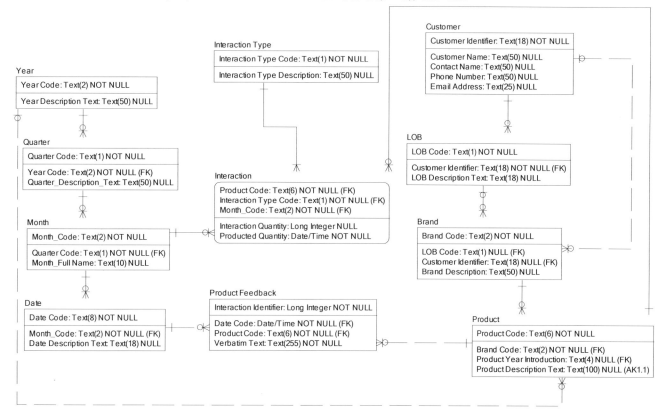

Applying the Data Model Scorecard®

Interaction Report for Product BB40 from May 2011

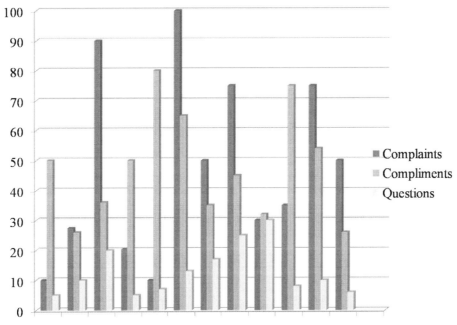

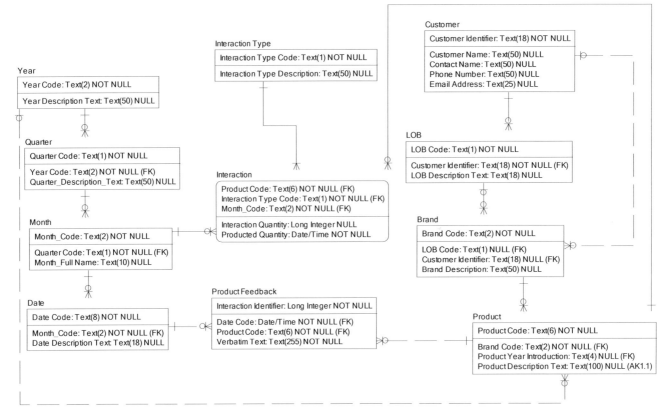

Interaction Type

Interaction Type Code: Text(1) NOT NULL
Interaction Type Description: Text(50) NULL

Customer

Customer Identifier: Text(18) NOT NULL
Customer Name: Text(50) NULL Contact Name: Text(50) NULL Phone Number: Text(50) NULL Email Address: Text(25) NULL

Year

Year Code: Text(2) NOT NULL
Year Description Text: Text(50) NULL

Quarter

Quarter Code: Text(1) NOT NULL
Year Code: Text(2) NOT NULL (FK) Quarter_Description_Text: Text(50) NULL

Interaction

Product Code: Text(6) NOT NULL (FK) Interaction Type Code: Text(1) NOT NULL (FK) Month_Code: Text(2) NOT NULL (FK)
Interaction Quantity: Long Integer NULL Producted Quantity: Date/Time NOT NULL

LOB

LOB Code: Text(1) NOT NULL
Customer Identifier: Text(18) NOT NULL (FK) LOB Description Text: Text(18) NULL

Month

Month_Code: Text(2) NOT NULL
Quarter Code: Text(1) NOT NULL (FK) Month_Full Name: Text(10) NULL

Brand

Brand Code: Text(2) NOT NULL
LOB Code: Text(1) NULL (FK) Customer Identifier: Text(18) NULL (FK) Brand Description: Text(50) NULL

Product Feedback

Interaction Identifier: Long Integer NOT NULL
Date Code: Date/Time NOT NULL (FK) Product Code: Text(6) NOT NULL (FK) Verbatim Text: Text(255) NOT NULL

Date

Date Code: Text(8) NOT NULL
Month_Code: Text(2) NOT NULL (FK) Date Description Text: Text(18) NULL

Product

Product Code: Text(6) NOT NULL
Brand Code: Text(2) NOT NULL (FK) Product Year Introduction: Text(4) NULL (FK) Product Description Text: Text(100) NULL (AK1.1)

Applying the Data Model Scorecard®

1. How well does the model capture the requirements?

ANYTHING YOU
WOULD CATCH
FOR
CORRECTNESS?

1.

2.

3.

4.

5.

2. How complete is the model?

ANYTHING YOU
WOULD CATCH
FOR
COMPLETENESS?

1.

2.

3.

4.

5.

#	Category	Total score	Model score	%
1	How well does the model capture the requirements?	15		
2	How complete is the model?	15		
3	How well do the characteristics of the model support the type of model?	10		
4	How structurally sound is the model?	15		
5	How well does the model leverage generic structures?	10		
6	How well does the model follow naming standards?	5		
7	How well has the model been arranged for readability?	5		
8	How good are the definitions?	10		
9	How consistent is the model with the enterprise?	5		
10	How well does the metadata match the data?	10		
	TOTAL SCORE	100		

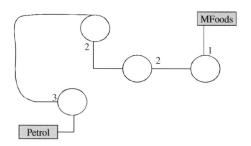

Module 3

Data Model Scorecard® Category #3: Model Type

Category Question: How well do the
characteristics of the model
support the type of model?

*This module is your
guide to:*   Understanding conceptual,
logical, and physical data
models

Category overview

How well do the characteristics of the model support the type of model?

model type

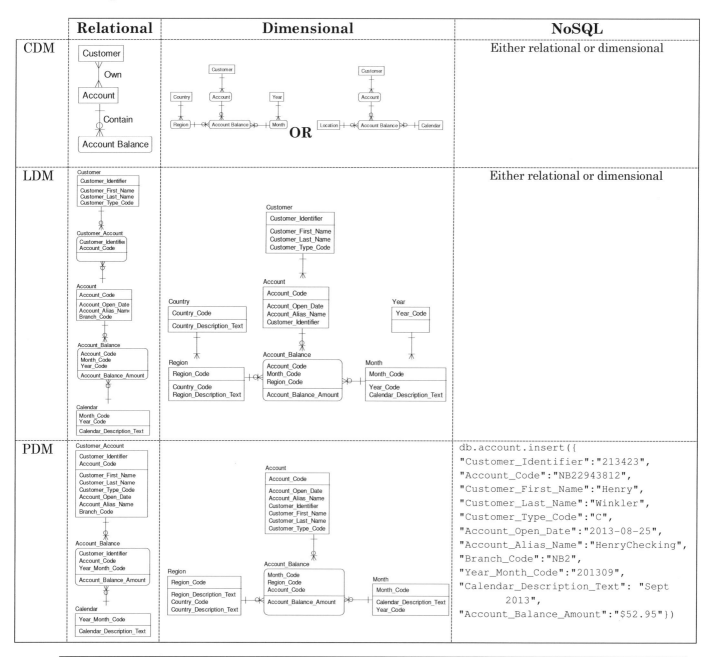

	Relational	Dimensional	NoSQL
CDM			Either relational or dimensional
LDM			Either relational or dimensional

PDM			`db.account.insert({`
			`"Customer_Identifier":"213423",`
			`"Account_Code":"NB22943812",`
			`"Customer_First_Name":"Henry",`
			`"Customer_Last_Name":"Winkler",`
			`"Customer_Type_Code":"C",`
			`"Account_Open_Date":"2013-08-25",`
			`"Account_Alias_Name":"HenryChecking",`
			`"Branch_Code":"NB2",`
			`"Year_Month_Code":"201309",`
			`"Calendar_Description_Text": "Sept`
			`     2013",`
			`"Account_Balance_Amount":"$52.95"})`

Category overview

How well do the characteristics of the model support the type of model?

EXPLANATION

This question ensures that the model type (conceptual, logical, or physical – and then either relational, dimensional, or NoSQL) of the model satisfies the criteria for this level of detail.

	Relational	Dimensional	NoSQL
Conceptual	Broad scope concepts and rules	Broad scope metrics and slicing	Either relational or dimensional
Logical	Normalized	All metrics and levels shown	Either relational or dimensional
Physical	Denormalized, views, indexes, etc.	Star schema or snowflake	Document, column, graph, etc.

CHALLENGE

During crunch times it is possible that one model might be created to represent both logical and physical views for example, and this can complicate the grading of this category. I once heard this type of model referred to as a "physio-logical" model.

CONCEPTUAL

High level, one inch equals 500 miles. We need to represent a very broad area on a "single piece of paper". Every entity and relationship must represent something basic and critical for that area we are modeling.

LOGICAL

Addresses the Business problem.

Fully-attributed, yet independent of technology. Every data element is assigned to an entity either based on existence and participation business rules, or by what makes sense to monitor part of the business. This is the business solution.

PHYSICAL

Addresses the Technical problem.

The logical data model compromised for technology. In addition, the software, hardware, and network are important factors to consider in building a model that works. Often the logical structure is changed to improve application performance or storage efficiencies. This is the technical solution. NoSQL (coined in 1998) is a catch-all for databases that are not using a relational database (a better term: NoRel).

Conceptual data model

Explanation and purpose

A conceptual data model (CDM) is a set of symbols and text that represents key concepts and their definitions and business rules for a defined business or application scope and for a particular audience.

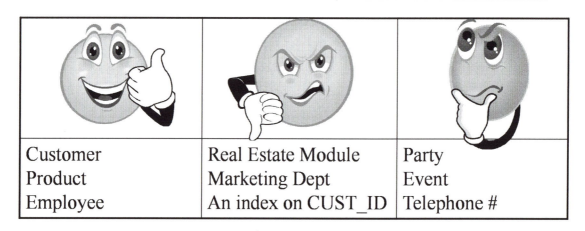

Customer Product Employee	Real Estate Module Marketing Dept An index on CUST_ID	Party Event Telephone #

Provides broad understanding!

Defines scope & direction!

Offers proactive analysis!

Low hanging fruit!

Builds rapport!

Just love those definitions!

Conceptual data model

Explanation and purpose

WHAT IS A CONCEPTUAL DATA MODEL?

A conceptual data model (CDM) is a set of symbols and text that represents key concepts and the rules binding these key concepts for a defined business or application scope and for a particular audience.

PROVIDES BROAD UNDERSTANDING

The conceptual data model ties subject areas together, and is able to visually show the dependencies and rules between these subject areas. CDMs are very broad in scope and therefore we can model entire departments or organizations, external concepts such as regulatory agencies or competitors, future architectures, etc.

DEFINES SCOPE AND DIRECTION

By visually showing subject areas and their business rules, we can more easily identify a subset of the model to analyze. For example, we can model the entire logistics department, and then scope out of this a particular logistics application that we would like to build.

OFFERS PROACTIVE ANALYSIS

By developing a conceptual understanding of the application, there is a strong chance we will be able to identify important issues or concerns that can save substantial time and money later on. Topics where prevention can occur include history requirements, functionality limitations, sourcing issues, etc.

"LOW HANGING FRUIT"

The conceptual data model takes a relatively minimal amount of time to build, and yet offers very large payoff in terms of business understanding and creating a solid foundation for design.

DEFINITIONS

If we can clearly and completely define Customer on a conceptual data model, imagine how much easier our lives would be at the logical and physical levels when there are hundreds of entities and data elements containing the term Customer.

Conceptual data model

Five ways of communicating

We can get very creative in telling the story on a conceptual data model. Think of your audience and the symbols that will be easiest for them to relate to.

Example 1: Using traditional modeling symbols (Information Engineering)

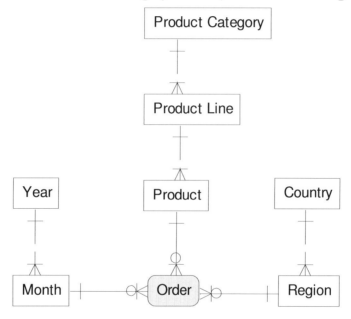

Example 2: Using Laura Reeves' Business Dimensional Model

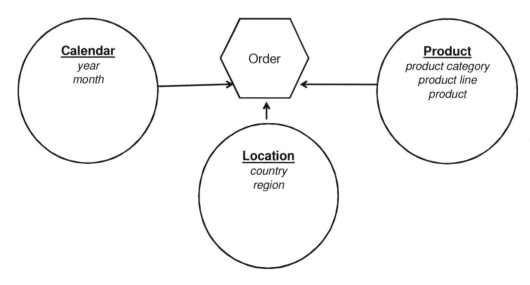

Conceptual data model

Five ways of communicating

Example 3: Fully Communication Oriented Information Modeling (FCO-IM)

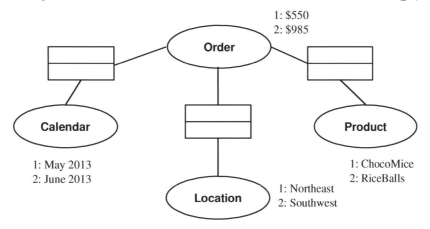

Example 4: Unified Modeling Language (UML)

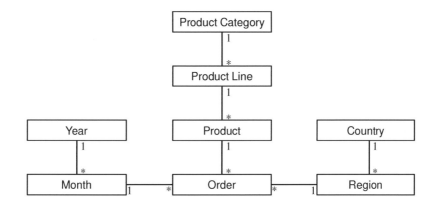

Example 5: Using the axis technique

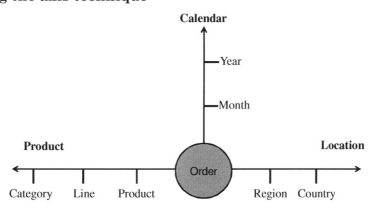

Conceptual data model

Actual examples

EXAMPLES

These are three actual CDM subsets from projects I have worked on. In Example 1, a university was chartered with building a data warehouse, and this CDM was built to provide the overall roadmap and list of definitions. In Example 2, I was given 30 minutes to explain a very complex part of SAP to an audience consisting of both technical and non-technical colleagues. In Example 3, I consolidated hundreds of terms and their definitions into a succinct CDM. The multiple definitions for facility were described neatly using this subtyping structure.

Example 1: University CDM

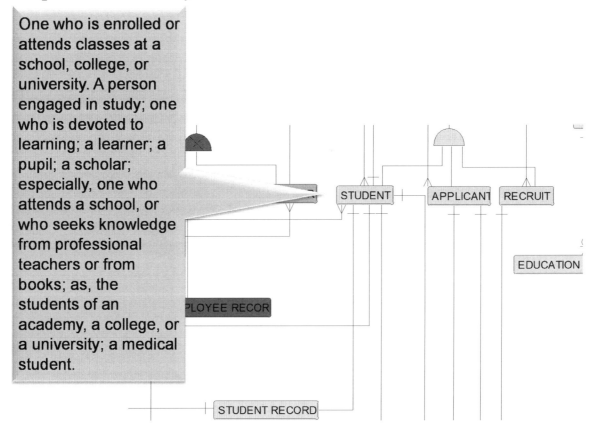

Conceptual data model

Actual examples

Example 2: SAP/R3 Classifications

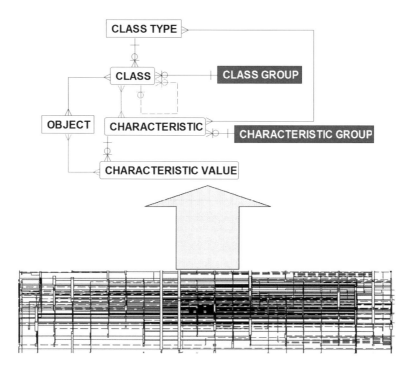

Example 3: Government Agency

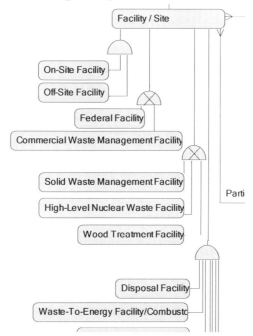

Conceptual data model

3 approaches to building a CDM

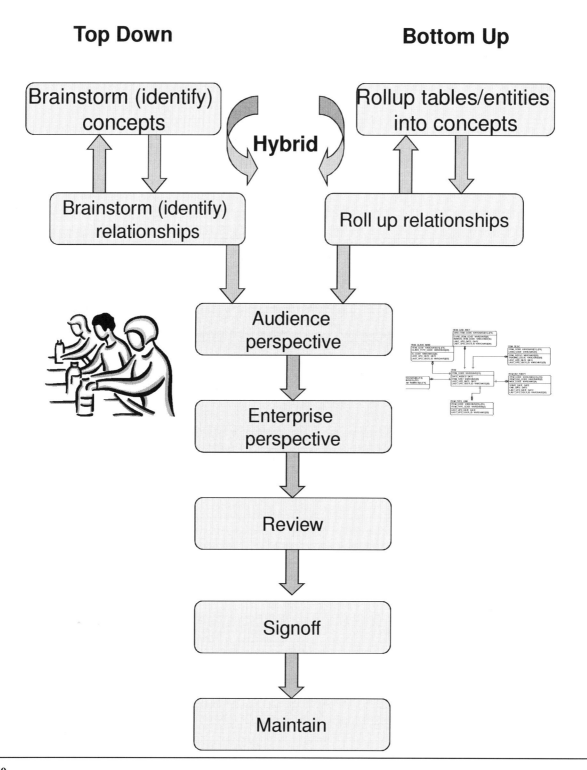

Top Down

Bottom Up

Brainstorm (identify) concepts

Hybrid

Rollup tables/entities into concepts

Brainstorm (identify) relationships

Roll up relationships

Audience perspective

Enterprise perspective

Review

Signoff

Maintain

Conceptual data model

3 approaches to building a CDM

BACKGROUND

There are three approaches to building a conceptual data model, and the approach taken depends on the available resources and the purpose of the model. If there are minimal business resources available and ample systems documentation, and the purpose of the model is to understand an existing application, a bottom-up approach is ideal. If a new system is being built from scratch and there are business experts eager to participate in the project, a top-down approach would be ideal. If a new system is being planned, or an upgrade to an existing system and business expertise is available and required, a hybrid approach is ideal.

BRAINSTORMING

In top-down and hybrid approaches, standard brainstorming techniques work quite well. I have found though, it is good to have something to start with, such as a generic model or a handful of subject areas you know will be on the list, such as Customer and Product. Remember, definitions are included here as well!

ROLLING UP

In bottom-up and hybrid approaches, we perform "data archeology" by examining sometimes hundreds of pages of documents and thousands of tables, and rolling them up into subject areas.

AUDIENCE PERSPECTIVE

This model needs to match the terminology of the business people involved in creating the model. Once they see their world in the boxes and lines, you can move on to the enterprise perspective.

ENTERPRISE PERSPECTIVE

Compare to an enterprise data model or common business knowledge or industry terms to ensure an enterprise perspective.

REVIEW

Make sure the model is reviewed for data modeling best practices as well as that it meets the requirements. If possible, apply the Data Model Scorecard®.

SIGNOFF

Easier said than done! Critical to the credibility of the model.

MAINTAIN

CDMs don't require the same frequency of maintenance as logical and physical, yet it still needs to be maintained to be valuable.

Conceptual data model

Challenges

Conceptual data model

Challenges

SCOPE

How do you know when you've modeled all the concepts you need? Two pointers can help here: you are always done with the model when the time is up (every modeling assignment must be timeboxed). The second point is if you are unsure whether something should be in scope or not, include it at least in the first iteration. It is always easier to take something out later than add it later.

CAN'T TOUCH THIS!

The conceptual data model is not real like a physical data model or set of database tables are real. It is often not thought of as a necessity in developing a system. As long as there are database tables the system could work. Therefore in many cases this model is difficult to justify.

LEVEL OF ABSTRACTION

It is very easy to make the business terms generic on a conceptual, but the tradeoff is that the audience may not be able to relate to any of the concepts!

RIGHT PEOPLE

Just like any project, it is important to have the right people involved. "Right people" in this context are those people who have the experience and enthusiasm to contribute to the models. Although at times people who don't have the experience (or the enthusiasm) will be the most important people you need to have in the room either because of perceived credibility to the project, or for political or budgeting reasons.

GOOD DEFINITIONS

Definitions can be extremely difficult to write at the conceptual level. Subject area definitions typically cross functions and you will frequently run into situations where experts from different departments see the same terms differently.

MAINTAIN

It takes a minimal amount of effort to maintain the domain and conceptual data models, but they still need to be maintained. Even a short lapse of time where the models are forgotten can negate their usefulness.

Conceptual data model

Now let's build a CDM!

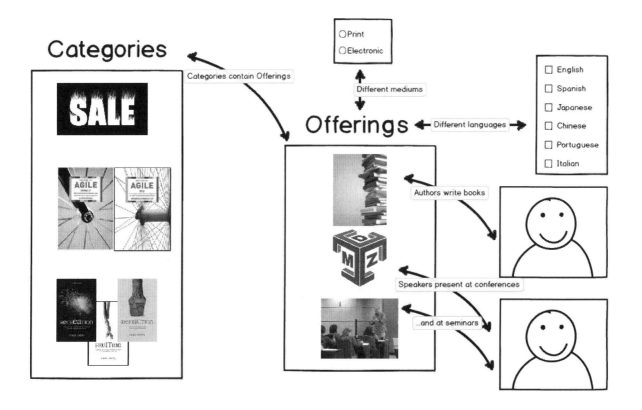

Technics Publications Offerings Camera Settings

Scope	Abstraction	Time	Function
__Project	__Bus Clouds	X Today	X Bus
X Program	__DB Clouds	__Tomorrow	__App
__Industry	X Ground		

Conceptual data model

Now let's build a CDM!

BACKGROUND

Based upon the prototype on the facing page, and a short overview of the Technics Publications business by its CEO, build a conceptual data model of their offerings. What camera settings should you use?

Your CDM:

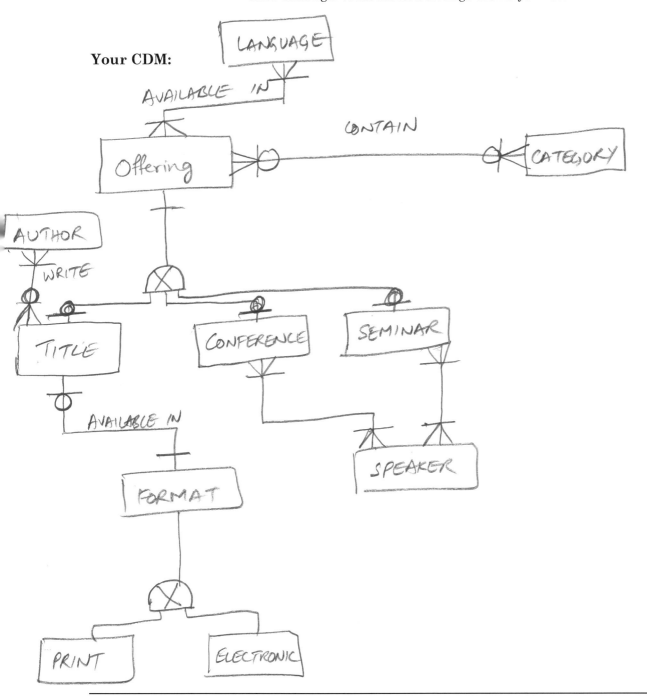

Logical data model

The logical data model is the business solution

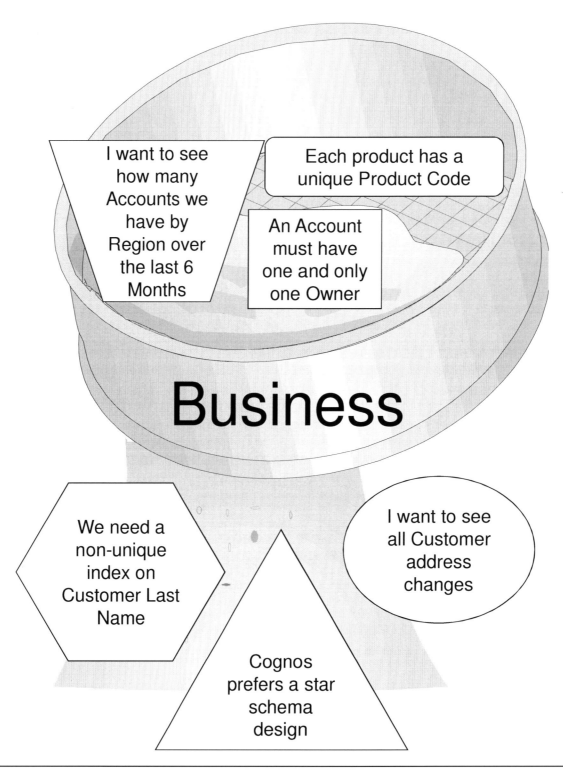

Logical data model

The logical data model is the business solution

DEFINITION

A logical data model (LDM) represents a detailed *business* solution. Business solution refers to focusing on solving a problem by understanding the characteristics of the data. The LDM is independent of technology. This means in capturing the business solution, we ignore all database and reporting software and hardware limitations. A logical data model of the order processing function for example, would look the same regardless of whether the application that is eventually built is built using IBM punch cards or Teradata!

RELATIONAL AND DIMENSIONAL

There are two types of logical data models: relational and dimensional. A logical relational model is a business solution of the data and rules of the *execution* of a business process. A logical dimensional data model is a business solution of the data and rules of the *evaluation* of a business process. Evaluation meaning the business is being monitored through metrics, such as Gross Sales Amount and Number of Customers.

WHAT IS LOGICAL?

Here are examples of what would be captured on an LDM:
- An Account must have one and only one Owner. (relational)
- I want to see how many Accounts we have by Region over the last 6 Months. (dimensional)
- No two products can have the same Product Code. (relational)
- I want to see Total Revenue by Customer, Product, and Region this Quarter as compared to last Quarter. (dimensional)

WHAT IS NOT LOGICAL?

Here are examples of what would <u>not</u> be captured on an LDM:
- We need a non-unique index on Customer Last Name, as this column will be retrieved often.
- Cognos prefers a star schema design so let's flatten each dimension into a single table.
- Microsoft Access will not be able to manage our Customer table so let's vertically partition contact details.
- I want to see all Customer address changes.

Logical data model
Logical relational data model

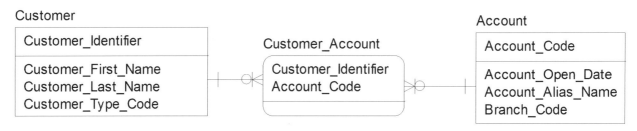

Customer

Customer_Identifier
Customer_First_Name Customer_Last_Name Customer_Type_Code

Customer_Account

Customer_Identifier Account_Code

Account

Account_Code
Account_Open_Date Account_Alias_Name Branch_Code

Logical data model
Logical relational data model

BACKGROUND

A logical relational model captures the business rules behind one or more business processes. For example, a logical data model of claims processing would capture the data elements that are mandatory on an insurance claim and the data rules on who can file claims (for example, a policyholder can file zero, one, or many claims).

This is the type of modeling that first came into being back in 1967 when Codd published his landmark paper distinguishing data from process. Relational models are heavily connected with mathematics. Set theory is the primary technique for building a logical relational data model. There are different levels of strictness within set theory, and each level represents another level of normalization, which will be discussed shortly.

❑ Business execution

❑ Scope = Concepts + Rules that describe a business process

❑ Designed to mimic how the business works

Logical data model
Logical dimensional data model

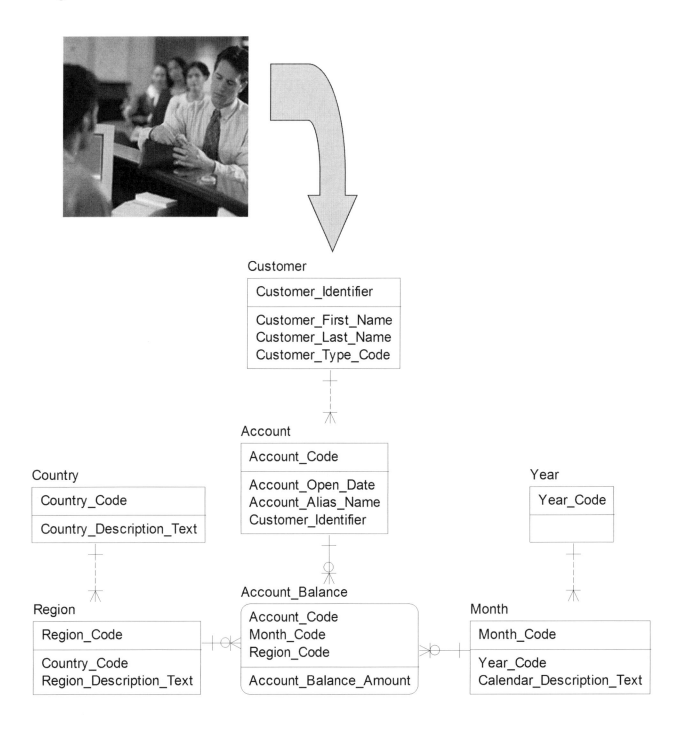

Logical data model

Logical dimensional data model

BACKGROUND

A logical dimensional data model is a business solution of the data and rules of the *evaluation* of a business process. Evaluation meaning the business is being monitored through metrics, such as Gross Sales Amount and Number of Customers.

A dimensional model is a data model whose only purpose is to allow efficient and user-friendly filtering, sorting, and summing of measures. The relationships on a dimensional model represent navigation paths instead of business rules as with the relational model. The scope of a dimensional model is a collection of related measures plus context that together address some business concern.

- ❑ Business evaluation (monitoring)
- ❑ Scope = Measure(s) + Context that address a business concern
- ❑ "Things I measure" go in the middle and "ways of looking at them" go in the surrounding boxes
- ❑ Designed for user friendliness and ease of manipulating numbers

Logical data model

Dimensional model components

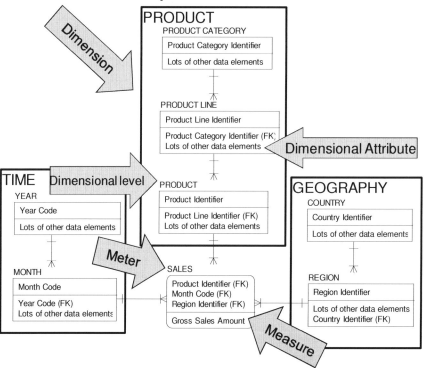

Requirements Statement	Measure(s)	Grain
I want to see total revenue by period, product, and region.		
Show me return amounts by order.		
What are gross sales of product brand for April?		
I need the percent change in member growth by demographics and month over the last five years.		
Get me the number of toys sold by child age appropriateness range, store number, and day of week.		

Logical data model

Dimensional model components

MEASURE

A measure is a data element that a set of business users need to 'see', and which can also be mathematically manipulated. Gross Sales Amount is an example of a measure.

METER

A meter is an entity containing a related set of measures. It is not a person, place, event, or thing, as we would expect on the relational model. Instead, it is a bucket of common measures. Common measures as a group address a business concern, such as Profitability, Employee Satisfaction, and Sales. The meter on the facing page is *Sales*. The meter is so important to the dimensional model that often the name of the meter is the name of the application.

DIMENSION

Things that get measured go in the middle and ways of looking at these things go in the surrounding boxes which are called dimensions. All the different ways of filtering, sorting, and summing measures are structured within dimensions. Dimensions are subjects whose only purpose is to add meaning to the measures. Dimensions are either hierarchies or lookups. *Gross sales amount* can be retrieved with any combination of month, product or region. Dimensions do not necessarily have to be hierarchies. Also, they usually appear in requirements statements after words such as 'by', 'for', and 'of'. If concepts are only related to each other through an event or transaction, then these concepts belong to separate dimensions.

DIMENSIONAL LEVEL

A dimensional level is one level within the hierarchy of a dimension, such as Country within the Geography dimension. Dimensional levels are created to allow easy drill up and down, and not built based on how the business works.

DIMENSIONAL ATTRIBUTE

The properties within a dimension, such as Country Code in the Country level of the Geography dimension. Note that sometimes numeric data elements can be dimensional attributes.

GRAIN

The grain is the meter's level of detail. It should be capable of answering all of the business questions within the scope of the dimensional model. It is generally a good practice to define the measures and grain as early as possible in the requirements process. The grain in this example is Month, Product, and Region.

Logical data model

Dimensional models are built for navigation

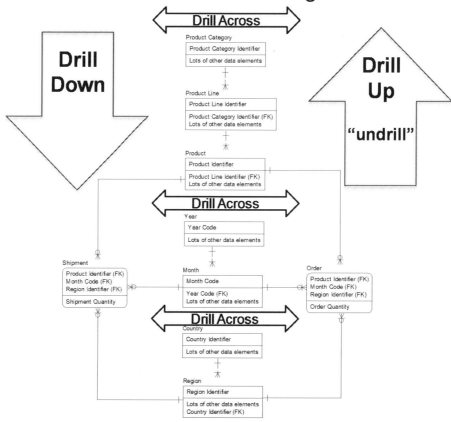

Requirements Statement	Drill Up, Drill Down, or Drill Across?
I want to see total revenue by period, product, and region. Then by country and year.	
What are gross sales of product brand for month? If I see a surprisingly low number I want to see gross sales by day.	
I need to see employee satisfaction by period, line of business and region. There is also a separate reporting initiative on employee productivity. I will eventually need to analyze the relationships between satisfaction and productivity.	

Logical data model

Dimensional models are built for navigation

DRILLING

Drilling is the process of changing the context of the measures. Changing the context means varying the dimensions that are used to view to measures, such as viewing the measures at a year level instead of at a month level, or at a region level instead of at a country level.

DRILLING DOWN

Drill down is when the context for the measure goes from higher level to lower level. For example, needing to see the measures at a month level and then at a day level.

DRILLING UP

Drill up is when the context for the measure goes from lower level to higher level. For example, needing to see the measures at a day level and then at a month level.

DRILLING ACROSS

Drill across is when there is a need to view measures from different dimensional models. The dimensions need to be built consistently to allow this type of analysis. Sometimes it is tempting to build relationships between meters or combine two or more meters into one. Be careful though – it is not worth the risk of erroneous results from measures that have no value for a given level of detail. For example, if there are order quantities yet no shipment quantities on a given day, what value would you put for shipment quantities? Zeros can cause confusion and the wrong results.

Logical data model
Measures monitor business processes

Transaction

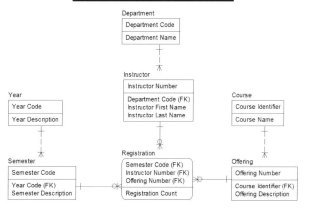

- Monitor events created from a business process
- Order Quantity, Customer Count, Gross Sales Amount
- Discrete
- Additive

Snapshot

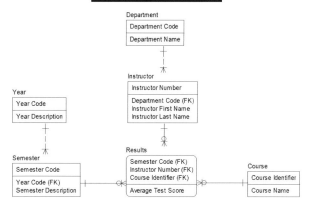

- Monitor impact of events created from a business process
- Account Balance Amount, Ozone Layer Thickness, Average Survey Question Score
- Compilation
- Semi- or Non-Additive

Accumulating

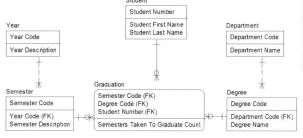

- Monitor progress of a business process
- Remaining Days Count, Settlement Days Count
- Progression
- Semi-Additive

Logical data model
Measures monitor business processes

BACKGROUND

Measures monitor business processes in one of three ways: Transaction, Snapshot, or Accumulating. It is important to understand the difference between these three because they have very different behaviors which can impact reporting results.

TRANSACTION

Transaction measures monitor events created from business processes, such as Order Quantity, Customer Count, and Gross Sales Amount. In terms of business intelligence maturity, transaction measures are a great place to start. An important property of transaction measures is that they are fully additive across all dimensions. For example, we can add Order Quantities at a day level to produce a meaningful result at a month level.

SNAPSHOT

Snapshot measures monitor the impact of events created from a business process, such as Account Balance Amount, Ozone Layer Thickness, and Average Survey Question Score. It is (at least theoretically) possible to produce snapshot measures by summing transaction measures. For example, to determine the Account Balance Amount we can sum the results of all individual account transactions such as deposits and withdrawals. However, would it be possible to determine the Ozone Layer Thickness by summing the cumulative results of everything that can affect the thickness of the ozone layer? Not likely. Snapshot measures are semi- or non-additive. As much as we would like to for example, we cannot sum our Account Balance Amount over a period of months (but we can sum our Account Balance Amount across all of our accounts).

ACCUMULATING

Accumulating measures monitor progress of a business process. Frequently the amount of days required to complete a certain business process step are tracked, such as Remaining Days Count or Settlement Days Count. What is very interesting about accumulating measures is that they can be updated. For example, today there are five days left and tomorrow there might be four days left to complete a business process step. Accumulating measures are semi- or non-additive, as we cannot sum the days remaining today and days remaining tomorrow and get a meaningful result.

Logical data model

Dimensional modeling Do's

Do only build dimensional models for measures	Customer Count ☑️ Top 50 Accounts 🚫 Actual comments 🚫 P & L statement 🚫
Do use relational for adhoc	"What products are for sale in the US?"
Do provide a richer grain if it will not impact performance, scope-creep, data quality validation, or user-friendliness	"Let's see, they want month level now, would they want day level a month from now?"
Do let creativity drive your dimensional structures	Brand Product Lot

Logical data model

Dimensional modeling Do's

DO ONLY BUILD DIMENSIONAL MODELS FOR MEASURES

Dimensional models should be built when there is a need to play with numbers. Metrics are data elements that can be mathematically manipulated, such as summed and averaged. The reason the dimensional model should be limited to numbers is because its design allows for easy navigation up and down hierarchy levels. By traversing hierarchy levels numbers need to be recalculated. For example, a Gross Sales Amount of $5 on a particular day might be $150 for a particular month in which that day belongs.

DO USE RELATIONAL FOR ADHOC

If there are no business requirements yet defined, dimensional models are difficult to build and will constrain the users. If the requirements are "Give me everything" or "I don't know what I want", it is a good practice to model relationally as this way the system has more flexibility. It is ok to use a dimensional structure however, when the adhoc requests are limited to the measures in a meter.

DO PROVIDE A RICHER GRAIN IF IT WILL NOT IMPACT PERFORMANCE, SCOPE-CREEP, DATA QUALITY VALIDATION, OR USER-FRIENDLINESS

This is a very controversial point among dimensional modelers. Do you design exactly for the questions the business needs answered, or do you add a more detailed grain to handle more detailed questions with the same measures? My belief is that it is ok to provide the richer grain as long as it does not impact performance (e.g. Will it take a lot longer to return results at a day level instead of at a month level?), scope-creep (e.g. Will the project take another month to finish because of the extra grain?), data quality (e.g. Will the business be responsible for checking an additional amount of data?), or user-friendliness (Is the dimensional model no longer easy to understand?). A critical factor in deciding whether to provide a lower grain (even down to an atomic grain) is architecture. Organizations with a bus architecture frequently go down to an atomic grain to avoid future rework.

DO LET CREATIVITY DRIVE YOUR DIMENSIONAL STRUCTURES

The relationships in a dimensional hierarchy do not have to mimic their relational counterparts. You can build dimensions to meet the way the business user thinks. For example, the concept of Lot includes product, shift, and plant. Yet in this example the business user wants to see Lot rolled up only under product.

Logical data model

Dimensional modeling Don'ts

Don't relate dimensions to each other	
Don't leave navigation paths empty	No optionality on relationships (lots of 99's!)
Don't mix grains	
Don't combine relational and dimensional on same <u>logical</u> model	

Logical data model

Dimensional modeling Don'ts

DON'T RELATE DIMENSIONS TO EACH OTHER

All relationships from dimensions must go through the meter. That is, you can never have relationships between different dimensions. You cannot show for example in the dimensional model on the facing page the rule capturing which products can be sold within which region, as this would require a relationship between *product* and *region*.

DON'T LEAVE NAVIGATION PATHS EMPTY

It is a good practice to avoid foreign key nulls on a dimensional model. If a specific Product does not roll up to a specific Product Line for example, using a default value instead of leaving the foreign key in Product empty will minimize reporting errors.

DON'T MIX GRAINS

Each meter must have a single grain. You want to avoid for example, relating both Product Line and Product to the Sales meter. The reason for this is when grains are mixed it becomes very easy to double and triple sum the measures. Creating summary tables or rolling up from Product to Product Line are better options.

DON'T COMBINE RELATIONAL AND DIMENSIONAL ON SAME LOGICAL MODEL

A logical model must be relational OR dimensional; it cannot have properties of both. When you get to the physical, one solution would be to combine them within the same schema. There are pros and cons though (like everything in the physical). Pros include meeting multiple needs within the same structure, cons include creating reporting complexity such as loops.

Logical data model
Additional dimensional modeling terminology

Conformed dimensions do not need to be identical with each other, they just need to be from the same superset.

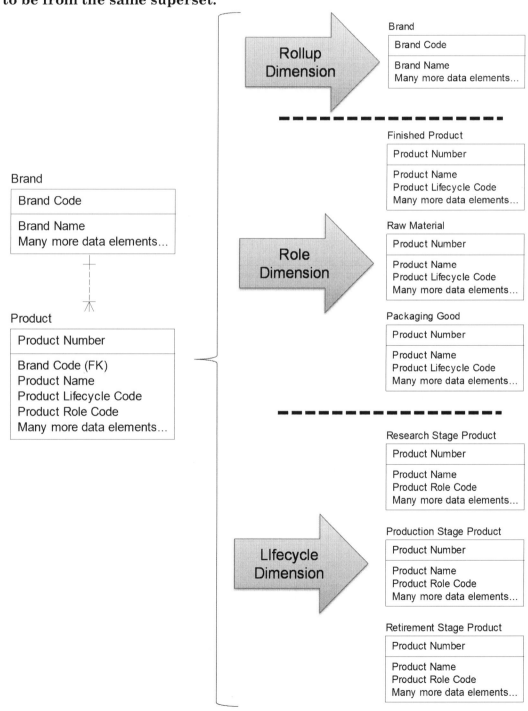

Logical data model
Additional dimensional modeling terminology

CONFORMED DIMENSION

A conformed dimension is a dimension that can be used by multiple business applications. It is built with the organization in mind, instead of just a particular application, to support drill across queries and enterprise consistency. In addition to using the exact dimension multiple times, conformed can also be a subset in the form of a rollup dimension (higher level in the hierarchy), a role dimension (more on roles in abstraction), or a lifecycle dimension (a certain phase of the dimension). Conformed dimensions allow the navigator the ability to ask questions that cross multiple marts.

FACTLESS FACT

A fact table that does not contain any facts is called a factless fact (good name, huh?). Factless facts count events by summing relationship occurrences between the dimensions. A factless fact in dimensional modeling has an associative entity as a counterpart on the relational modeling side. Usually on the physical dimensional model, there is a count measure added to the factless fact which always contains the value '1'. It is quicker to sum a field than it is easier to count relationship occurrences. Attendance is a factless fact in the model below. It resolves the many-to-many-to-many relationship that exists between the dimensions.

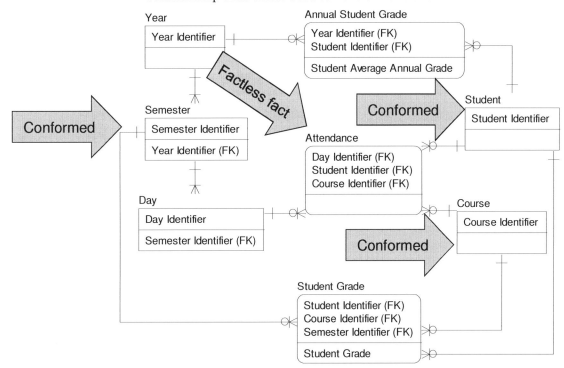

Logical data model

Additional dimensional modeling terminology

BRIDGE TABLE

A bridge table resolves a many-to-many relationship from the dimension to the meter. In other words, a given meter instance may need to refer to more than one dimension instance. Bridge tables can be shown as the typical resolution of a many-to-many on a logical, but may need a different physical structure depending on reporting tools.

BEHAVIORAL DIMENSION

A dimension that is created based upon measurements. Measurement ranges are grouped together in the dimension, such as by sales amounts or performance. This type of dimension is ideal when the users recognize the same set of bands, and they are stable. "How many customers do we have with sales between $500,000 and $750,000?" Student Grade Point Average Range is an example of a behavioral dimension in the model below.

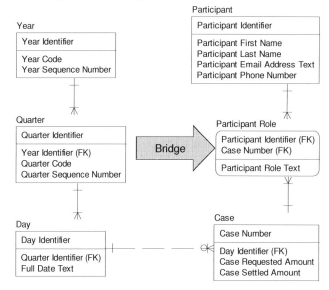

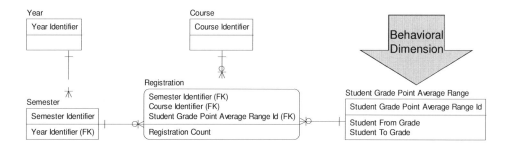

Logical data model

Thought-provoking dimensional model quotes

EARLY DIMENSIONAL BATTLES

Two articles that are worthwhile reads:
- "A Dimensional Modeling Manifesto", by Ralph Kimball (www.dbmsmag.com/9708d15.html)
- "The Problem with Dimensional Modeling", by Bill Inmon (www.billinmon.com/library/articles/artdimmd.asp)

The dimensional model is the only viable technique for achieving both user understandability and high query performance in the face of ever-changing user questions.
Ralph Kimball, DBMS Magazine, August 1997

The dimensional modelers have crafted a fine hammer. Now everything looks like a nail to them.
Bill Inmon, DM Review, May 1998

The data warehouse is nothing more than the union of all the data marts.
Ralph Kimball, Dec 1997

You can catch all the minnows in the ocean and stack them together and they still do not make a whale.
Bill Inmon, DM Review, May 1998

We want the Inmon approach in the Kimball timeframe.

Logical data model

Fun with dimensional modeling

My dimensional logical data model:

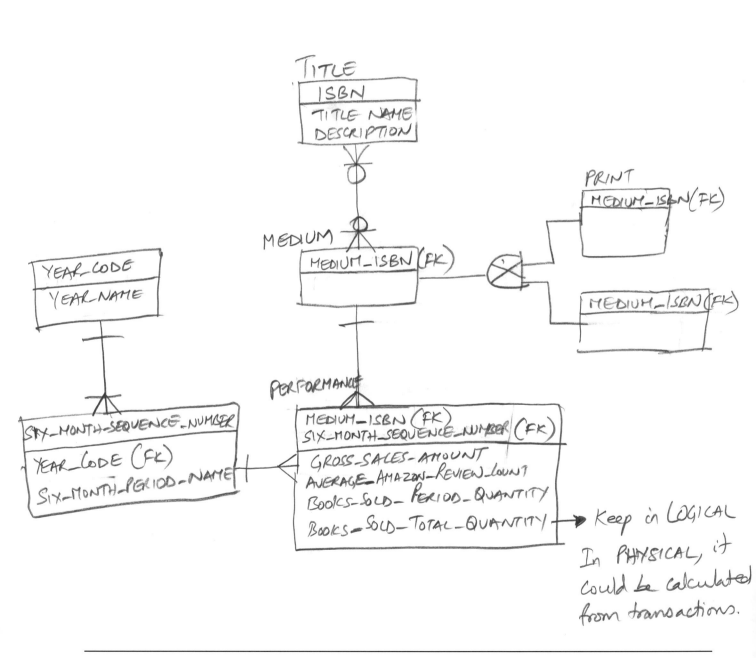

Logical data model

Fun with dimensional modeling

EXPLANATION Steve would like to reward the author of the *best* book every six months with a $100 Amazon gift card. Build him a dimensional logical model, based on this answer to an interview question, "What do you need?"

> An author can directly influence how well their title does across all medium (Kindle, print, etc.), and therefore every six months when I pay royalties, I would like to reward the author(s) of the title that does best across four key performance indicators: gross sales over last six months, the number of copies that sold (across all medium) over the last six months, the number of copies that sold (across all medium) since publication date, and the average Amazon review across all Amazon sites.

Logical data model

Relational modeling is all about normalizing

Logical data model

Relational modeling is all about normalizing

BACKGROUND

When I turned 12, I received a trunk full of baseball cards as a birthday present from my parents. I was delighted, not just because there may have been a Hank Aaron or Pete Rose buried somewhere in that trunk, but because I loved to organize the cards. I categorized each card according to year and team.

Normalization is a process of applying rules to render simple and stable something that is complex. I was normalizing the baseball cards according to year and team. We can normalize the data elements within our organizations, with a different set of rules yet with the same goal of simplifying and stabilizing something complex. Just as those baseball cards lay unsorted within that trunk, our companies have huge numbers of data elements spread throughout departments and applications. The rules applied to normalizing the baseball cards entailed first sorting by year, and then by team within a year. The rules for normalizing our data elements can be boiled down to sorting them according to their correct primary and foreign keys. The end result is a simple and stable view of how a business area or application works, or should work.

In analyzing the data elements for the correct primary and foreign keys, we are forced to understand the rules governing the way a business works. We analyze each data element in order to understand not only what it is, but also how it relates to every other data element in our model. By asking questions and finding answers, we develop a strong understanding of the content of the model.

To identify the correct primary and foreign keys, we need to apply a series of more granular rules. The rules are grouped into levels according to their specificity. Each level is considered a separate normal form, starting with first normal form, which is the least specific, and concluding with fifth normal form, the most specific. The full set of normalization levels is the following:
- first normal form (1NF)
- second normal form (2NF)
- third normal form (3NF)
- Boyce/Codd normal form (BCNF)
- fourth normal form (4NF)
- fifth normal form (5NF)

If a model is in 5NF, it is also in 4NF, BCNF, and so on. That is, the higher levels of normalization subsume the lower rules.

Logical data model

Normalization benefits

Logical data model
Normalization benefits

STRONGER UNDERSTANDING

Normalization forces us to understand the content of what is being modeled. We learn how each data element relates to every other data element. Before normalization, we may have a fairly good understanding of a particular data element (such as its definition and domain), but we most likely lack knowledge about the way in which this data element relates to every other data element in the model.

GREATER APPLICATION STABILITY

Normalization leads to a model that mimics the way in which the business works. As the business goes about its daily operations, the application receives data according to the rules that govern the business. The model underlying the application has been structured with the knowledge that these rules can govern, and therefore the system runs smoothly as long as the rules in the business match the rules documented throughout the normalization process. If, for example, more than one person can own an account, the model—and, therefore, the application—will accommodate this fact.

LESS DATA REDUNDANCY

Each level of normalization removes a certain kind of *data redundancy* from the model. Data redundancy occurs when the same information appears more than once in the same model. As redundancy is removed, changing the data becomes a quicker process, because there is less of it to update or insert. If *person's last name* appears four times on a model and Mary's last name changes, the application would have to ensure that all four occurrences of Mary's last name get updated correctly.

BETTER DATA QUALITY

By reducing redundancy and by enforcing data rules through relationships, the data are less likely to get out of synch or violate business rules. Also, a considerable number of rules, therefore, are enforced on the model. If an account must have at least one account owner, the model will prevent accounts with invalid or missing account owners from occurring.

FASTER BUILDING OF NEW MODELS

Normalization ensures correct primary and foreign keys. As a result, data elements are assigned to their most appropriate entity. All data elements that require *account identifier* for uniqueness appear in *account*. There is a degree of common sense applied to the place in which data elements reside, and therefore it becomes easier to identify and reuse normalized structures on a new model. The result is more consistency across models and less time developing applications.

Logical data model

Normalization in a nutshell

Make sure every data element is <u>single-valued</u> and <u>depends</u> <u>completely</u> and <u>only</u> on its primary key.

Single-valued:

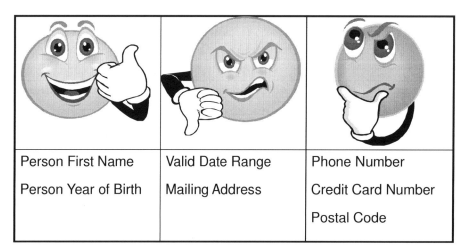

Person First Name Person Year of Birth	Valid Date Range Mailing Address	Phone Number Credit Card Number Postal Code

<u>Dependency</u> = no more than one value of each data element comes back for each primary key value

ISBN	Title	Subtitle	Author	Price
9780977140060	Data Modeling Made Simple	A Practical Guide for Business and IT Professionals	Steve Hoberman	$44.95
9781935504047	Building the Unstructured DW	Architecture, Analysis, and Design	Bill Inmon Krish Krishnan	$44.95
9781935504290	The Hidden Corporation	A Data Management Security Novel	David Schlesinger	$18.95

<u>Completely</u> = minimal primary key

<u>Only</u> = no derived data

Logical data model

Normalization in a nutshell

IN ONE SENTENCE   Normalization is a formal process of asking business questions. It is an organization technique. Chris Date once said, "The principles of database design are nothing more than formalized common sense." When we normalize we need to make sure every data element is single-valued and depends completely and only on its primary key. An easy (and humorous) way to remember this is with this slogan: "Every data element depends on the key, the whole key, and nothing but the key, so help me Codd!"

SINGLE-VALUED   A data element must contain only one piece of information. Sometimes it is easy to identify data elements that need to be split apart into two or more other data elements, and sometimes it can be tricky. Where it gets tricky is when the data element theoretically could be split apart, but does anyone from the business really ever need to see it in separate pieces? This is the important question to ask. Postal Code could be multi-valued for example, depending on your perspective of this field. The first digit in Zip Code for example, covers region. The next two digits specify a Facility (there are over 900 facilities in the United States).

DEPENDENCY   'Dependency' means that for a given primary key value, will it always return at most one of every data element that is identified by this key? If a Customer Identifier value of '123' for example, returns three Customer Last Names ('Smith', 'Jones', and 'Roberts'), this violates the dependency definition.

COMPLETELY   'Completely' means that the minimal set of data elements is present in the primary key. If for example, there are two data elements in an entity's primary key yet only one is needed for uniqueness, normalization requires this situation to be fixed.

ONLY   'Only' means that each data element must depend directly on the primary key and nothing else. For example, if derived data depends on the components of the data element and not directly on the primary key, this situation violates normalization.

Logical data model

Starting with chaos

Employee

Employee Identifier
Department Code
Phone Number 1
Phone Number 2
Phone Number 3
Employee Name
Department Name
Employee Start Date
Employee Vested Indicator

How do we identify an Employee? What about a Department? What do those phone numbers really mean?

Logical data model

Starting with chaos

BACKGROUND

The term *chaos* can be applied to any unorganized pile, including data elements. We may have a strong understanding of each of the data elements, such as their name and definition. We lack knowledge about how the data elements fit together. We understand each piece of the puzzle, but we do not yet understand the connections between the pieces. In our example with the business card, how do the data elements *address* and *telephone number* connect? Just as we need to determine the appropriate place for each piece within our puzzle, we need to determine the appropriate place for each data element within our model.

EXAMPLE

The Employee example on the facing page is our starting point. We might have great definitions for each of these data elements but what is lacking is how they relate to each other. Hence the chaos.

Always a good idea to look at some data!

Emp Id	Dept Cd	Phone 1	Phone 2	Phone 3	Emp Name	Dept Name	Emp Start Date	Emp Vested Ind
123	A	973-555-1212	678-333-3333	343-222-1111	Henry Winkler	Data Admin	4/1/2012	N
789	A	732-555-3333	678-333-3333	343-222-1111	Steve Martin	Data Admin	3/5/2007	Y
565	B	333-444-1111	516-555-1212	343-222-1111	Mary Smith	Data Warehouse	2/25/2006	Y
744	A	232-222-2222	678-333-3333	343-222-1111	Bob Jones	Data Admin	5/5/2011	N

Logical data model

Normalization steps

FIRST NORMAL FORM (1NF)

1NF states that every non-key data element must depend on its primary key. Another way of looking at 1NF is that for a given primary-key value, we can identify at most one of every data element that depends on that primary key. If a *customer identifier* value of 123 brings back both Smith and Jones as *customer last name* values, we have not identified the correct primary key.

Two activities will ensure that a valid primary key is assigned to each entity:
- Move repeating data elements to a new entity.
- Separate *multi-valued* data elements.

Employee

Employee Identifier
Department Code

Employee Phone Number
Organization Phone Number
Department Phone Number
Employee First Name
Employee Last Name
Department Name
Employee Start Date
Employee Vested Indicator

1NF Questions to ask:
- Does it make business sense to parse Employee Name?
- How about Phone Number? How about Employee Start Date?
- Is Phone Number really a repeating group? What is the significance of 1, 2, and 3?

SECOND NORMAL FORM (2NF)

2NF states that we must remove non-key data elements not dependent on the whole primary key. As we noted earlier, non-key data elements are all data elements except for primary, foreign, and alternate keys. A data element that depends on only part of the primary key is called a partial key dependency. We want to make sure our primary keys are correct, and we want to remove any partial key dependencies.

Logical data model

Normalization steps

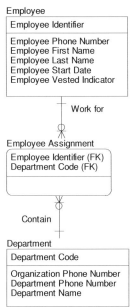

Employee

Employee Identifier
Employee Phone Number
Employee First Name
Employee Last Name
Employee Start Date
Employee Vested Indicator

Work for

Employee Assignment

Employee Identifier (FK)
Department Code (FK)

Contain

Department

Department Code
Organization Phone Number
Department Phone Number
Department Name

2NF Questions to ask:

- Can an Employee work for more than one Department?
- Is the Employee Start Date the date the Employee started work for the Organization or for the Department?

THIRD NORMAL FORM (3NF)

3NF states that we must remove non-key data elements not dependent on the whole primary key. A data element that depends on only part of the primary key is called a partial key dependency. We want to make sure our primary keys are correct, and we want to remove any partial key dependencies.

3NF Questions to ask:

- How do you derive Employee Vested Indicator?

Employee

Employee Identifier
Employee Phone Number
Employee First Name
Employee Last Name
Employee Start Date

Work for

Employee Assignment

Employee Identifier (FK)
Department Code (FK)

Contain

Department

Department Code
Organization Phone Number
Department Phone Number
Department Name

Logical data model

The Normalization Hike – 10 steps to the summit!

5NF **4NF**	10. Look for hidden business rules in the primary keys of entities with three or more identifying relationships
BCNF **3NF** **2NF**	9. Remove data elements not directly dependent on primary key 8. Remove data elements not dependent on whole primary key
1NF	7. Resolve many-to-many relationships 6. Remove repeating data elements 5. Separate multi-valued data elements 4. Validate initial rules 3. Refine scope 2. Sort data elements 1. Build a conceptual data model

Logical data model

The Normalization Hike – 10 steps to the summit!

JUST LIKE HIKING

There is a trail near our house we hike quite often. It takes time and effort to reach the summit, which is a beautiful lookout point over the surrounding towns and countryside. As data modelers, we go through a similar trek during every design. We start off at the bottom of a trail, ready for an adventure, with little understanding of how the data elements relate to each other. As we progress along the trail--huffing, puffing, and sweating--we get to higher elevations, and our view improves. We normalize--first normal form, second normal form, and third normal form--each additional degree of normalization taking us to a higher level of understanding. When we eventually arrive at fifth normal form, we have developed a complete understanding and appreciation of the application. The Normalization Hike is an informal set of rules for progressing to the lookout point in fifth normal form. One organization calls this mountain "Hober-Hill".

NORMALIZATION REALIZATION

Many years ago, I was normalizing trying to think through again how 2NF differs from 3NF. It suddenly occurred to me that it doesn't really matter what the difference is between 2NF and 3NF! What does matter is that model at the end is completely normalized. I started drafting informal (yet complete steps) to normalizing and I arrived at these 10 steps. The Normalization Hike's two main goals are:

- **Describe the levels of normalization in a succinct and practical way.** The Normalization Hike provides a less technical and theoretical explanation of normalization than your standard explanation. For example, this tool avoids words such as "determinate" and "join-dependency". There is no need in our finished design to distinguish 2NF from 3NF.
- **Provide the visual.** The Normalization Hike is a progression we go through whenever we do a design. Just like any long hike with a challenging destination, the more we progress along the trail, the greater our understanding and appreciation, and the more sweat and effort goes into arriving at the final normalized logical design. This visual is very effective for explaining the value of normalization and the effort that normalization requires.

REGARDLESS OF APPROACH

Whether you are starting with a list of source system data elements, a set of business requirements, or a completely clean slate, you can apply the Normalization Hike. Normalization is all about asking business questions – each level you go you ask more questions until there is complete business understanding.

Logical data model

One of my favorite topics: Desserts!

DESSERT DATA MART

A large restaurant chain wants to build a dessert data mart. Below are some sample desserts along with the general requirement of knowing which desserts are most popular. On the facing page is the list of data elements we will be normalizing. In a bottom-up modeling approach, this list would most likely come from source system files and tables. In a top-down modeling approach, this list would come from requirements documents and meetings with the business users.

Some sample desserts:

VANILLA BEAN CHEESECAKE
Cheesecake made with real vanilla beans, baked in a vanilla graham-cracker crust. Layered with white chocolate mousse and white chocolate shavings. Served with whipped cream and a fresh strawberry.

WARM APPLE CRISP
Apples simmered with cinnamon and brown sugar, then sprinkled with oatmeal crumbles. Topped with hot caramel sauce.

OREO® MADNESS
Two giant Oreo® cookies sandwiched with vanilla ice cream and topped with chocolate and caramel sauces.

Logical data model
Starting with Chaos – Data Element Listing

Name	Definition
Order	
Order Number	The unique number assigned to each order within a restaurant. This is usually but not always the number preprinted on the upper right hand corner of each check.
Restaurant Code	Links back to the restaurant and combines with Order Number to uniquely identify an Order.
Order Amount	The total amount of the order that the customer needs to pay for their meal. Does not include sales tax or gratuity.
Order Payment Time	When the order was paid. Notice this is not the time when the customers sat down. It is only when we received payment. (Format: YYYYMMDDHHMM)
Item Code 1	Links back to the Item.
Quantity 1	How many of the item has been ordered.
Total Amount 1	Calculated based on multiplying Quantity by List Price.
Item Code 2	Links back to the Item.
Quantity 2	How many of the item has been ordered.
Total Amount 2	Calculated based on multiplying Quantity by List Price.
Item Code 3	Links back to the Item.
Quantity 3	How many of the item has been ordered.
Total Amount 3	Calculated based on multiplying Quantity by List Price.
Dessert	
Dessert Code	The unique code assigned to each dessert. This value is independent of time, meaning the same dessert offered each October will have the same dessert code.
Dessert Name	The full name of the dessert that appears on the menu.
Dessert Description	The text that appears under the name on the menu describing the dessert.
Dessert Price Amount	The price of this dessert. This is the list price from the menu, not including tax.
Restaurant	
Restaurant Code	Unique identifier for a restaurant. Every manager knows their restaurant code.
Restaurant Region Code	The code within a region of the United States. EXAMPLE: NE = Northeast
Restaurant Region Name	The name of the region within the United States.
Restaurant Owner 1 Name	The owner of the restaurant.
Restaurant Owner 1 Ownership Percent	A number from 1 to 100, describing the percent that the owner owns in the restaurant.
Restaurant Owner 2 Name	The second owner, if applicable, for the restaurant.
Restaurant Owner 2 Ownership Percent	A number from 1 to 100, describing the percent that the owner owns in the restaurant.
Restaurant Owner 3 Name	The third owner, if applicable, for the restaurant.
Restaurant Owner 3 Ownership Percent	A number from 1 to 100, describing the percent that the owner owns in the restaurant.

Logical data model

1. Build a conceptual data model

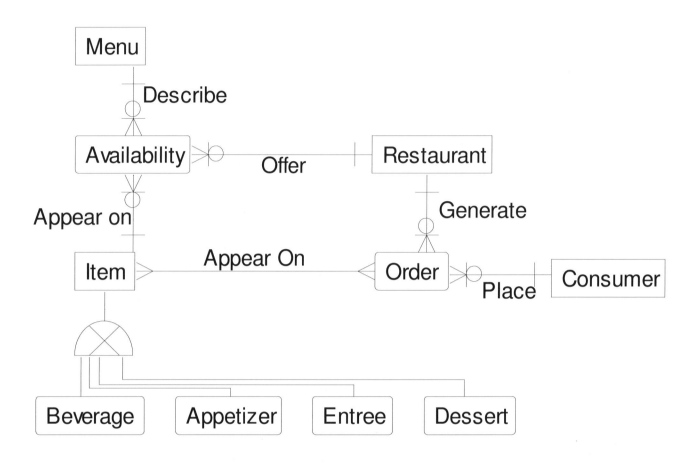

- Each Menu can describe many Items offered at many Restaurants.
- Each Restaurant may offer many Items on many Menus.
- Each Item may appear on many Menus in many Restaurants.
- Each Item may be a Beverage, Appetizer, Entrée, or Dessert.
- Each Restaurant may generate many Orders.
- Each Order must be generated by one Restaurant.
- Each Item must appear on many Orders.
- Each Order must contain many Items.
- Each Consumer may place many Orders.
- Each Order must be placed by one Consumer.

Logical data model

1. Build a conceptual data model

ABOUT THIS STEP

My first step is to build a conceptual data model. Note that the scope of this model might change (and most likely will) as we progress up the mountain. If we have an enterprise data model or an existing conceptual data model of this area, we need to use that instead of starting the conceptual data model from scratch.

MENU

A list of items available at a restaurant.

ITEM

An edible substance that is offered to consumers for a published price.

DESSERT

A course that typically comes at the end of a dinner, usually consisting of sweet food but sometimes of a strongly flavored one, such as some cheeses. Often, the dessert is seen as a separate meal or snack rather than a course, and may be eaten some time after the meal.

CONSUMER

An individual who dines in one of our restaurants.

ORDER

A request to purchase Items for an agreed price.

AVAILABILITY

Captures whether an Item is available for purchase from a given Menu in a given Restaurant.

RESTAURANT

An establishment for dining.

QUESTIONS AT THIS STEP

- What is within the scope of the project?
- What is outside the scope?
- What are the enterprise-wide definitions and terms?
- Where will the data come from?

Logical data model

2. Sort data elements

ABOUT THIS STEP

This step involves assigning data elements to conceptual entities, much the same way that I first sorted the baseball cards by year. In deciding which bucket an entity belongs in, also read and most likely refine the definitions. You do not have to get this step 100% right. If I chose incorrectly, this will get fixed as part of the normalization steps we will go through on the following slides.

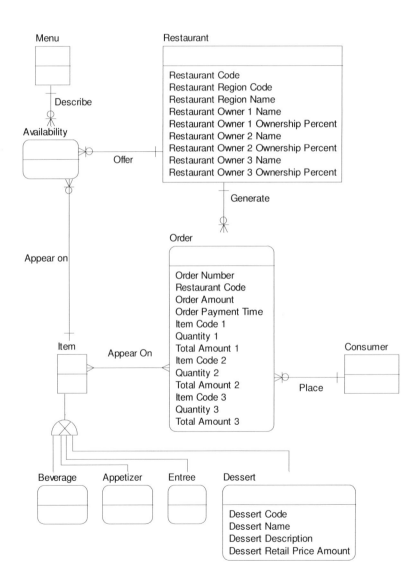

Logical data model

3. Refine scope

ABOUT THIS STEP
Those entities shown in gray have been considered out-of-scope in this example. Scope includes deciding what is at a supertype level and what is at a subtype level. Questions to answer at this step include:

- What is unique to desserts, and what is common across all items?
- Do we need to know anything about Menu? Is any information available?
- Do we need to just focus on desserts, or are other types of items also relevant?
- What is in scope? What is out of scope?

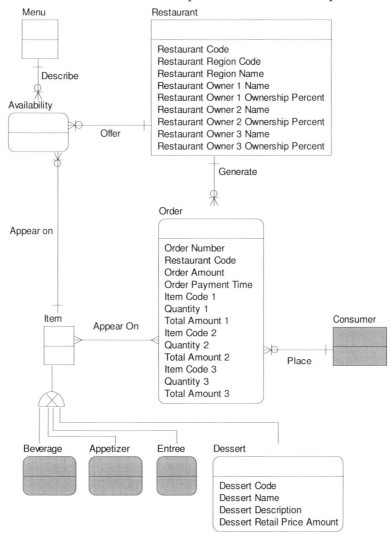

Logical data model

4. Validate initial rules

ABOUT THIS STEP   Business rules come from many places, such as from business users, source system experts, ERP packages and requirements documents. Business rules need to consistently represent either the way the world works today, or the way we are changing it to work in the future.

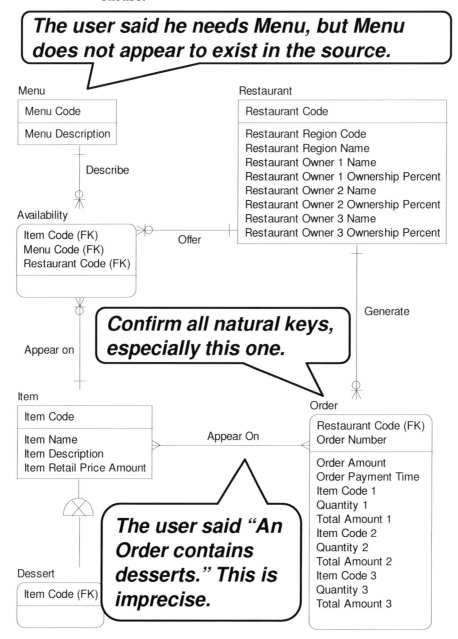

Logical data model

5. Separate multi-valued data elements

ABOUT THIS STEP *Multi-valued* means that within the same data element we are storing at least two distinct values. In other words, we need to ensure that each data element is atomic and contains only one value. For example, *name* may contain both a first name and last name. *First name* and *last name* can be considered distinct data elements, and therefore "John Smith" stored within *name* is multi-valued, because it contains "John" and "Smith." Enforce class words at this point. Class words are the high level domain of the data element, such as Name, Date, Identifier, and Code.

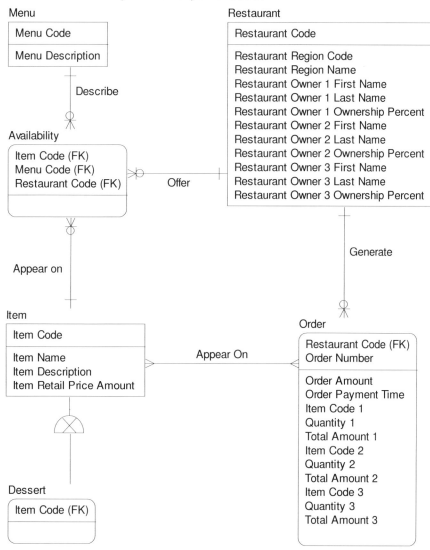

Logical data model

6. Remove repeating data elements

ABOUT THIS STEP

A repeating data element occurs when two or more of the same data element exists within the same entity. Repeating data elements fix the number of values an entity instance can have. If a data element is repeated three times in an entity, we can have at most three occurrences of this data element for a given entity instance. We cannot have four and we waste space if we have only one or two. Therefore, we need to move the data element that is repeating to a new entity.

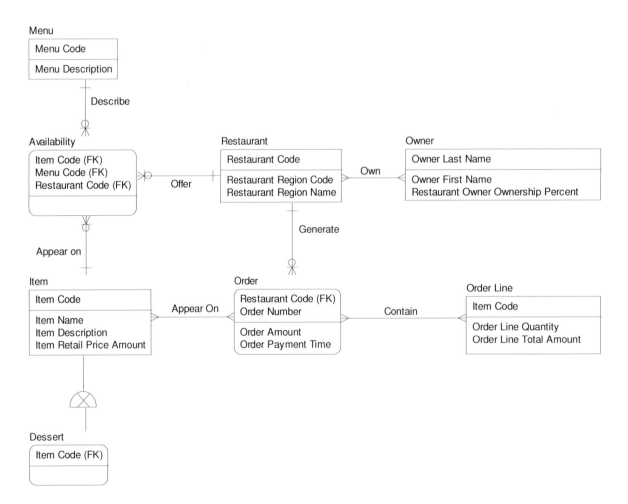

Logical data model

7. Resolve many-to-many relationships

ABOUT THIS STEP   Wherever there are many-to-many relationships on our model, we need to replace them with associative entities. Associative entities are entities that at a minimum contain the data element foreign keys from the two entities that made up the many-to-many relationship. In coming up with a label for one side of an associative entity, pretend the associative entity does not exist and create a label as if you were reading from one kernel entity to the other.

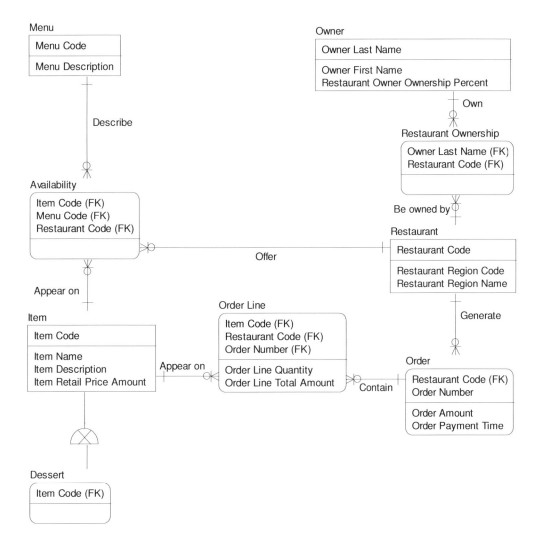

Logical data model

8. Remove data elements not dependent on whole primary key

ABOUT THIS STEP   We need to make sure that each entity contains the minimal primary key. Partial key dependencies must be resolved.

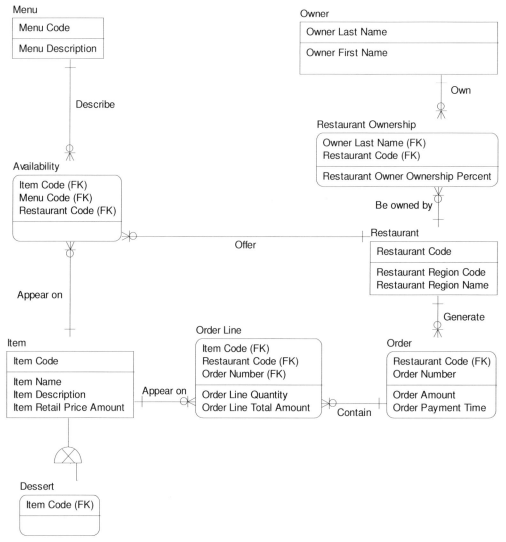

Logical data model

9. Remove data elements not directly dependent on primary key

ABOUT THIS STEP   Here we remove hidden dependencies. Each non-key data element must be directly dependent on the primary key, and not directly dependent on any other non-key data elements within the same entity. Violations most commonly fall into either derived data or decodes embedded with codes in non-lookup entities.

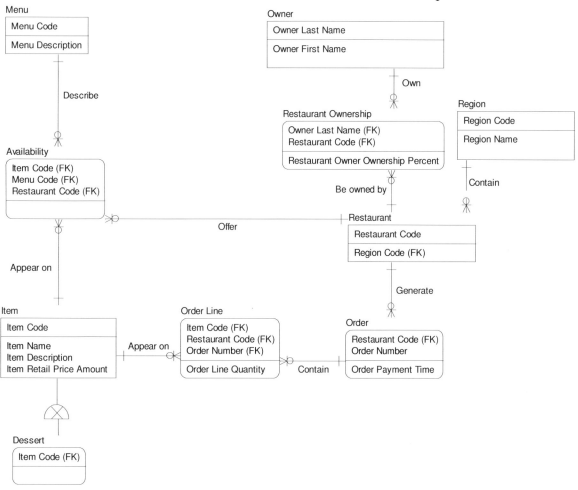

Logical data model

Covering Boyce-Codd Normal Form (BCNF) in steps 8 & 9

Student #	Course #	Student Last Name	Course Name	Date Enrolled
123	789	Jones	Literature	9/1/11
58	789	Smith	Literature	9/15/11
58	567	Smith	Acting 101	2/25/11
123	567	Jones	Acting 101	3/5/11
123	90	Jones	Juggling	4/1/11

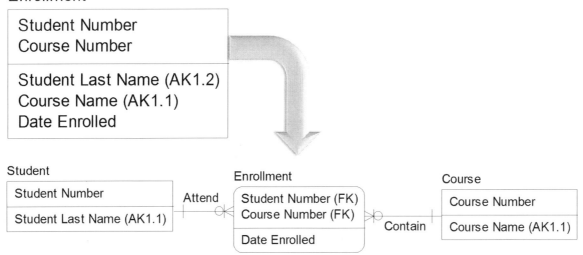

Enrollment

| Student Number |
| Course Number |
| Student Last Name (AK1.2) |
| Course Name (AK1.1) |
| Date Enrolled |

Student
| Student Number |
| Student Last Name (AK1.1) |

Attend

Enrollment
| Student Number (FK) |
| Course Number (FK) |
| Date Enrolled |

Contain

Course
| Course Number |
| Course Name (AK1.1) |

EXPLANATION OF BCNF

Raymond Boyce and Edgar Codd defined BCNF in 1974 to be a model with no overlapping candidate keys. A candidate key is one or more data elements that uniquely identify a record. Therefore a candidate key can be either a primary or alternate key (and nothing else). To arrive at an overlapping situation, at least one of the candidate keys must be composite. Composite means that the key contains more than one data element. 3NF applies the dependency rules to non-key data elements. BCNF applies the dependency rules to primary and alternate key data elements. If we simply ignore whether the data elements are key or not we can automatically apply 3NF and BCNF. Notice that in Steps 8 and 9 there is no reference to key or non-key. Therefore simply applying Steps 8 and 9 will cover 3NF and BCNF.

Logical data model

10. Look for hidden business rules in the primary keys of entities with three or more identifying relationships

ABOUT THIS STEP

Sometimes instead of a many-to-many relationship we might find ourselves with a many-to-many-to-many relationship (and even more complex). In these situations ask yourself "Are business rules hiding in the primary key of these complex associative entities?" If the answer is "yes", show these rules. Showing these rules increases model integrity and removes redundancies from the model. In the model below, there are rules between Menu and Restaurant and also between Menu and Item that we now show. Not all Restaurants offer all Menus and not all Menus contain all Items and these are the rules which are now enforced on the model.

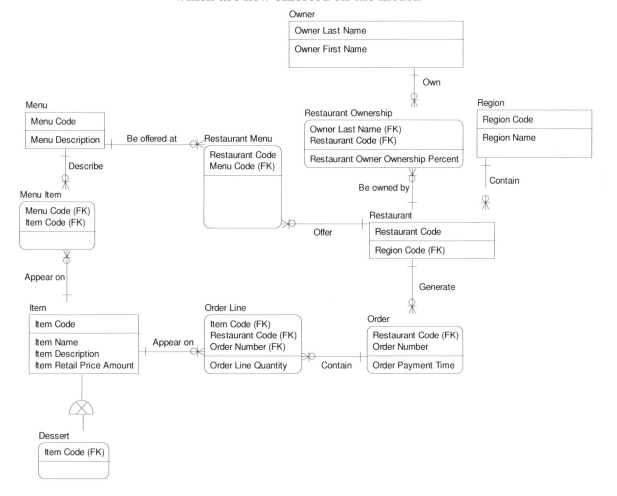

Logical data model

10. Look for hidden business rules in the primary keys of entities with three or more identifying relationships

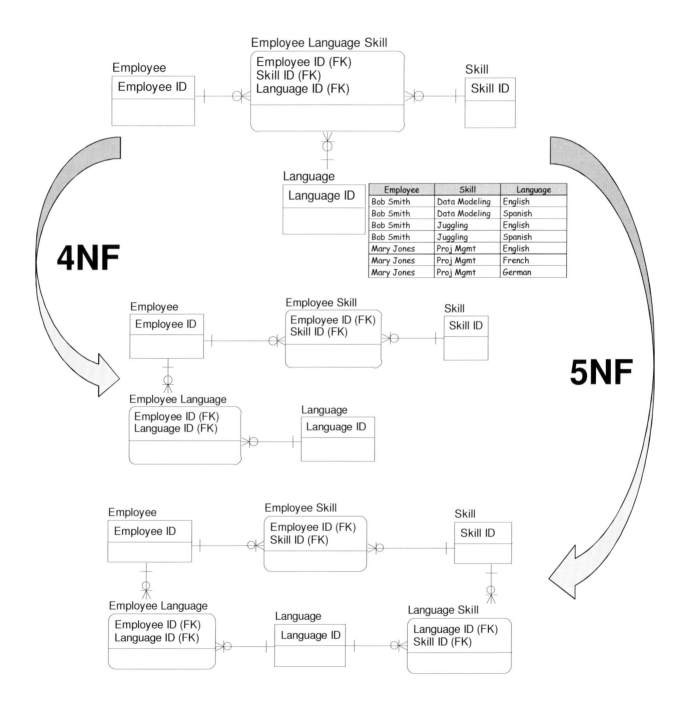

Logical data model

10. Look for hidden business rules in the primary keys of entities with three or more identifying relationships

EXAMPLE

By breaking apart Employee Language Skill we are able to remove data redundancies and enforce more business rules.

QUESTION AT THIS STEP

Are Language and Skills independent of each other?

ABOUT 4NF AND 5NF

Both Fourth Normal Form (4NF) and Fifth Normal Form (5NF) require showing the business rules in primary keys. 4NF requires showing any hidden rules and 5NF adds to this showing when everything relates to everything else. Examples of both are shown on the facing page.

As long as we show the rules in the large complex primary keys, our model is in 5NF.

Logical data model

Is there life after 5NF?

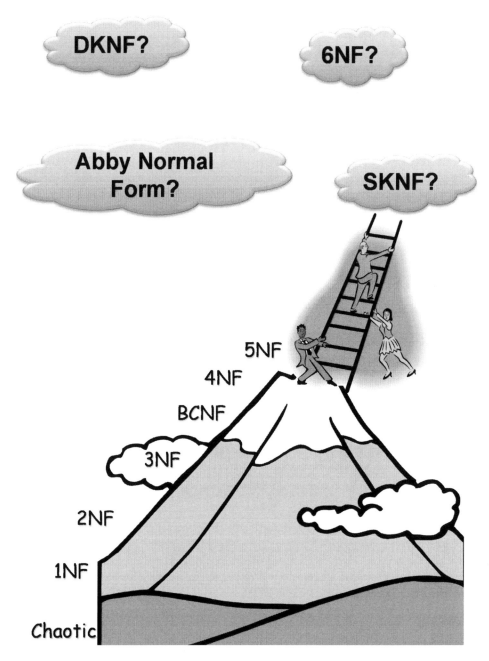

Make sure every data element is single-valued and depends completely and only on its primary key, and make sure there are no hidden business rules in any primary keys

Logical data model

Is there life after 5NF?

BACKGROUND

If you were going to summarize the different levels of normalization, you can cover up through 5NF with this statement: "Make sure every data element is single-valued and depends completely and only on its primary key, and make sure there are no hidden business rules in any primary keys."

There are higher levels of normalization than 5NF, such as Sixth Normal Form (6NF), Superkey Normal Form (SKNF), Domain Key Normal Form (DKNF), and others. 6NF was defined by Chris Date in 2002, and can informally be summarized as, keep breaking your data model down into smaller and smaller pieces until you can't put it back together again. This leads to a majority of entities having a single data element in their primary key and a single data element that depends on this primary key.

I have read the formal definition to SKNF (Date, 2004) several times and cannot decipher how it differs from 5NF. Chris Date says in his book *Database Design and Relational Theory*, "SKNF falls strictly between 4NF and 5NF."

DKNF was defined by Ronald Fagin in 1981 to require that all data elements have a precise domain set defined (could be a format, list, or range domain). This means for example, that if you have a data element called Gender Code, it is connected with an appropriate domain, such as {Male, Female}. I consider this a good modeling practice that should be applied for any type of modeling (not just through the normalization process).

Logical data model

Now let's build a LDM!

SAMPLE SURVEY:

COMMENT CARD

Server _____ Date _____

At Publyk House, we want you to have a truly enjoyable and memorable experience each time you visit our restaurant. Please take a moment to share your comments, suggestions or questions about our food, service and ambiance. Your comments are intended for private use to make your experience as enjoyable as possible.

Were you greeted properly?

POOR ☐ 1 ☐ 2 ☐ 3 ☐ 4 ☐ 5 EXCELLENT

How was your server?

POOR ☐ 1 ☐ 2 ☐ 3 ☐ 4 ☐ 5 EXCELLENT

How was the atmosphere?

POOR ☐ 1 ☐ 2 ☐ 3 ☐ 4 ☐ 5 EXCELLENT

How was the price/value?

POOR ☐ 1 ☐ 2 ☐ 3 ☐ 4 ☐ 5 EXCELLENT

What is your favorite menu item & your least favorite? Why? _____
_____
_____

How did you hear about us? _____

Do you plan on coming back? ☐ Yes ☐ No

Would you recommend us to a friend? ☐ Yes ☐ No

If you would like to receive promotional e-mails, including new menu items, please write down your email address:

_____

Your comments: _____
_____
_____
_____

Logical data model

Now let's build a LDM!

BACKGROUND

You are hired as the data modeler for an organization that is producing a survey data entry and analysis system. A sample survey form appears on the facing page. Using this form, your knowledge of surveys in general, and the results of a brief interview with the business user, build a fully normalized logical data model for the survey application.

SUBJECT

SUBJECT_ID

SURVEY

SURVEY_ID

MENU

SUBJECT_ID
MENU_ID
MENU-NAME

SERVER

SUBJECT_ID
SERVER_ID
SERVER_NAME

MENU ITEM

MENU_ID
MENU-ITEM_ID

INQUIRY

INQUIRY_ID
SERVER_ID
MENU-ITEM_ID

SURVEY RESPONSE

SURVEY_ID
INQUIRY_ID

RATING   QUESTION   FREE FORM

Physical data model

The physical data model is the technical solution

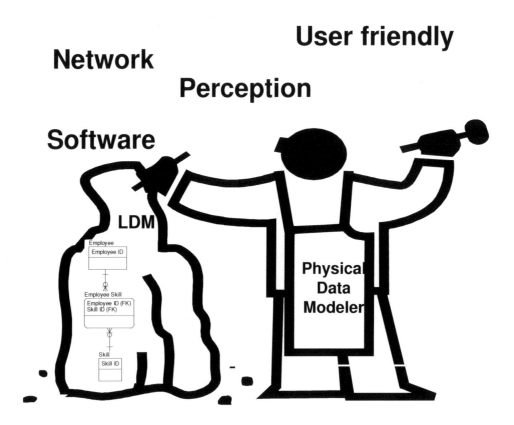

Physical data model

The physical data model is the technical solution

BACKGROUND

The logical data model represents a business solution. The physical data model represents a technical solution. The technical solution needs to take into account all of the software and hardware and networking components of the application. Physical data models based upon the same logical data model will vary greatly if one is for an application to be run on FoxPro and another is for an application to be run on Teradata, for example. A physical data model designed for FoxPro will vary quite a bit from its logical data model to compensate for the lack of scalability and robustness present in FoxPro. Teradata, however, is a much more powerful platform. As a result, a physical data model designed for Teradata will more closely resemble the logical.

A way to summarize the physical data model is that it accounts for the realities which are not of concern on the logical. The logical is an ideal model; the physical model incorporates compromises to make things work efficiently.

PHYSICAL DATA MODELING TECHNIQUES

Denormalization is a term that is applied exclusively to physical relational models, because you can't denormalize something unless it has already been normalized. However, the denormalization techniques can be applied to dimensional models as well, you just can't use the term 'denormalization'.

	Relational	Dimensional
Denormalization	☑	"Flattening"
Indexing	☑	☑
Views	☑	☑
Partitioning	☑	"Snowflaking"

Physical data model

Denormalization overview

Denormalization is the process of selectively violating normalization rules and reintroducing redundancy into the model.

| Pros | Cons |

Update time

Space

User friendly

Stunt growth

Performance

Data quality

In the reality in which we design very large databases, selective denormalization is often required – but it is important to initiate the design from a clean (normalized) starting point and use an engineering approach for choosing denormalization.

Stephen Brobst, Chief Technology Officer, Teradata

*Denormalization is dangerous.
Use it as a last resort.*

Physical data model

Denormalization overview

BACKGROUND

Denormalization is the process of selectively violating normalization rules and reintroducing redundancy into the model. Carefully and objectively consider what is gained and lost for each situation.

INTRODUCES DATA QUALITY PROBLEMS

By having the same value appear multiple times, we substantially increase opportunities for data quality issues when those values change. Imagine, for example, if we failed to update all *employee* instances of a company name change if company information is denormalized into *employee*. Also, denormalizing reduces the number of relationships and therefore reduces the amount of referential integrity on our model. Denormalizing company information into *employee* means we can no longer enforce the rule that each *employee* must work for a valid company.

STUNTS GROWTH OF THE APPLICATION

When we denormalize, it can become harder to enhance structures to meet new requirements, because before we add data elements or relationships we need to understand all the hidden rules on the physical data model that were shown on the logical data model. If *year* and *month* are denormalized into *day*, we can quickly retrieve year and month information when viewing a particular day. However, it would be very challenging to expand this denormalized time structure to add *week*, for example. We would have to sort through all the redundant data and then add new redundant data for *week*.

TAKES UP MORE SPACE

In a table with a small number of records, extra storage space incurred by denormalization is usually not substantial. However, in tables with millions of rows, every character could require megabytes of additional space. You might be thinking that space is cheap. It is true that space is becoming cheaper every day. However, I recently had to purchase more storage space for one of my projects, and I was amazed at the amount of time required to go through the budgeting process and red tape to actually receive the storage space. Space was cheap, but time was not.

INCREASES UPDATE, DELETE, AND INSERT TIME

When we repeat the value of a data element, we can usually reduce retrieval time. However, if we have to change the value that we are repeating, we need to change it wherever it occurs. If we are repeating *company* information for each *employee*, for example, and a *company name* value is changed, we will need to make this update for each *employee* instance that works for this company.

Physical data model

Denormalizing techniques

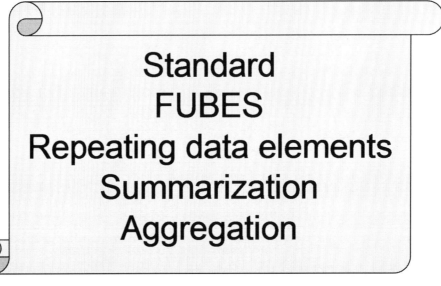

Standard
FUBES
Repeating data elements
Summarization
Aggregation

Normalized model with sample data

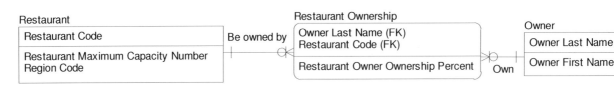

Restaurant

| Restaurant Code |
| Restaurant Maximum Capacity Number Region Code |

Be owned by

Restaurant Ownership

| Owner Last Name (FK) Restaurant Code (FK) |
| Restaurant Owner Ownership Percent |

Own

Owner

| Owner Last Name |
| Owner First Name |

Restaurant Code	Max	Region
AB	150	NE
RE	225	SW
DE	75	SE

Last Name	Restaurant Code	Owner Percent
Winkler	AB	50
Murphy	AB	50
Martin	RE	100
Martin	DE	50
Murphy	DE	50

Last Name	First Name
Winkler	Henry
Martin	Steve
Murphy	Eddie

Physical data model

Denormalizing techniques

BACKGROUND

Once you decide you need to denormalize, there are 5 different techniques that can be used.

STANDARD

The standard method is the most common of the five denormalization techniques. The parent entity in the relationship disappears, and all the parent's data elements and relationships are moved to the child entity. Recall the child entity is on the many side of the relationship and contains the foreign key back to the parent entity, which appears on the one side of the relationship.

FUBES

FUBES (fold up but easily separate) is an acronym I made up for a technique that combines the standard method of denormalizing with also allowing access to just the parent data elements. There is an additional data element that contains a level code and additional instances for each of the parents.

REPEATING DATA ELEMENTS

In the repeating data elements technique, the same data element or group of data elements is repeated two or more times in the same entity. Also known as an *array*, a repeating group requires fixing the number of times something can occur.

SUMMARIZATION

Summarization is used when there is a need to report on higher levels of granularity than what is captured on the logical data model.

AGGREGATION

Aggregation is when you are combining two or more entities into one where a one-to-one relationship exists between the entities. You do not incur the redundancy from the Standard technique.

Physical data model

Denormalization technique: Standard

Option 1: Get rid of Restaurant

Restaurant Ownership

| Owner Last Name (FK) |
Restaurant Code
Restaurant Owner Ownership Percent
Restaurant Maximum Capacity Number
Region Code

Own

Owner

Owner Last Name
Owner First Name

Last Name	Restaurant Code	Owner Percent	Max	Region
Winkler	AB	50	150	NE
Murphy	AB	50	150	NE
Martin	RE	100	225	SW
Martin	DE	50	75	SE
Murphy	DE	50	75	SE

Last Name	First Name
Winkler	Henry
Martin	Steve
Murphy	Eddie

Option 2: Get rid of Owner

Restaurant

Restaurant Code
Restaurant Maximum Capacity Number
Region Code

Be owned by

Restaurant Ownership

| Owner Last Name |
Restaurant Code (FK)
Restaurant Owner Ownership Percent
Owner First Name

Restaurant Code	Max	Region
AB	150	NE
RE	225	SW
DE	75	SE

Last Name	Restaurant Code	Owner Percent	First Name
Winkler	AB	50	Henry
Murphy	AB	50	Eddie
Martin	RE	100	Steve
Martin	DE	50	Steve
Murphy	DE	50	Eddie

Physical data model

Denormalization technique: Standard

BACKGROUND   Standard denormalization is the traditional way of denormalizing. The parent data elements and relationships get folded up into the child entity.

WHEN TO USE   The standard way of denormalizing is ideal for the following situations:
- When you need to maintain the flexibility that existed on the normalized model. We still could support the many-to-many between Restaurant and Owner.
- When a majority of the time the retrieval required is only at the lowest level.
- When a user-friendly structure is required. At least one relationship has been removed making it less complicated for users to navigate (assuming users have access to the underlying structures which is a large assumption).

EXAMPLE   There are three options, two on the facing page and one below.

Option 3: Get rid of both Restaurant and Owner

Restaurant Ownership

| Owner Last Name |
| Restaurant Code |

| Restaurant Owner Ownership Percent |
| Restaurant Maximum Capacity Number |
| Region Code |
| Owner First Name |

Last Name	Restaurant Code	Owner Percent	Max	Region	First Name
Winkler	AB	50	150	NE	Henry
Murphy	AB	50	150	NE	Eddie
Martin	RE	100	225	SW	Steve
Martin	DE	50	75	SE	Steve
Murphy	DE	50	75	SE	Eddie

We can model Option 3 as a *document*, e.g. MongoDB:

```
db.RestaurantOwnership.insert(
{"OwnerLastName" : "Winkler",
"RestaurantCode" : "AB",
"RestaurantOwnerOwnershipPercent" : "50",
"RestaurantMaximumCapacityNumber" : "150",
"RegionCode" : "NE",
"OwnerFirstName" : "Henry"},
{"OwnerLastName" : "Murphy",
"RestaurantCode" : "AB",
"RestaurantOwnerOwnershipPercent" : "50",
"RestaurantMaximumCapacityNumber" : "150",
"RegionCode" : "NE",
"OwnerFirstName" : "Eddie"})
```

Physical data model

Denormalization technique: FUBES

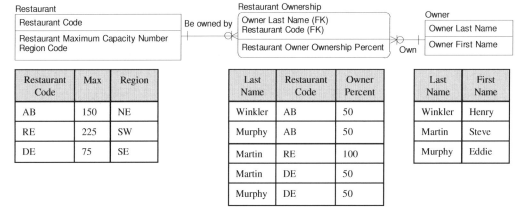

Restaurant Ownership

Restaurant Ownership Identifier
Restaurant Code Restaurant Owner Ownership Percent Restaurant Maximum Capacity Number Region Code Owner Last Name Owner First Name **Restaurant Ownership Level Code**

Rest Owner-ship ID	Rest Code	Owner Percent	Max	Region	Last Name	First Name	Level Code
123	AB	50	150	NE	Winkler	Henry	Ownership
124	AB	50	150	NE	Murphy	Eddie	Ownership
125	RE	100	225	SW	Martin	Steve	Ownership
126	DE	50	75	SE	Martin	Steve	Ownership
127	DE	50	75	SE	Murphy	Eddie	Ownership
128	AB		150	NE			Rest
129	RE		225	SW			Rest
130	DE		75	SE			Rest
131					Winkler	Henry	Owner
132					Murphy	Eddie	Owner
133					Martin	Steve	Owner

Physical data model

Denormalization technique: FUBES

BACKGROUND

Fold Up But Easily Separate (FUBES) is when you denormalize two or more tables together, yet still have the ability to access individual instances from each of the entities. You can use FUBES when you would like everything from the Standard option, but also want to be able to access all entities instances that have been denormalized. FUBES requires that a level or type code be added to the entity so that each of the entity instances can be retrieved.

WHEN TO USE

FUBES should be chosen when there is value in denormalizing yet there is a still a need to access parent instances. Having an instance for each parent allows us to achieve better report performance as we can directly tie to parent levels without having to roll up from the child. We can store sales at a year level for example and save the query time of summarizing daily level sales up into a year level.

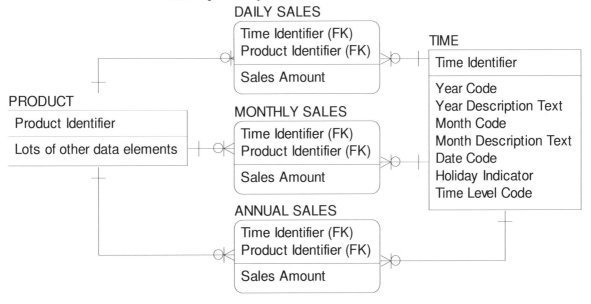

Time Identifier	Year Code	Month Code	Date Code	Time Level Code
1	2011			Year
2	2011	Jan		Month
3	2011	June		Month
4	2011	June	6/1/2011	Date
5	2011	June	6/1/2011	Date

Physical data model

Denormalization technique: Repeating data elements

BACKGROUND

The repeating data elements technique is when you copy one or more data elements from one entity into one or more other entities. It is done primarily for performance because by repeating data elements across entities we can reduce the number of joins needed to return results.

WHEN TO USE

The repeating-group technique is useful in the following situations:

- **When it makes more sense to keep the parent entity instead of the child entity.** It can make more sense when the parent entity is going to be used more frequently than the child or if there are rules and data elements useful to preserve in the parent entity format.
- When an entity instance will never exceed the fixed number of data elements added.
- **When you need a spreadsheet.** We would repeat the one or more data elements that appear in the spreadsheet column headers. This can lead to producing the report in less time than by stringing together a large number of entity instances.

Option 1:

Owner

Owner Last Name
Owner First Name Restaurant Code 1 Restaurant Maximum Capacity Number 1 Region Code 1 Restaurant Owner Ownership Percent 1 Restaurant Code 2 Restaurant Maximum Capacity Number 2 Region Code 2 Restaurant Owner Ownership Percent 2 Restaurant Code 3 Restaurant Maximum Capacity Number 3 Region Code 3 Restaurant Owner Ownership Percent 3

Option 2:

Restaurant

Restaurant Code
Restaurant Maximum Capacity Number Region Code Restaurant Owner Ownership Percent 1 Owner Last Name 1 Owner First Name 1 Restaurant Owner Ownership Percent 2 Owner Last Name 2 Owner First Name 2 Restaurant Owner Ownership Percent 3 Owner Last Name 3 Owner First Name 3

Physical data model

Denormalization technique: Repeating data elements

EXAMPLE

At the end of a given month, the oldest value is removed and a new value is added. This is called a rolling 12 months. Faster performance and a more user-friendly structure led us to adding repeating groups in this example and purposely violating 1NF.

DIMENSIONAL
TECHNIQUE

In dimensional modeling terms, this is called a pivoted fact table. A set of metrics become a single row instead of multiple rows. Very similar to a spreadsheet.

SALES SUMMARY REPORT

| Product Identifier |
| Month Code |
| Year Code |

| Current Month - 1 Total Sales Amount |
| Current Month - 2 Total Sales Amount |
| Current Month - 3 Total Sales Amount |
| Current Month - 4 Total Sales Amount |
| Current Month - 5 Total Sales Amount |
| Current Month - 6 Total Sales Amount |
| Current Month - 7 Total Sales Amount |
| Current Month - 8 Total Sales Amount |
| Current Month - 9 Total Sales Amount |
| Current Month - 10 Total Sales Amount |
| Current Month - 11 Total Sales Amount |
| Current Month - 12 Total Sales Amount |
| Lots of other sales report data elements |

Physical data model

Denormalization technique: Summarization

BACKGROUND A summary table contains information at a higher level of granularity than exists in the business. In our restaurant and owner example, we are storing quantities instead of the actual values.

WHEN TO USE Extra redundancy from the summary tables not only takes up more space but leads to extra development effort. It takes a greater time of the batch processing window to populate summary tables, so make sure the value is greater than the cost. Summary structures are more common with transaction data.

Restaurant

Restaurant Code
Restaurant Maximum Capacity Number Region Code Owner Quantity

Restaurant Code	Maximum	Region	Owner Quantity
AB	150	NE	2
RE	225	SW	1
DE	75	SE	2

Owner

Owner Last Name
Owner First Name Restaurant Quantity

Last Name	First Name	Restaurant Quantity
Winkler	Henry	1
Martin	Steve	2
Murphy	Eddie	2

Physical data model

Denormalization technique: Summarization

EXAMPLE

The summary tables in this example allow the user to answer high-level questions without spending time figuring out how to do it with very low-level tables. The response time is also much quicker because of the highly summarized nature of the data. The only difference between a summary fact table and a base fact table is the level of grain. A base fact table contains the lowest level within a data mart, and a summary table contains a higher level of grain.

HIGHEST LEVEL OF SUMMARIZATION

The highest level of summarization is to ignore one or more dimensions altogether. In the example below, if the user ignores the time dimension and just queries on the sales of products, this would be an example of a very high level of summarization.

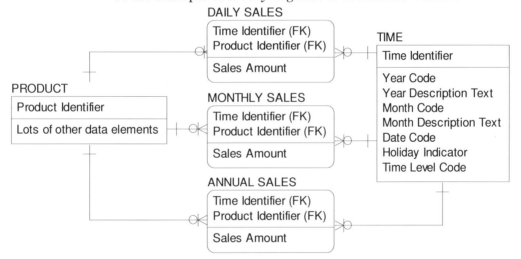

You can also summarize by ignoring one or more dimensions

Physical data model
Denormalization technique: Aggregation

Relational example:

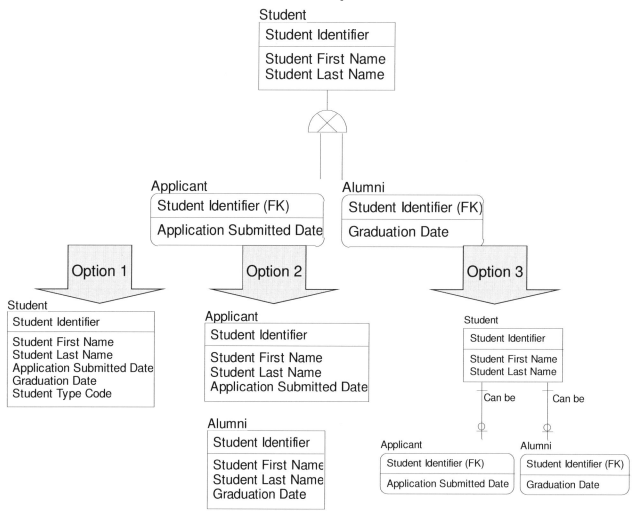

Physical data model
Denormalization technique: Aggregation

BACKGROUND

Aggregation is when you combine two or more tables together that have a one-to-one relationship. Option 1 is called rolling up, Option 2 is rolling down, and Option 3 which is identity (not a aggregation technique but shown here for completeness), is when the subtype symbol is replaced with one-to-one relationships.

DIMENSIONAL TECHNIQUE

A merged fact is when fact tables from different marts are combined into a single structure (see below for example). Fact tables with the same grain are combined to reduce database overhead and allow users to answer even more business questions. If fact tables do not have the same grain, or are sparsely populated, zeros (or worse nulls) can appear as measurement values which can cause confusion on the reporting side. "Why are there zero shipments on Tuesday, April 1st, 2012?"

WHEN TO USE

Rolling up is ideal when extra flexibility is required or when the subtypes are representing a lifecycle where subtypes can move through the different stages in the lifecycle. Rolling down is usually ideal for reporting situations where the supertype can be too generic. It is also used in situations where there are very little common properties across the subtypes. Identity preserves the most rules however performance can suffer.

Dimensional example:

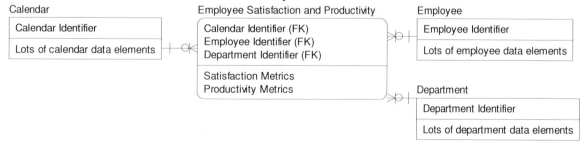

Fun with aggregation

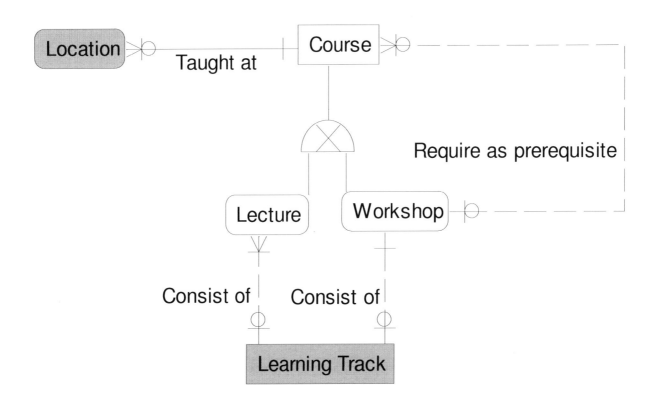

Rolling Down

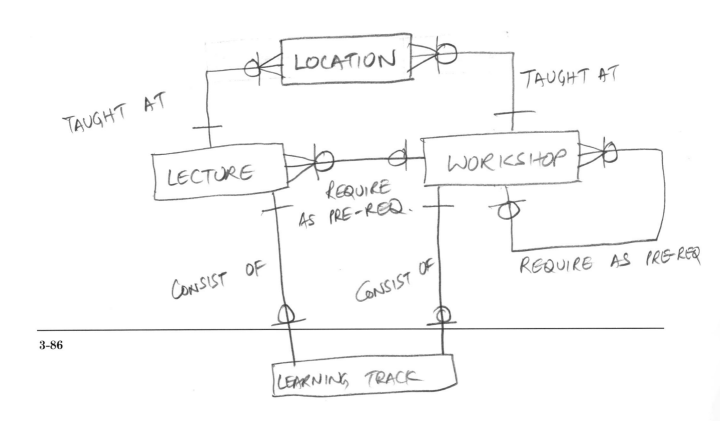

Fun with aggregation

CHALLENGE

Rolling down: Remove the supertype entity and copy all of the data elements and relationships from the supertype to each of the subtypes.

Rolling up: Remove the subtypes and copy all of the data elements and relationships from each subtype to the supertype. Also add a type code to distinguish the subtypes.

Identity: Convert the subtype symbol into a series of one-to-one relationships, connecting the supertype to each of the subtypes.

For this Challenge, create these three physical data models.

Rolling Up

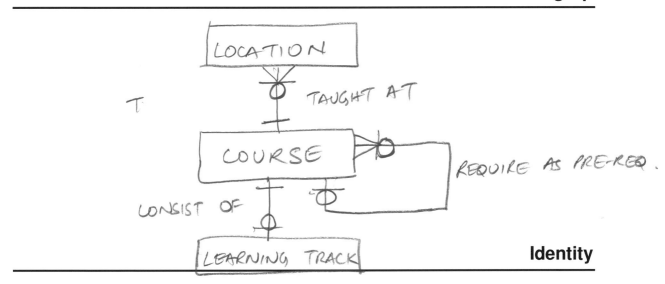

Identity

Physical data model

Indexing

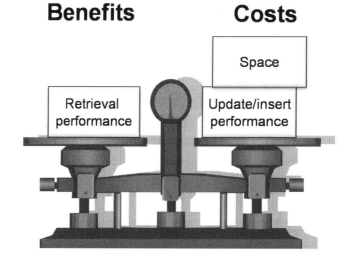

An index is a value and a pointer to instances of that value in a table.

Benefits   **Costs**

Space

Retrieval performance   Update/insert performance

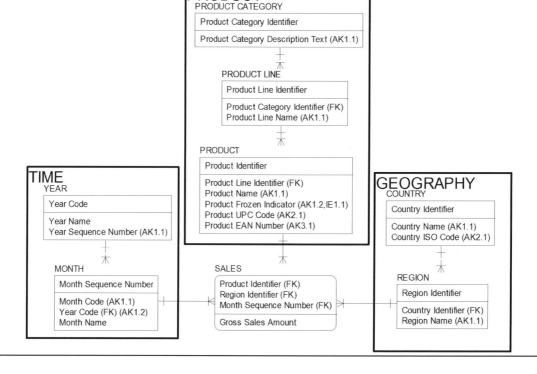

PRODUCT
PRODUCT CATEGORY

Product Category Identifier
Product Category Description Text (AK1.1)

PRODUCT LINE

Product Line Identifier
Product Category Identifier (FK) Product Line Name (AK1.1)

PRODUCT

Product Identifier
Product Line Identifier (FK) Product Name (AK1.1) Product Frozen Indicator (AK1.2,IE1.1) Product UPC Code (AK2.1) Product EAN Number (AK3.1)

TIME
YEAR

Year Code
Year Name Year Sequence Number (AK1.1)

MONTH

Month Sequence Number
Month Code (AK1.1) Year Code (FK) (AK1.2) Month Name

SALES

Product Identifier (FK) Region Identifier (FK) Month Sequence Number (FK)
Gross Sales Amount

GEOGRAPHY
COUNTRY

Country Identifier
Country Name (AK1.1) Country ISO Code (AK2.1)

REGION

Region Identifier
Country Identifier (FK) Region Name (AK1.1)

Physical data model

Indexing

EXPLANATION An index is a value and a pointer to instances of that value in a table.

EXAMPLE In the example on the facing page, the primary, alternate and foreign keys were indexed. Note that if a key contains more than 1 data element, they are indexed by the order in which the keys appear. A composite index is an index on at least two data elements. The order the data elements appear is the order in most cases on how they are indexed. In the Product table for example, there is a composite index on the alternate key Product Name and Product Frozen Indicator.

Here are some questions that can be asked against this structure:
- What was our Gross Sales Amount for all Frozen products from the Northeast in January 2007?
- What 3 products generated the most sales from Canada in 2008? Show their UPC.
- What was the Gross Sales Amount for our Dark Chocolate line in 2007?

Physical data model

Views

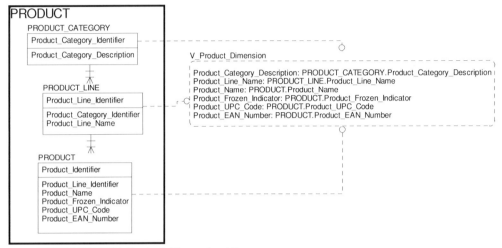

CREATE VIEW V_Product_Dimension AS
        SELECT PRODUCT_CATEGORY.Product_Category_Description,
PRODUCT_LINE.Product_Line_Name, PRODUCT.Product_Name,
PRODUCT.Product_Frozen_Indicator, PRODUCT.Product_UPC_Code,
PRODUCT.Product_EAN_Number
        FROM PRODUCT_CATEGORY, PRODUCT_LINE, PRODUCT
        WHERE PRODUCT_CATEGORY.Product_Category_Identifier =
PRODUCT_LINE.Product_Category_Identifier AND
PRODUCT_LINE.Product_Line_Identifier = PRODUCT.Product_Line_Identifier

Benefits

- No denormalization of the PDM
- Minimizes ETL load time while presenting multiple fresh views
- Multiple views of the same data, without physical data replication

Costs

- As the complexity of the view definitions increases, performance and usability decreases
- Denormalization usually better performance

Physical data model

Views

BACKGROUND

A view is a virtual table. It is a "view" into one or many tables or other views that contain or reference the actual data elements. We can use views in almost all situations where we are considering denormalization. Views can offer the same benefits as denormalization *without the drawbacks associated with data redundancy and loss of referential integrity*. A view can provide user-friendly structures over a normalized structure, thereby preserving flexibility and referential integrity. A view will keep the underlying normalized model intact and at the same time present a denormalized or summarized view of the world to the business.

STANDARD VIEW

The standard view runs the SQL to retrieve data at the point when a data element in the view is requested. It can take quite a bit of time to retrieve data depending on the complexity of the SQL and the data volume.

INSTANTIATED VIEW

Instantiated views can match and even sometimes beat retrieval speed from actual tables because they are generated at some predetermined time and stored in system cache.

Every database package has a different name for this type of view. For example,
- Oracle: Materialized view
- DB/2: Materialized query table
- SQL server: Indexed views
- Teradata: Join index (or aggregate join index)

EXAMPLE

A view is shown on the model as a rectangle with rounded corners and outlined by a dotted line. There is SQL query language behind the view.

Physical data model

Partitioning

Partitioning is when a database table is split up into two or more tables. Vertical partitioning is when data elements are split up, and horizontal is when rows are split up.

SALES

Product Identifier
Month Code
Year Code
Region Identifier
Gross Sales Amount

Could horizontally partition by Year

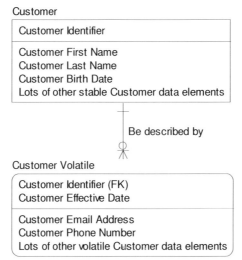

Customer

Customer Identifier
Customer First Name
Customer Last Name
Customer Birth Date
Lots of other stable Customer data elements

Be described by

Customer Volatile

Customer Identifier (FK)
Customer Effective Date
Customer Email Address
Customer Phone Number
Lots of other volatile Customer data elements

Could vertically partition by moving volatile data elements into their own table

Physical data model

Partitioning

BACKGROUND

Partitioning is when a database table is split up into two or more tables. Vertical partitioning is when data elements are split up and horizontal is when rows are split up. It is common for both horizontal and vertical to be used together. That is, when splitting rows apart we in many cases learn that certain data elements only belong with one set of rows.

Partitioning can be used as a reactive technique, meaning that even after an application goes live, the designer might choose to add partitioning after monitoring performance and space and determining that an improvement is needed.

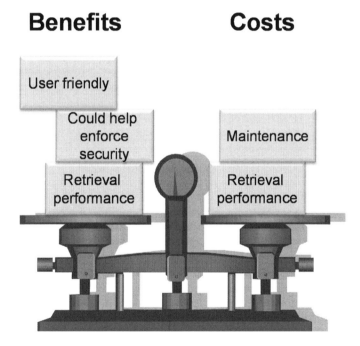

Physical data model

Star schema vs. Snowflake

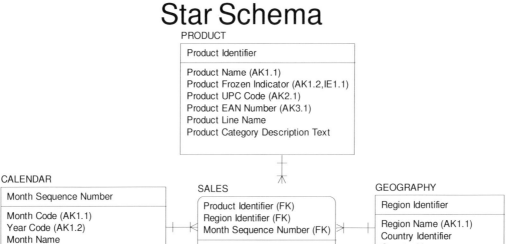

Star Schema

PRODUCT

Product Identifier
Product Name (AK1.1)
Product Frozen Indicator (AK1.2,IE1.1)
Product UPC Code (AK2.1)
Product EAN Number (AK3.1)
Product Line Name
Product Category Description Text

CALENDAR

Month Sequence Number
Month Code (AK1.1)
Year Code (AK1.2)
Month Name
Year Name
Year Sequence Number

SALES

Product Identifier (FK)
Region Identifier (FK)
Month Sequence Number (FK)
Gross Sales Amount

GEOGRAPHY

Region Identifier
Region Name (AK1.1)
Country Identifier
Country Name
Country ISO Code

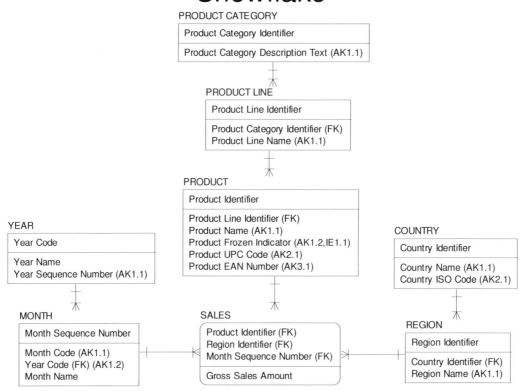

Snowflake

PRODUCT CATEGORY

Product Category Identifier
Product Category Description Text (AK1.1)

PRODUCT LINE

Product Line Identifier
Product Category Identifier (FK)
Product Line Name (AK1.1)

PRODUCT

Product Identifier
Product Line Identifier (FK)
Product Name (AK1.1)
Product Frozen Indicator (AK1.2,IE1.1)
Product UPC Code (AK2.1)
Product EAN Number (AK3.1)

YEAR

Year Code
Year Name
Year Sequence Number (AK1.1)

COUNTRY

Country Identifier
Country Name (AK1.1)
Country ISO Code (AK2.1)

MONTH

Month Sequence Number
Month Code (AK1.1)
Year Code (FK) (AK1.2)
Month Name

SALES

Product Identifier (FK)
Region Identifier (FK)
Month Sequence Number (FK)
Gross Sales Amount

REGION

Region Identifier
Country Identifier (FK)
Region Name (AK1.1)

Physical data model

Star schema vs. Snowflake

STAR SCHEMA

A star schema is when each set of tables that make up a dimension is flattened into a single table. Notice I used the phrase "flattened" instead of "denormalized" because a dimensional model is never normalized to begin with, but instead separated into different tables by hierarchy level. The meter is called a fact table in the physical, and appears in the center of the model with each of the dimensions relating to the meter at the lowest level of detail. A star schema is relatively easy to create and implement, and visually appears elegant and simplistic to both IT and the business.

SNOWFLAKE

We "snowflake" due to a number of factors including if having one flattened table takes up too much space, if the ETL effort is too great, or if the usage patterns dictate. I read in a recent data modeling article the following quote: "A snowflake schema is a star schema with fully normalized dimensions...A snowflake schema can be produced from a star schema by normalizing each dimension table." This is not usually a true statement. Snowflaking is a physical design practice where tables are broken out from dimension structures due to space and performance issues. Sometimes the tables (called outriggers) are broken out following the rules of normalization but more than likely they are broken out by different levels or rates of change. An advantage of the snowflake representation is that it explicitly shows the hierarchy structure of each dimension, which can help show how the data can be sensibly analyzed. Sometimes the snowflaked model can even contain more tables then the original logical dimensional model.

CHOICES, CHOICES, CHOICES

There are a number of factors to consider in deciding whether to go the star schema or snowflake route. Consider how the data will be most frequently accessed, and consider performance and space implications carefully (not just for today but also for 5-10 years in the future). Most dimensional models are star schemas, and are usually snowflaked due to data volatility or summarization requirements.

Dimension tables are traditionally wide (lots of columns) and fact tables are traditionally deep (lots of rows). Avoid structures that are both deep and wide.

Physical data model

Additional physical dimensional modeling terminology

Degenerate dimension

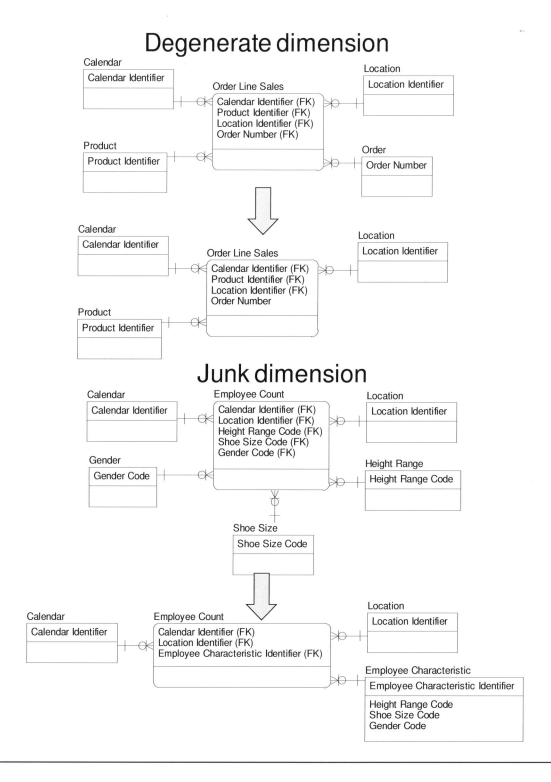

Junk dimension

Physical data model

Additional physical dimensional modeling terminology

DEGENERATE DIMENSION	A degenerate dimension is a dimension whose data element(s) have been moved to the fact table. A degenerate dimension is most common when the original dimension contained only a single data element such as a transaction identifier. The modeler needs to carefully consider filter and storage space implications.

JUNK DIMENSION

A junk dimension containing all the possible combinations of a small and somewhat related set of indicators and codes. Factors to consider in creating junk dimensions are:

- **Usage**. Make sure the dimensions folded into a single table are often queried together by the business. This is the most important factor.
- **Number of dimensions in the fact table**. If you have too many dimensions (where "too many" is determined by technology limitations), there is a good chance the design might be more efficient with a junk dimension.
- **Size of junk dimension**. If an outer join produces too many rows (where "too many" is determined by technology limitations), you might consider restructuring or not using the junk dimension.

Junk dimensions can either be populated with all possible combinations during initial load, or can be populated as values come in during normal load times. The decision depends on the stability and volume of the data.

Slowly changing dimensions

Explanation

- An SCD is every reference subject area in the data warehouse
- It is not limited just to dimensions
- It reminds us that we need to decide how to handle data changes
- We need to ask
  - Which data elements within this entity can change?
  - For those that can change, do you only need the original, or only the current, or everything, or somewhere in between?

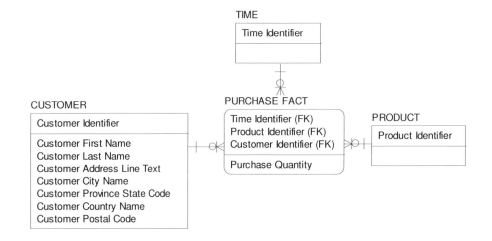

Slowly changing dimensions

Explanation

In the physical dimensional model, we need to consider history requirements. Transaction data and reference data behave very differently from each other in terms of value updates. Transaction data occurs very frequently and usually once they occur they are not updated (e.g. once an order has been delivered you can no longer change its properties such as Order Quantity). Reference data on the other hand, is much less volumous but values can change more often (e.g. people move to different addresses, product names change, and sales departments have reorganizations).

In the data warehouse environment, every reference subject area becomes a slowly changing dimension (SCD). This term has been coined by Ralph Kimball, and an SCD is any subject area (both relational and dimensional) whose values can change over time. There are four ways to handle these data changes: Type 0 stores only the original, Type 1 stores no history, Type 2 stores all history, and Type 3 stores some history.

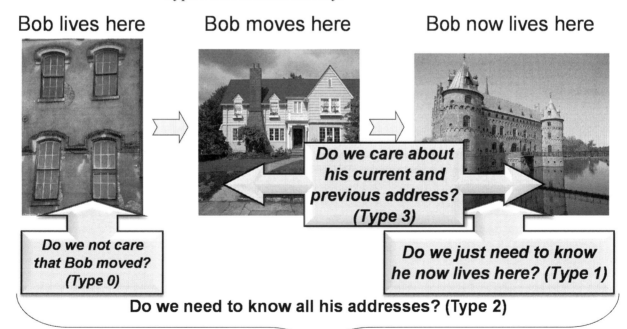

Slowly changing dimensions

Type 0

EXPLANATION   Type 0 means only the original information is kept. It is useful for data that does not change, such as calendar.

> Don't update

> Ignore else Insert

> Ideal when data does not change

EXAMPLE:

- Bob moves 5 times. We only store his original address.
- How much did we sell to Bob over the last 3 years?

Slowly changing dimensions

Type 1

EXPLANATION   Type 1 means only the most current information is kept.

> No history
>
> Update else Insert
>
> Useful to correct errors
>
> Easiest to implement
>
> Least expensive for CPU and storage
>
> Ideal if no history required

EXAMPLE:

- Bob moves 5 times. We only store the 5th time, where he currently lives
- How much did we sell to Bob over the last 3 years?

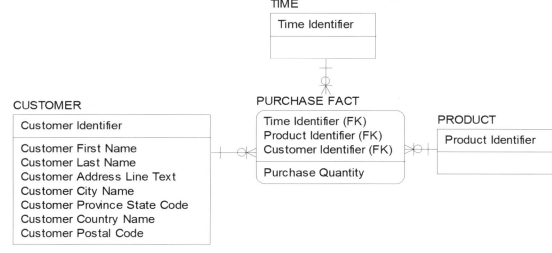

CUSTOMER

ID	FIRST	LAST	ADDRESS	
123	Steve	Smith	10 Main	
456	Bob	Jones	~~15 Park~~	25 Elm

PURCHASE FACT

CUST	TIME	PROD	QTY
123	789	122	500
456	987	675	1000
456	356	278	750

Slowly changing dimensions

Type 2

EXAMPLE:

- Bob moves 5 times. We store all 5 times as separate rows, along with when he moved and why for each move.
- How much did we sell to Bob when he lived at 14 Main Street?
- Which of Bob's addresses had the most sales?

- New surrogate key -

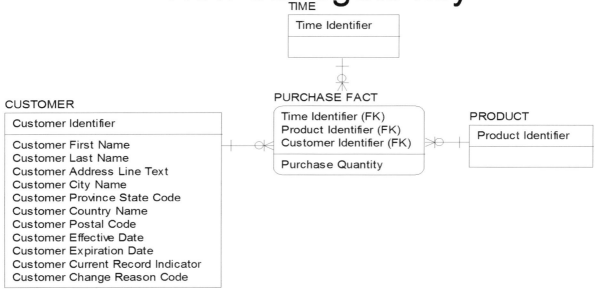

CUSTOMER

ID	FIRST	LAST	ADDRESS	EFF	EXP	CURR	REASON
123	Steve	Smith	10 Main	4/1/2010	9/9/3000	Y	
456	Bob	Jones	15 Park	6/15/2007	~~9/9/3000~~	~~Y~~	
					7/12/2012	N	5
899	Bob	Jones	25 Elm	7/13/2012	9/9/3000	Y	

Slowly changing dimensions

Type 2

EXPLANATION   Type 2 allows you to represent the entire environment at a point in time (aka Chronology or Audit).   The dimension foreign key is no longer a reference data instance, but a reference data instance at a particular point in time. It becomes a time machine.

- Original surrogate key & date -

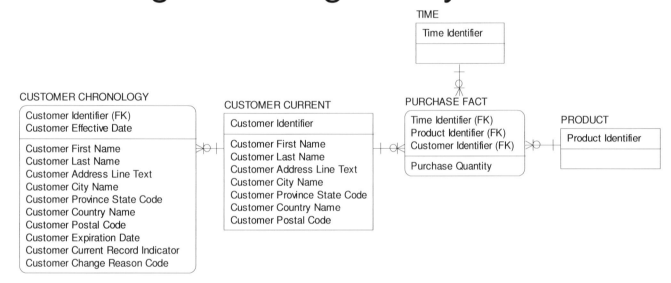

CUSTOMER CHRONOLOGY

ID	FIRST	LAST	ADDRESS	EFF	EXP	CURR	REASON
123	Steve	Smith	10 Main	4/1/2010	9/9/3000	Y	
456	Bob	Jones	15 Park	6/15/2007	~~9/9/3000~~	~~Y~~	
					7/12/2012	N	5
456	Bob	Jones	25 Elm	7/13/2012	9/9/3000	Y	

Slowly changing dimensions

Type 3

> Store some changes on some columns

> History is usually original or previous

> Columns instead of rows

> Least used

EXAMPLE:

- Bob moves 5 times. We store the address details from his original address and his most current.

- How much did we sell to Bob when he lived at his original address?

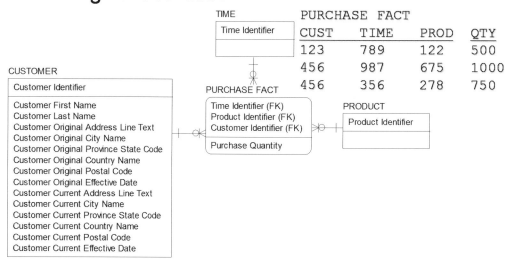

TIME

Time Identifier

PURCHASE FACT

CUST	TIME	PROD	QTY
123	789	122	500
456	987	675	1000
456	356	278	750

CUSTOMER

Customer Identifier

Customer First Name
Customer Last Name
Customer Original Address Line Text
Customer Original City Name
Customer Original Province State Code
Customer Original Country Name
Customer Original Postal Code
Customer Original Effective Date
Customer Current Address Line Text
Customer Current City Name
Customer Current Province State Code
Customer Current Country Name
Customer Current Postal Code
Customer Current Effective Date

PURCHASE FACT

Time Identifier (FK)
Product Identifier (FK)
Customer Identifier (FK)

Purchase Quantity

PRODUCT

Product Identifier

CUSTOMER

ID	FIRST	LAST	ORIG	EFF	CURR	EFF
123	Steve	Smith	10 Main	4/1/2010	10 Main	4/1/2010
456	Bob	Jones	15 Park	6/15/2007	25 Elm	7/13/2012

Slowly changing dimensions

Type 3

EXPLANATION
Type 3 is very useful when there is a need to store "some" history, such as current and previous, or current and original. History is stored in columns instead of rows, similar to an array or repeating groups structure. Type 3 is frequently chosen for purely technology reasons such as to simplify development, save storage space, or increase query performance.

Applying the Data Model Scorecard®

Interaction Report for Product BB40 from May 2011

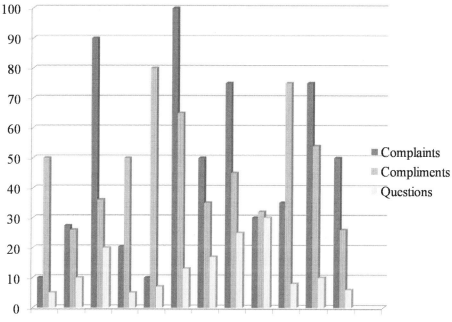

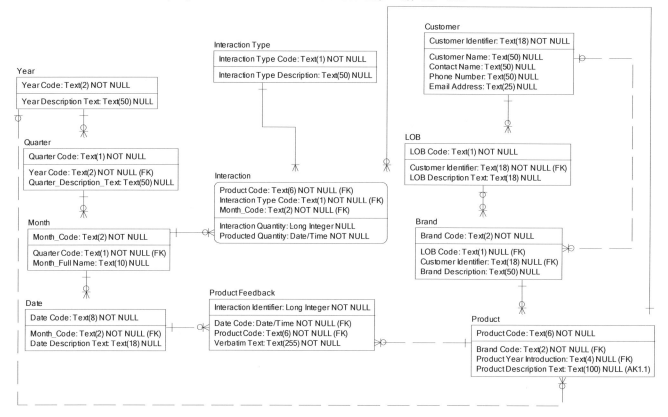

Applying the Data Model Scorecard®

3. How well do the characteristics of the model support the type of model?

EXPLANATION

This question ensures that the model type (conceptual, logical, or physical – and then either relational or dimensional) of the model satisfies the criteria for this level of detail.

ANYTHING YOU WOULD CATCH IN THE MODEL ON THE FACING PAGE FOR THIS CATEGORY?

1.

2.

3.

4.

5.

6.

7.

8.

9.

10.

#	Category	Total score	Model score	%
1	How well does the model capture the requirements?	15		
2	How complete is the model?	15		
3	How well do the characteristics of the model support the type of model?	10		
4	How structurally sound is the model?	15		
5	How well does the model leverage generic structures?	10		
6	How well does the model follow naming standards?	5		
7	How well has the model been arranged for readability?	5		
8	How good are the definitions?	10		
9	How consistent is the model with the enterprise?	5		
10	How well does the metadata match the data?	10		
	TOTAL SCORE	100		

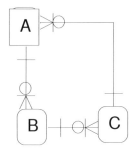

Module 4

Data Model Scorecard® Category #4: Structure

Category Question: How structurally sound is the model?

This module is your guide to: Applying acceptable modeling principles

Category overview

How structurally sound is the model?

The structure category focuses on data modeling and database best practices. It validates the design practices employed to build the model. Unlike the Model Type category, the Structure category does not distinguish conceptual from logical from physical, or relational from dimensional. Unlike the Correctness and Completeness categories, the Structure category allows us to completely overlook the actual subject matter being modeled. Having null primary and alternate keys, circular relationships, entities containing no data elements, the same data element defined differently across entities – these are all examples of structure violations. Many of the potential problems from this category are quickly and automatically flagged by our modeling and database tools.

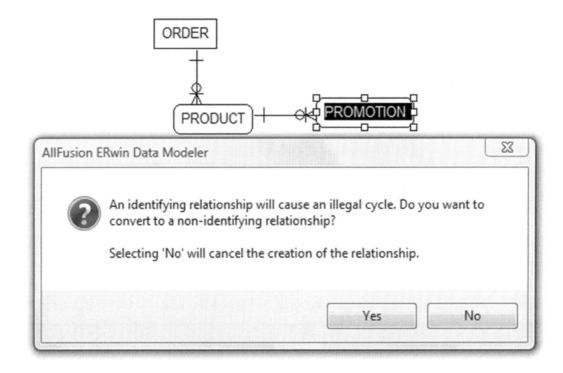

Structural soundness catches

20 examples

NULL CANDIDATE KEYS

An alternate or primary key that can be empty. Even though some databases permit null alternate keys, this is not a best practice.

EMPTY ENTITIES

On a logical or physical data model, an entity should have at least one data element. I have seen this on models, where the empty entity was a "placeholder for future use", or the data elements were unknown.

STANDALONE ENTITIES

With few exceptions, an entity should have at least one relationship. One exception would be a common code table.

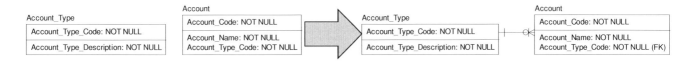

CIRCULAR RELATIONSHIPS

A "Catch-22" situation, where no entity instances can be created because of mandatory relationships which start and end at the same entity.

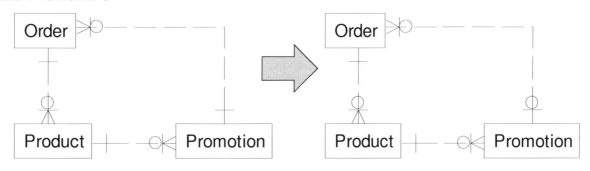

Structural soundness catches

20 examples

MISSING LENGTH

The formatting is provided but the length is missing.

Promotion

Promotion_Code: CHAR(5) NOT NULL
Promotion_Description: VARCHAR() NOT NULL Promotion_Start_Date: DATE NOT NULL Promotion_End_Date: DATE NULL Promotion_Type_Code: CHAR() NULL

Promotion

Promotion_Code: CHAR(5) NOT NULL
Promotion_Description: VARCHAR(250) NOT NULL Promotion_Start_Date: DATE NOT NULL Promotion_End_Date: DATE NULL Promotion_Type_Code: CHAR(3) NULL

DIFFERENT FORMAT OR LENGTH

If there are two or more data elements with the same name, but their format or length is different.

Savings_Account

Account_Number: CHAR(8) NOT NULL
Account_Name: CHAR(50) NOT NULL

Checking_Account

Account_Number: CHAR(18) NOT NULL
Account_Name: VARCHAR(50) NULL

Savings_Account

Account_Number: CHAR(8) NOT NULL
Account_Name: CHAR(50) NOT NULL

Checking_Account

Account_Number: CHAR(8) NOT NULL
Account_Name: CHAR(50) NOT NULL

DEFAULT FORMAT

Many modeling tools use default formats, such as char(18) and varchar(10).

Checking_Account

Account_Number: CHAR(18) NOT NULL
Account_Name: VARCHAR(10) NULL

Checking_Account

Account_Number: CHAR(8) NOT NULL
Account_Name: CHAR(50) NOT NULL

Structural soundness catches

20 examples

PARTIAL KEY RELATIONSHIPS

A relationship between two entities where only part of the primary key from the parent entity is migrated to the child entity.

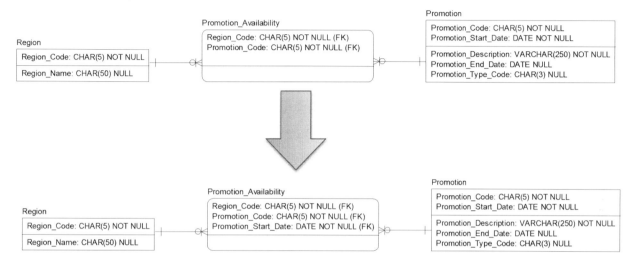

RELATIONSHIP MISSING AN END

A dangling relationship that ends in space, and is not connected on both sides.

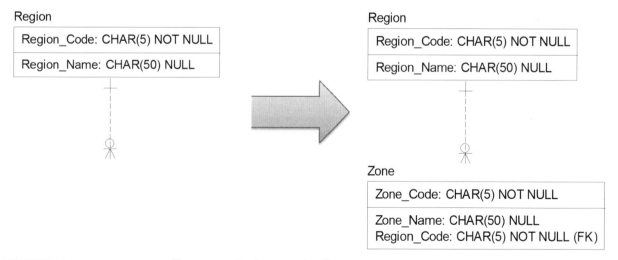

ENTITIES WITH THE SAME NAME

For example, having the Customer entity twice in the same model.

Structural soundness catches

20 examples

DUPLICATE RELATIONSHIPS

Two or more relationships that appear to be redundant with each other. There might be a business reason for this, but it should be questioned because it can easily be a human error that causes this situation.

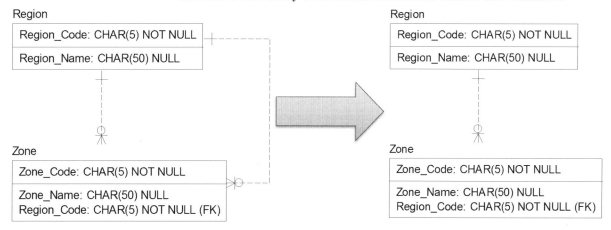

DEFINITION INCONSISTENCY

These data elements appear more than once on the same model, yet have a different definition.

Menu.Price: This is the retail amount of an item offered for purchase in our restaurant.

Order_Line.Price: This is the actual amount of an item in our restaurant. For example, the restaurant manager might have adjusted the price in reaction to a customer complaint.

Menu.Retail_Price: This is the retail amount of an item offered for purchase in our restaurant.

Order_Line.Actual_Price: This is the actual amount of an item in our restaurant. For example, the restaurant manager might have adjusted the price in reaction to a customer complaint.

RESERVED WORDS

These data elements have a SQL-reserved word as their name. A reserved word is a term used within a database to perform database actions (e.g. Select or Table), and therefore having a reserved word as a name can lead to confusion in the database.

Structural soundness catches

20 examples

SUBTYPE WITH DIFFERENT PK THAN SUPERTYPE

This subtype has a different primary key than its supertype.

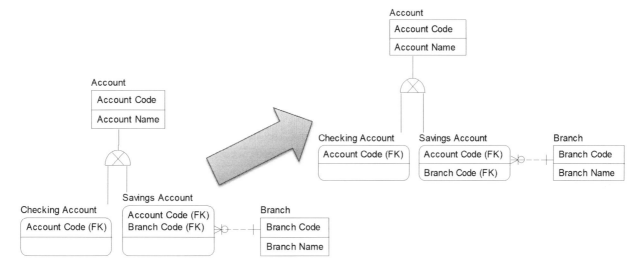

SUBTYPE WITH MORE THAN ONE SUPERTYPE

If a subtype has more than one supertype, there will definitely be a primary key issue and an inheritance issue.

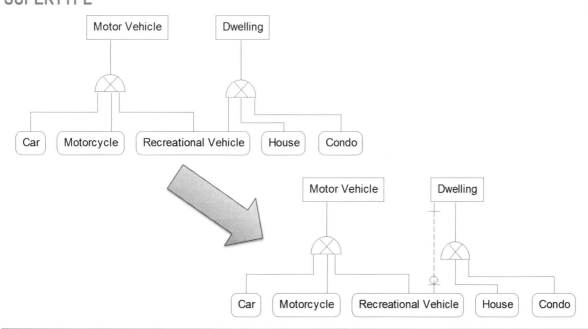

Structural soundness catches

20 examples

MANDATORY RELATIONSHIP ASSOCIATED WITH NULL FK

A relationship is defined as mandatory yet associated with a null foreign key.

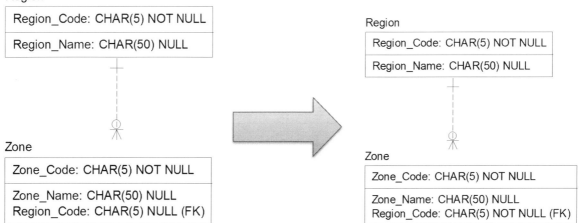

OPTIONAL RELATIONSHIP ASSOCIATED WITH NOT NULL FK

This is the opposite of the situation above. There is a relationship that should be optional but the foreign key is defined as mandatory (not null).

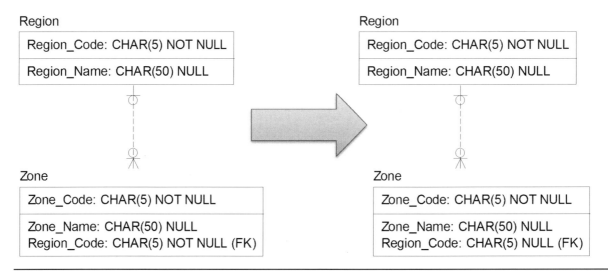

Structural soundness catches

20 examples

REDUNDANT INDEX

Extraneous indexes should be caught in this category.

Account

Account_Code: NOT NULL (IE1.1)
Account_Name: NOT NULL Account_Type_Code: NOT NULL

Account

Account_Code: NOT NULL
Account_Name: NOT NULL Account_Type_Code: NOT NULL

DUPLICATE DATA ELEMENTS

Having the same data element in the same entity more than once, and not being a repeating group.

Account

Account_Code: NOT NULL
Account_Name: NOT NULL Account_Name_: NOT NULL Account_Type_Code: NOT NULL

Account

Account_Code: NOT NULL
Account_Name: NOT NULL Account_Type_Code: NOT NULL

DECIMAL CANDIDATE KEY

A primary or alternate key with a decimal format will cause join issues.

Region

Region_Code: DEC(15,4) NOT NULL
Region_Name: CHAR(50) NULL

Region

Region_Code: CHAR(5) NOT NULL
Region_Name: CHAR(50) NULL

Structural soundness catches

How many structural soundness violations can you find?

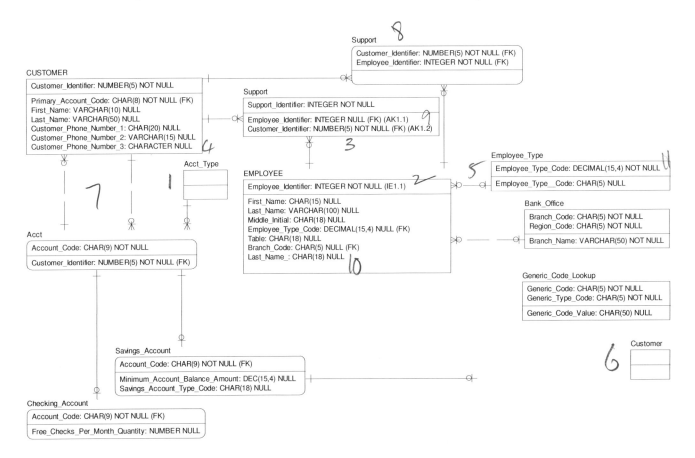

#	
1.	Empty entity
2.	Invert Entry (dupe index) for Primary key
3.	NUMBER (5) ?
4.	CHARACTER data type ?
5.	Employee-Type-Code repeated (different data types)
6.	Hanging entity

Structural soundness catches

How many structural soundness violations can you find?

7.	Circular relationship
8.	Dupe Support entities
9.	NULL alternate key
10.	Last_Name repeated
11.	DECIMAL primary key → <u>not</u> recommended.
12.	
13.	
14.	
15.	
16.	
17.	
18.	
19.	
20.	

Applying the Data Model Scorecard®

Interaction Report for Product BB40 from May 2011

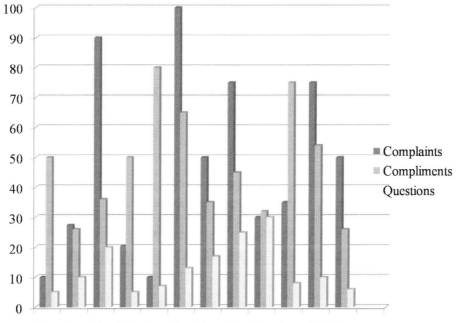

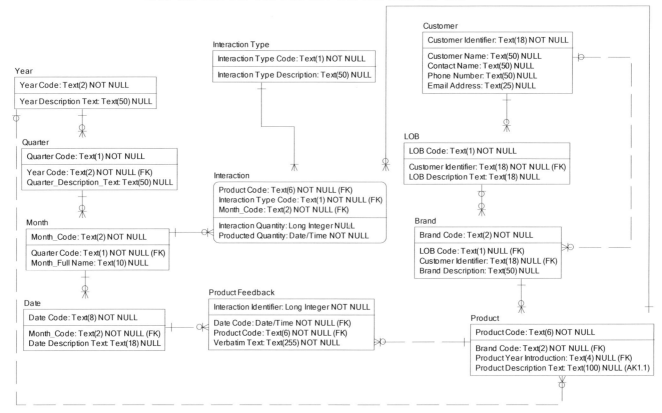

Applying the Data Model Scorecard®

4. How structurally sound is the model?

EXPLANATION

The structure category focuses on data modeling and database best practices. It validates the design practices employed to build the model.

ANYTHING YOU
WOULD CATCH IN
THE MODEL ON
THE FACING PAGE
FOR THIS
CATEGORY?

1.

2.

3.

4.

5.

6.

7.

8.

9.

10.

#	Category	Total score	Model score	%
1	How well does the model capture the requirements?	15		
2	How complete is the model?	15		
3	How well do the characteristics of the model support the type of model?	10		
4	How structurally sound is the model?	15		
5	How well does the model leverage generic structures?	10		
6	How well does the model follow naming standards?	5		
7	How well has the model been arranged for readability?	5		
8	How good are the definitions?	10		
9	How consistent is the model with the enterprise?	5		
10	How well does the metadata match the data?	10		
	TOTAL SCORE	100		

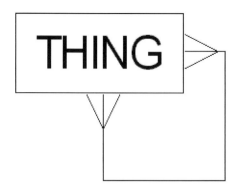

Module 5

Data Model Scorecard® Category #5: Abstraction

Category Question: How well does the model leverage generic structures?

This module is your guide to: Determining the optimal use of generic concepts

Category overview

How well does the model leverage generic structures?

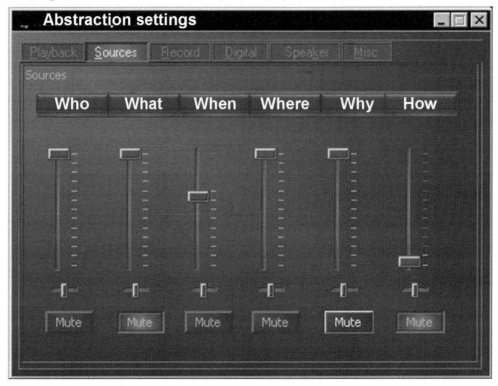

abstraction

Confirms an appropriate use of abstraction on the model

Customer is now Party/Role ("Who?")

Finished Good is now Product ("What?")

Month is now Time ("When?")

Mailing Address is now Location ("Where?")

Order is now Event ("Why?")

Invoice Receipt is now Document ("How?")

Category overview

How well does the model leverage generic structures?

EXPLANATION
This category confirms an appropriate use of abstraction on the model. One of the most powerful tools a data modeler has at their disposal is abstraction, the ability to increase the types of information a design can accommodate using generic concepts. Going from Customer Location to a more generic Location for example, allows the design to more easily handle other types of locations, such as warehouses and distribution centers. Abstraction can be properly applied (or abused!) at the entity, relationship, and data element levels.

PURPOSE
To have the right level of flexibility.

CHALLENGE
You need to know how to phrase "what if" scenarios, and find people in the business who can answer these questions. For example, if you are considering the "Who" concept, and currently you only have Customer on your model, someone needs to confirm that in the not so distant future you will have other types of party roles, such as Employee and Supplier.

Also, you (or your management) will need to know how to weigh the potential value of abstraction with the effort required implementing an abstract structure. As a modeler I thought abstraction was the most amazing concept – then, I volunteered to take over a development project and my first assignment was to implement an abstract structure I designed! It was very painful and I learned that flexibility always comes with a price!

VOLUME CONTROL
I visualize the abstraction setting as a volume control, where the greater the volume, the greater the use of abstraction. For example, if we are considering "who" is important to your organization, little or no volume would lead to "Customer" and turning the volume all the way to max would lead to "Party".

Power of abstraction

Abstraction explanation

A logical data modeling process where we redefine data elements, relationships, and/or entities into more generic structures

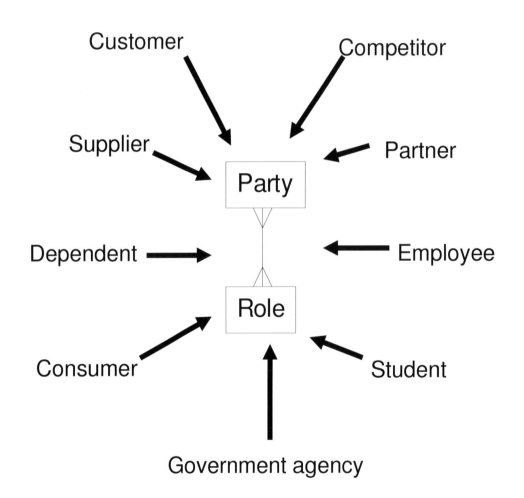

Power of abstraction

Abstraction explanation

BACKGROUND

For artists, abstraction is a tool. It lets them efficiently capture and represent complex topics. We data modelers are artists, and abstraction is an efficient tool at our disposal also.

The data modeler is responsible not only for correctly representing the requirements of an application, but also for having the foresight to design flexible structures in areas where requirements may change in the near future.

Abstraction is part of the logical data modeling process and is usually performed after normalizing. Abstraction brings flexibility to your logical data models by redefining and combining some of the data elements, entities, and relationships within the model into more generic terms. Abstraction is the removal of details in such a way as to broaden applicability to a wide class of situations while preserving the important properties and essential nature from concepts or subjects. By removing these details, we remove differences and therefore change the way we view these concepts or subjects, including seeing similarities that were not apparent or even existent before.

For example, instead of having separate *customer* and *employee* entities, there may be situations in which it would be valuable to have the generic *person* entity. *Person* can include concepts that may need to be added to an application in the near future. If *contractor* is required by an application that is built upon a model that already uses *person*, many (or even all) of the data elements and relationships assigned to *person* might also be applicable for *contractor*, and therefore the model and application will experience few or no changes.

Power of abstraction

Abstraction example

Customer	Supplier	Employee
First name	Company name	First name
Last name	Contact first name	Last name
Phone number	Contact last name	Work phone number
Fax number	Phone number	Home phone number
Tax id	Fax number	Mobile number
First order date	Credit Rating	Social Security #
DUNS #	First PO Date	Email address
	DUNS #	Hire date
		Clock #

- ☑ An Employee can be assigned to many Customers
- ☑ A Customer can contact many Employees
- ☑ An Employee manages the relationship with many Suppliers
- ☑ A Supplier can contact many Employees

Power of abstraction

Abstraction example

BACKGROUND

Create an abstract data model using these entities, data elements, and business rules. For this example we are keeping the relationships simple. But in real life there could be many more details. For example, the relationship between Employee and Customer can be an Account Manager relationship, a Customer Service relationship, a Call Upon relationship, or many other types of business relationships.

Power of abstraction

Where abstraction fits

1. Normalize

2. Apply the <u>Abstraction Safety Guide</u> in this order:

a. Data Elements

b. Entities

c. Relationships

3. Document in detail

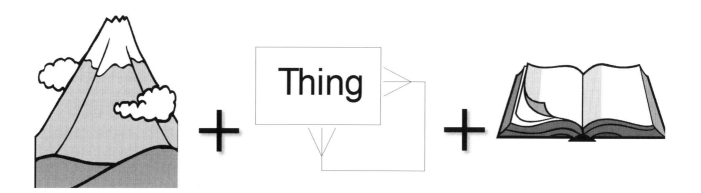

Power of abstraction

Where abstraction fits

SEQUENCE

I recommend starting with data elements. Once we start with data elements and abstract where appropriate, we can more easily see what is common across entities.

After data elements, we can abstract entities and relationships. Entities next because they can open the door to abstract more data elements, entities, or relationships. Then relationships. Note that after abstracting each of these, there might still be some opportunities for abstracting at any of these three levels that were not apparent or did not exist in the first iteration. This is because when we abstract we sometimes open up new opportunities we did not think of before.

Here is our model after Step 1 (normalization) is applied:

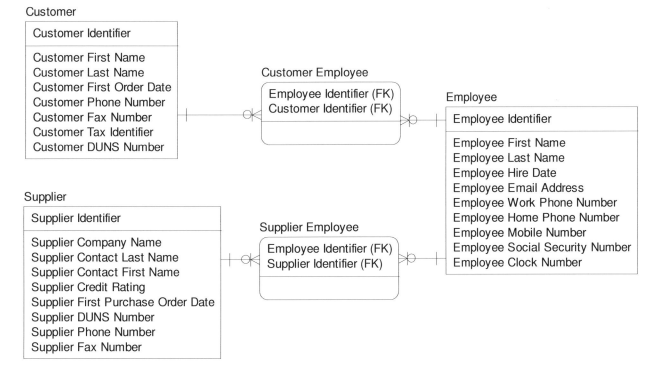

Power of abstraction

Abstraction Safety Guide (ASG)

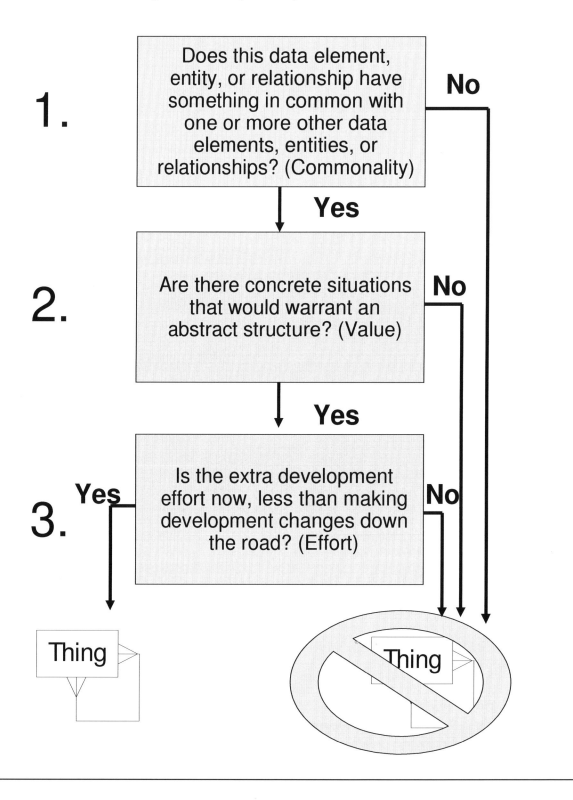

1. Does this data element, entity, or relationship have something in common with one or more other data elements, entities, or relationships? (Commonality)

No **Yes**

2. Are there concrete situations that would warrant an abstract structure? (Value)

No **Yes**

3. Is the extra development effort now, less than making development changes down the road? (Effort)

Yes **No**

Thing

Thing

Power of abstraction

Abstraction Safety Guide (ASG)

BACKGROUND

The Abstraction Safety Guide contains three questions to decide where to abstract:

Does this data element, entity, or relationship have something in common with one or more other data elements, entities, or relationships? If yes, are there concrete situations that would warrant an abstract structure? If yes, is the extra development effort now, less than making development changes down the road?

If the answer to all 3 is "Yes!", abstract!

COMMONALITY

The first of these three questions asks, "Do we have a match anywhere on our model?" Did we find two or more entities, relationships, or data elements that appear to share a common trait? This is the detective work when we scan our model in search of anything that might appear to match something else. Remember playing the card game Concentration when you were a child? You would put a deck of picture cards face down on a table and then turn over two to see if they match. It is the same concept on the data model. If we don't find a match, we move on.

VALUE

Now that we have found several potential candidates for abstraction, we need to ask for each of these, "Are there concrete situations that would warrant an abstract structure?" In other words, is there value in abstracting? Many times when we abuse abstraction and over-abstract, we avoid asking this question. In determining the value of abstraction, ask the business experts questions like "Would your application need additional types of....?", and fill in the end of this question with what you are considering to abstract. For example, "Would your application need additional types of order lifecycle dates?"

EFFORT

The final question is around the effort involved in implementing the abstract structure. After determining that there is value in having such an abstract structure, we now need to answer the question, "Is the extra development effort now, substantially less than the development effort down the road?" This is a very tricky question, because it depends on who you ask. If you ask the data modeler (probably yourself) or anyone from the data administration team, the answer will probably be a resounding "Yes, it is worth the effort now." That is because we are looking ahead for the next requirement that can take advantage of these abstract structures. We are looking beyond just the current application. But who really needs to answer the question is the individual or department that pays the bills for the current application.

Power of abstraction

Abstracting the data elements

Before   After

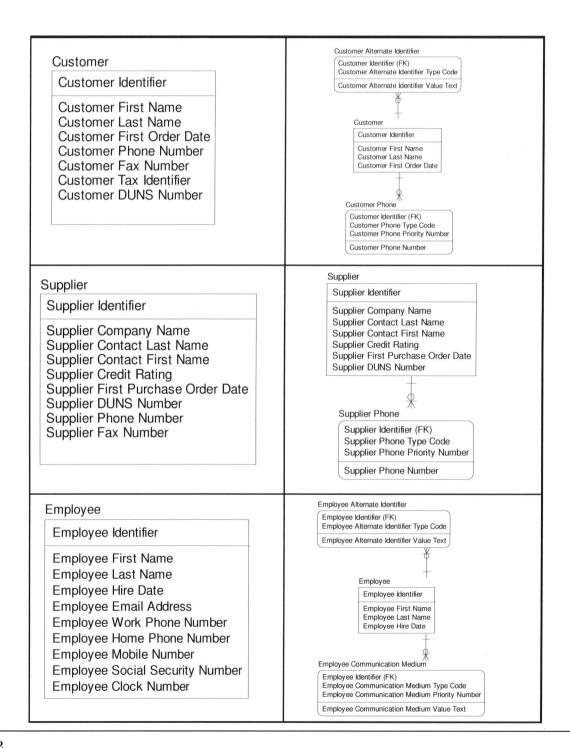

Power of abstraction

Abstracting the data elements

CUSTOMER

Phone and Fax number have become abstracted into Customer Phone where the Customer Phone Type is "Phone" or "Fax", and Customer Phone Number is the actual phone number. The same idea is applied to the Tax id and DUNS# in Customer Alternate Identifier.

SUPPLIER

Here Phone and Fax are abstracted into Supplier Phone using the same idea we saw with Customer. Notice that there is only a single alternate identifier for Supplier, DUNS #, therefore there was no need to create the Alternate Identifier abstract structure.

EMPLOYEE

Employee mimics the Customer structure with Employee Phone containing Phone Number and Pager Number, and Employee Alternate Identifier containing Social Security Number and Clock Number. As an additional abstraction step, we can include email address with the phone concept to create Communication Medium. We are taking "baby steps" and so we first abstracted the phone information and then realized that email address and phone numbers are really just different ways of communicating with someone.

Here is the model after abstracting the data elements:

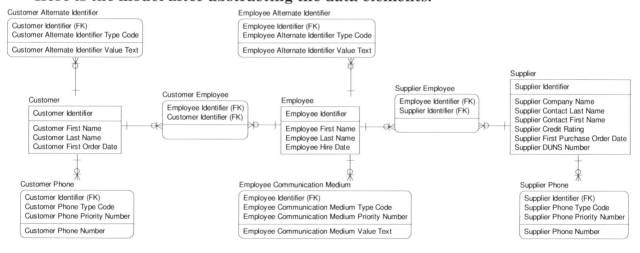

Power of abstraction

Parties and roles

> Party is a person or organization of interest to the enterprise. It is similar to the concept of "Who?". That is, who is important to the business?

Roles are necessary to achieve the holistic picture

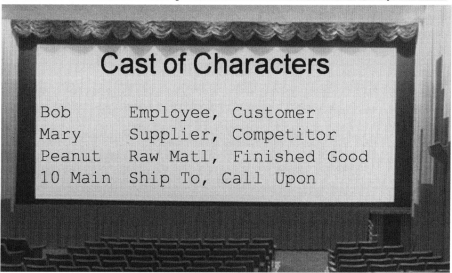

Cast of Characters

Bob	Employee, Customer
Mary	Supplier, Competitor
Peanut	Raw Matl, Finished Good
10 Main	Ship To, Call Upon

Two types of roles

- Event-independent roles
  - Member
  - Provider
- Event-dependent roles
  - A Claim turns the Provider into the Primary Care Physician
  - A Claim turns the Member into the Claimant

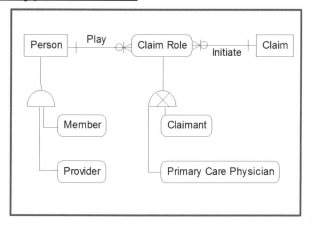

Power of abstraction

Parties and roles

INTRODUCING PARTY

Party is a person or organization of interest to the enterprise. It is similar to the concept of "Who?". That is, who is important to the business? Party is a very popular abstract entity in many organizations. All companies have people and organizations that can play different roles and Party is a very good way to encompass all of their common properties. Do you use Party in your organization? It can be called a more serious term such as Business Partner, Involved Party, and even Ephemeral Being!

LOVE/HATE RELATIONSHIP WITH PARTY

People have a love/hate relationship with Party. Those that love it admire its flexibility. Those that hate it despise its vagueness. In the example on the facing page, Party was not admired and therefore we used Person with an overlapping subtype to encompass the role concept.

ABOUT ROLES FROM WILLIAM KENT

"At the beginning of a mystery, we need to think of the murderer and the butler as two distinct entities, collecting information about each of them separately. After we discover that 'the butler did it', have we established that they are the same entity? Shall we require the modeling system to collapse their two representatives into one?"

EVENT-INDEPENDENT VS. EVENT-DEPENDENT ROLES

Event independent roles are parts a party, product, or location can play regardless of what daily business events occur (e.g. Customer, Provider, Member). Event dependent roles on the other hand, are directly impacted by daily business events. Bob the Provider for example, can become Bob the Primary Care Physician when the 'Claim Received' business event occurs.

Power of abstraction

Adding Party and Role to our example

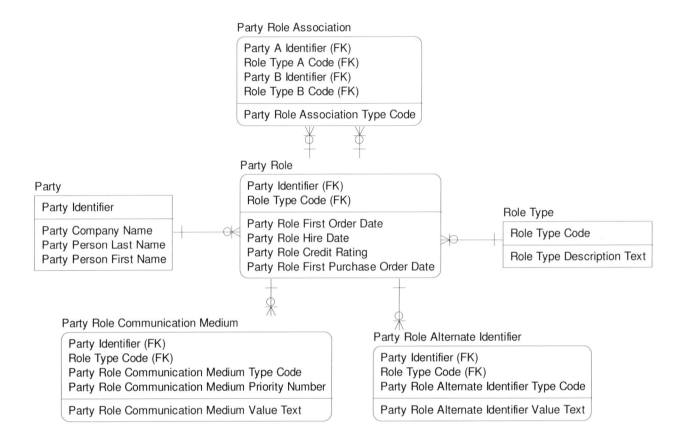

Party Role Association

Party A Identifier (FK)
Role Type A Code (FK)
Party B Identifier (FK)
Role Type B Code (FK)
Party Role Association Type Code

Party Role

Party Identifier (FK)
Role Type Code (FK)
Party Role First Order Date
Party Role Hire Date
Party Role Credit Rating
Party Role First Purchase Order Date

Party

Party Identifier
Party Company Name
Party Person Last Name
Party Person First Name

Role Type

Role Type Code
Role Type Description Text

Party Role Communication Medium

Party Identifier (FK)
Role Type Code (FK)
Party Role Communication Medium Type Code
Party Role Communication Medium Priority Number
Party Role Communication Medium Value Text

Party Role Alternate Identifier

Party Identifier (FK)
Role Type Code (FK)
Party Role Alternate Identifier Type Code
Party Role Alternate Identifier Value Text

EXAMPLE

Note that in many cases entities and relationships are abstracted at the same time. This is because once we abstract an entity we can move all of the common data elements and relationships up to the more abstract level. So in this example the relationship from Employee to Supplier and from Employee to Customer got abstracted to the Party Association level when we introduced the Party concept.

Power of abstraction

Adding subtyping to our example

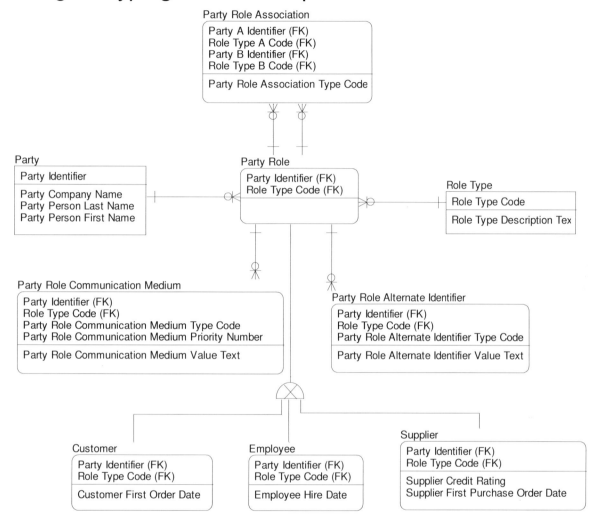

ADDING SUBTYPES Here we added subtypes to our abstract model to capture some of the information that was lost when we first abstracted. Note that the data elements specific to a particular entity are now shown in that entity. For example, Customer First Order Date is now shown in the Customer entity.

CREATIVITY How else could we have modeled our Party example using subtypes?

Power of abstraction

Adding metadata entities to our example

ADDING METADATA ENTITIES

Metadata entities are entities on our model that contain as values metadata for business entities on our design. They do not contain business values like the other entities we deal with (Customer, Employee, etc.). Metadata entities become extremely important when we abstract because they allow us to put back the domain integrity we lost by abstracting back into our design.

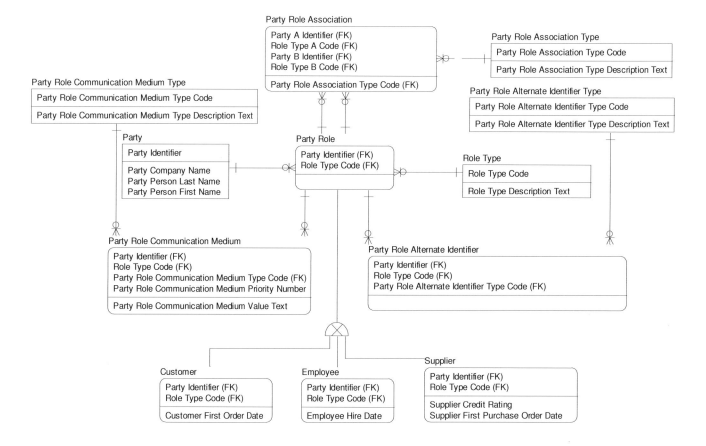

Party Role Communication Medium Type	
Code	Description
01	Phone
02	Fax
03	Mobile
04	Email

Party Role Alternate Identifier Type	
Code	Description
01	Tax Identifier
02	DUNS
03	Social Security Number
04	Clock Number

Party Role Association Type	
Code	Description
01	Customer Employee
02	Supplier Employee

Power of abstraction

Abstraction vs. Normalization

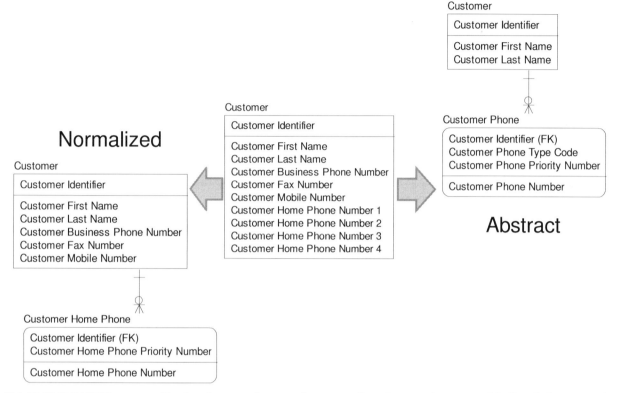

BACKGROUND

Both abstraction and normalization strive to add flexibility to the design, but normalization makes sure existing business requirements have minimal redundancy and maximum flexibility, while abstraction does this for future requirements. Normalization applies to the values, abstraction applies to the types.

EXAMPLE

For example, if a Customer can have two or more home phone numbers, we will normalize home phone number into its own entity and define a one-to-many relationship between the entities Customer and Customer Home Phone. This reduces the redundancy of having Customer Home Phone 1 Number, Customer Home Phone 2 Number, and so on, in the Customer entity. Normalizing home phone number lets us represent any number of home phone numbers for a customer without any design or development changes. However, if we abstract Customer Home Phone Number into Customer Phone Number, we can now handle multiple additional types of phone numbers that we could not previously, such as fax, cell, and pager phone numbers.

Power of abstraction

Pros of abstraction

> *A tactician knows what to do when something needs doing. A strategist knows what to do when nothing needs doing.*
> Savielly Tartakover

INCREASES APPLICATION STABILITY

A new association type was required in our Sales Organization structure. Due to using an abstract association concept, there were no database changes needed. We just added a new row.

FACILITATES INTEGRATION AND ENTERPRISE ARCHITECTURE

You can bring disparate source systems or subject areas together, such as storing customer locations and warehouses in the abstract Location structure. Abstraction automatically provides *structure* integration, and could assist business teams with providing true *data* integration.

REDUCES DESIGN TIME

We were able to create a global integration model in less than a week. Instead of listing every possible location in our business, we were able to abstract to a concept called "Location". We drew our relationships to Location, that otherwise would have been associated to a number of Location's subtypes, which would have taken a much longer time to analyze.

FORCES GREATER UNDERSTANDING OF ENTITIES

Before grouping separate entities together, we need to understand each entity and what it has in common with other entities, hence increasing our understanding.

CREATES NEW BUSINESS OPPORTUNITIES

I know of a global furniture company that was able to identify new sales opportunities after viewing their customers and employees and vendors as roles and parties.

ABSOLVES THE MODELER FROM CAPTURING SOME BUSINESS RULES

Sometimes this is a good thing, especially if the data modeler does not know all of the rules, or if rules can change over time. This can also be a bad thing, causing frustrating data quality problems. The end result is that the data modeler is pushing the work to a different team member – usually the developer.

Power of abstraction

Cons of abstraction

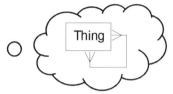

MODEL BECOMES VAGUE AND IMPRECISE

You need more explanation and documentation. I was once on an airplane reviewing an abstract model for a meeting, when a young girl sitting next to me asked me what I was doing. I was so happy she took an interest in my diagram, that I explained to her the data modeling basics along with the purpose of this particular model. Her next question was "What's a Business Party?" Good question!

FEWER RULES IN THE DATABASE

If a customer has to have a phone number, the only way to enforce this business rule in our current abstract Communication Medium Type structure is through code. The responsibility falls more on the developer than on the data modeler.

GREATER DEVELOPMENT EFFORT

If the source or target of an abstract structure is not abstract, it is usually a time consuming and complex development effort to populate or extract data from an abstract structure.

PERFORMANCE ISSUES

It can take the software tools longer to find the data if they are first looking for row values to find other row values.

DIFFICULT TO JUSTIFY LONG TERM BENEFITS TO A PROJECT-FOCUSED TEAM

If you are working with a project that has been pulling extra hours to deliver on time, the last thing that the project manager wants to hear is that the database structure's flexibility will require several additional weeks of work, yet the company may benefit from this flexibility over the next 3-5 years.

REPORTING TOOLS CAN HAVE DIFFICULTY WITH ABSTRACTION

Many reporting tools need columns to tie to (and not rows) and therefore they don't work well with abstraction. Some tools let you build views to hide abstraction and present columns for the reporting tool.

CAUSES STEWARDSHIP GAPS

Imagine trying to find a business professional to be responsible for Party or Thing!

Patterns and industry models

3 levels of patterns

> **Abstract modeling patterns that can replace application-specific sections on the model**

BACKGROUND

The more we abstract, the more we realize that the same rather tiny abstraction building blocks or components keep appearing in our designs, with very slight variations. You need to first understand your application before you can successfully apply these components.

GOALS

- **Creates designs faster.** By knowing that these patterns exist and when to use them, you can simply 'plug them in' to your model. For example, there is a pattern for alternate identifiers. As soon as you apply the 3 questions and identify several alternate identifiers in your logical data model, you can use the alternate identifier abstract structure in your design. This can drastically decrease modeling time because you don't have to create new abstract structures. Note you also can reuse definitions and other types of metadata from these components. For example, once you define the Alternate Identifier entity, you should be able to reuse the definition of this entity wherever Alternate Identifier is reused.

- **Saves development time.** If you continually reuse the same designs, there is a very good chance you will be able to reuse other parts of the software lifecycle as well. You will be able to reuse potentially some of the code and reporting and mapping and population logic. For example, if you have programming code to populate the alternate identifier structures for customer, you can probably reuse a large portion of this code to populate the alternate identifier structures for supplier.

- **Improves consistency across data models.** By using the same patterns over and over again you increase the consistency across your models. This leads to greater understanding and integration between your applications. For example, if the alternate identifier abstract concept is structured the same in three different models, someone very familiar with only one of the models would be able to understand this concept in all three models. This helps reduce the loss of business meaning that abstraction can introduce. After someone is explained the alternate identifier concept once, they will understand alternate identifier everywhere it appears.

Patterns and industry models

3 levels of patterns

BACKGROUND

John Giles' book **The Nimble Elephant: Agile Delivery of Data Models using a Pattern-based Approach**, defines three levels of patterns: elementary, assembly, and integration. The two diagrams below are from **The Nimble Element**.

ELEMENTARY

Elementary patterns are the "nuts and bolts" of data modeling. They include structures such as hierarchy patterns, and class word abstractions. From the **Nimble Elephant**: "They are handy (and even essential) design patterns, but they are too technical to excite most business people."

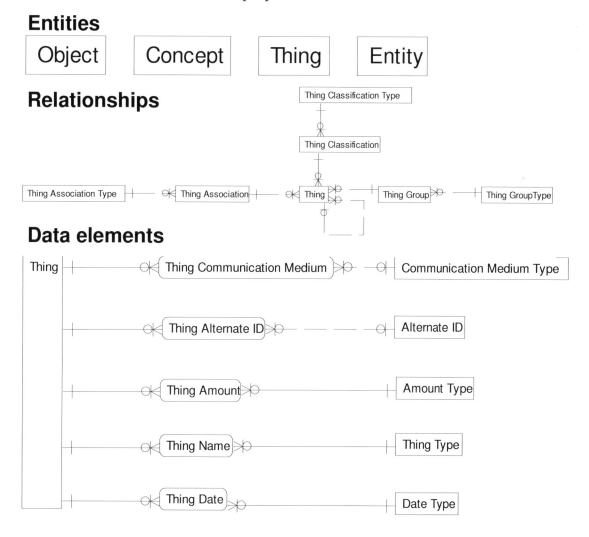

Entities

| Object | Concept | Thing | Entity |

Relationships

Data elements

Patterns and industry models

3 levels of patterns

ASSEMBLY

Assembly patterns are the building blocks that represent generic business concepts, such as the Party/Role structure mentioned earlier, as well as several other business concepts such as Location, Document, and Agreement. Business people can understand them, and they are often the subject of published data model patterns that can give the modeler proven, robust, extensible, and implementable designs. Think "who", "what", "when", "where", "why", "how", etc.

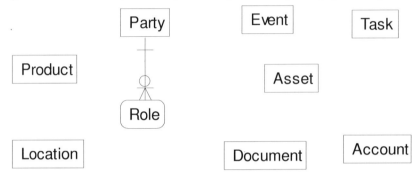

INTEGRATION

From the **Nimble Elephant**: "Integration patterns (or "patterns of patterns") provide the framework for linking the assembly patterns in common ways." This includes standard ways of relating the assembly patterns. The model below is an example of linking the assembly patterns.

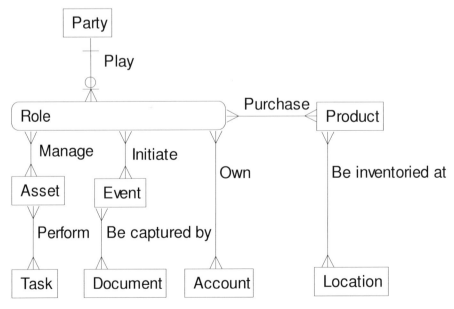

Patterns and industry models

About industry models

Subset of Teradata's Manufacturing CDM

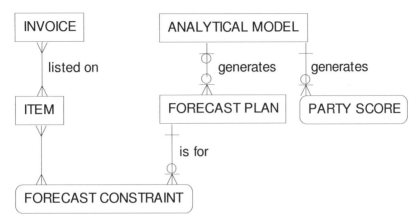

EXPLANATION	An industry model is a prebuilt data model that captures how an organization in a particular industry works or should work.
COMPETITIVE ADVANTAGE	Use of an industry model is still at its "competitive advantage" stage and not yet at its "competitive necessity" stage. A relatively small number of organizations are using them. For example, in our EDM survey, 18 out of 22 (82%) organizations built their own EDM.
INDUSTRY CONSORTIUMS	<ul><li>National Retail Federation's Association of Retail Technology Standards (ARTS)</li><li>Global Justice XML Data Model</li><li>ACCORD life, annuity and other insurance model</li><li>PPDM/PODS for GEO utilities</li><li>Health Level Seven (HL7) Reference Information Model (RIM)</li><li>New Generation Operation and Support (NGOSS) Shared Information Data Model (SID)</li></ul>
VENDOR MODELS	<ul><li>Teradata</li><li>IBM</li><li>ADRM</li></ul>

Actual implementations

Data warehouse and Reference database

Data Warehouse

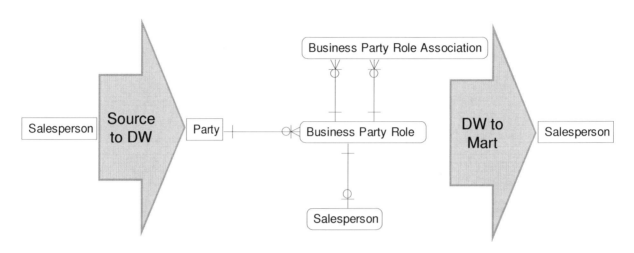

Reference Database

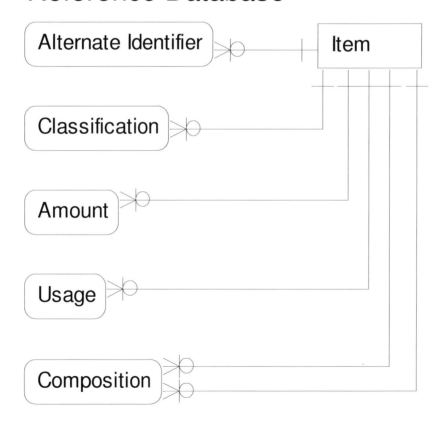

Actual implementations

Data warehouse and Reference database

DATA WAREHOUSE

This is how the Sales Organization subject area was designed. This model was a failure because although the structures were implemented generically, the code was implemented to only consider sales organization, so new types of Parties could not easily be accommodated.

REFERENCE DATABASE

This is how an Item reference database was designed. Notice how abstraction is applied to data elements and relationships. There is an Alternate Identifier table very similar to our earlier example, which contains other ways to uniquely identify an Item (e.g. UPC). There is also a Classification table to capture the groupings or categories an item can belong to and the hierarchy between these groupings or categories. The Amount table abstracts standard amounts associated with an item, such as list price and weight.

This model was a success because all of the interfaces were abstracted to reflect the abstract database, so that any new change was a non-event through the whole system, and therefore the application required very little maintenance.

Applying the Data Model Scorecard®

Interaction Report for Product BB40 from May 2011

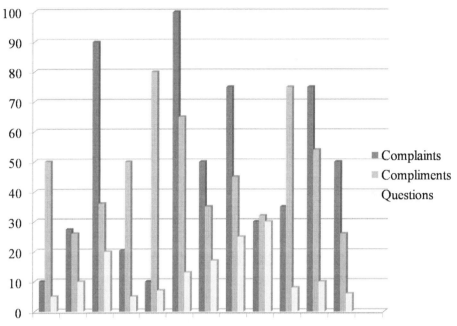

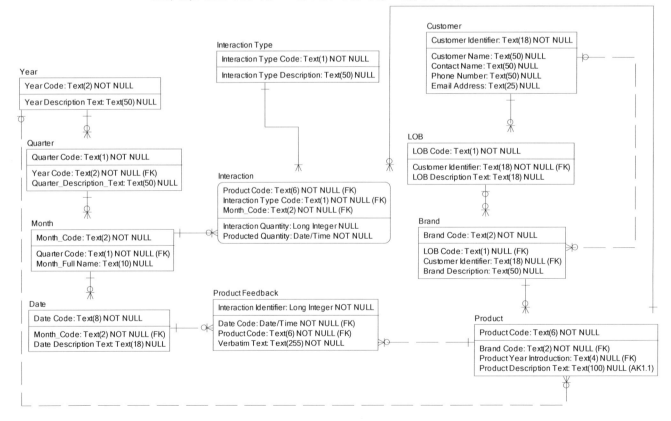

Applying the Data Model Scorecard®

5. How well does the model leverage generic structures?

EXPLANATION

This category confirms an appropriate use of abstraction on the model. One of the most powerful tools a data modeler has at their disposal is abstraction, the ability to increase the types of information a design can accommodate using generic concepts.

ANYTHING YOU WOULD CATCH IN THE MODEL ON THE FACING PAGE FOR THIS CATEGORY?

1.

2.

3.

4.

5.

6.

7.

8.

9.

10.

#	Category	Total score	Model score	%
1	How well does the model capture the requirements?	15		
2	How complete is the model?	15		
3	How well do the characteristics of the model support the type of model?	10		
4	How structurally sound is the model?	15		
5	How well does the model leverage generic structures?	10		
6	How well does the model follow naming standards?	5		
7	How well has the model been arranged for readability?	5		
8	How good are the definitions?	10		
9	How consistent is the model with the enterprise?	5		
10	How well does the metadata match the data?	10		
	TOTAL SCORE	100		

3 questions to cross safely to the other side:
1. When (if at all) should a standard allow for an entity or data element to have more than one name?
2. At what point (if any) would you postpone the deployment of a new system for not following naming standards?
3. Who in your organization is responsible for *enforcing* naming standards?

Module 6

Data Model Scorecard® Category #6: Standards

Category Question: How well does the model follow naming standards?

This module is your guide to: Using consistent naming standards

Category Overview

How well does the model follow naming standards?

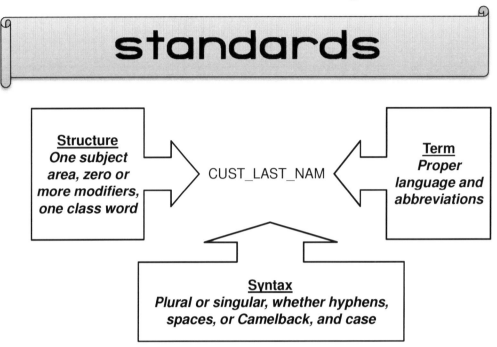

EXPLANATION

Correct and consistent naming standards are extremely helpful for knowledge transfer and integration. New team members who are familiar with similar naming conventions on other projects will avoid the time to learn a new set of naming standards. This category focuses on naming standard structure, term, and syntax.

STRUCTURE

Structure means the building blocks of a name. A popular standard for data element structure is one Prime, zero, one, or many Modifiers, and one Class Word. A prime is a concept that is basic and critical to the business. A modifier qualifies this prime and a class word is the high-level domain for a data element. Examples of class words are Quantity, Amount, Code, and Date.

TERM

Term includes proper spelling and abbreviation. An abbreviations list can be used to name each logical and physical term.

SYNTAX

Syntax includes whether the term should be plural or singular, whether hyphens, spaces, or Camelback (i.e. initial upper case such as CustomerLastName) should be used, and case (i.e. upper case, initial upper case, or lower case).

Category Overview

Structure

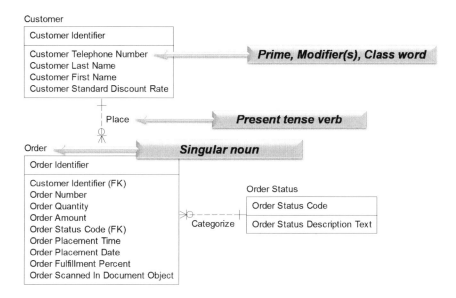

BACKGROUND

Naming structure refers to the types of terms that make up an entity, data element, or relationship name. For structure, the key word is 'type', as we are not referring to terms such as 'Customer' but instead types such as nouns, verbs, and modifiers.

ENTITY

An entity name is a noun. It is not a property of the noun (i.e. a data element), but the noun itself. Customer is an entity name, but Customer Last Name is not.

DATA ELEMENT

A popular standard for data element structure is one Prime, zero, one, or many Modifiers (aka Descriptors), and one Class Word. A prime is a concept that is basic and critical to the business. A modifier qualifies this prime and a class word is the high-level domain for a data element. Examples of class words are Quantity, Amount, Code, and Date.

Category Overview

Structure (continued)

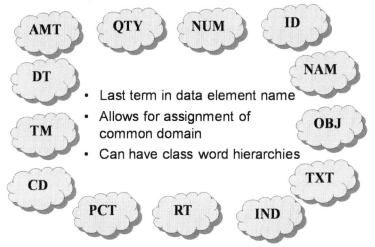

- Last term in data element name
- Allows for assignment of common domain
- Can have class word hierarchies

COMMON CLASS WORDS

- Amount (AMT). Numeric value expressing a quantity of monetary currency; when denominated in other than U.S. Dollars, an *Amount* field must be accompanied by a *Code* class element which identifies the currency.
- Code (CD). Symbols used to represent one other attribute, the decode.
- Date (DT). Alphanumeric value representing a month, day, and year.
- Identifier (ID). A data element used to completely or partially identify a table.
- Indicator (IND). A flag used by the business to show which of two conditions apply. Where there are more than two possible conditions, or where a third *(not sure or unknown)* condition may exist the *Code* class word should be used.
- Name (NAM). Word or phrase that designates a person, place, or thing.
- Number (NUM). An alphanumeric value that cannot be mathematically manipulated. Often NUM is used for business identifiers, such as employee number, serial number, part number, and telephone number.
- Percent (PCT). The numeric ratio of two numbers, multiplied by 100.
- Object (OBJ). Image, document, multimedia, BLOB (Binary Large OBject).
- Quantity (QTY). A non-monetary accumulation (either positive or negative) of some unit. Includes the count of a number of things, such as number of customers.
- Rate (RT). Numeric value representing the quotient of two numbers. PCT is multiplied by 100, RT is not.
- Text (TXT). Information, primarily in the form of words, stored as a unit.
- Time (TM). Alphanumeric value representing the time of day; hour, minutes, and seconds.

Category Overview

Term

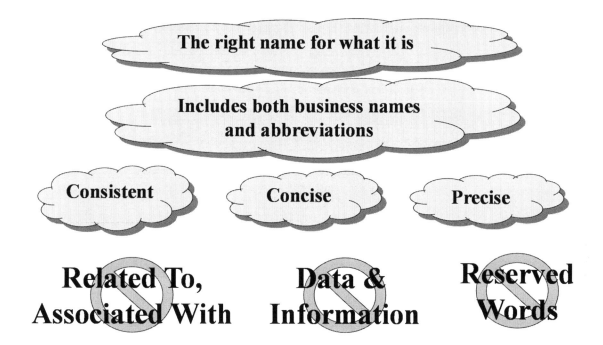

BACKGROUND	Term refers to proper spelling and abbreviation. Traditionally logical names are spelled out completely and physical names contain some form of abbreviation. An abbreviations list can be used to name each physical term.
SPECIFIC TO ENTITIES	Reflect the thing the entity represents, rather than any medium on which it is handled. For example, when naming an entity to describe the event oriented data associated with the receipt of a complaint from a student, use something like Student Complaint, rather than Student Complaint Letter.
SPECIFIC TO RELATIONSHIPS	Use meaningful names. Names like "related to" or "associated with" do not add enough meaning to the name to be useful when communicating the relationship to others.

Category Overview

Syntax

**How terms
are
separated**

Case

CUSTOMER LAST NAME?
CustomerLastName?
Customer_Last_Name?
Customer Last Name?
customerLastName?
Customer-Last-Name?
CUSTOMER-LAST-NAME?
customer last name?
customer_last_name?

BACKGROUND

Syntax refers to whether the term should be plural or singular, whether hyphens, spaces, or Camelback (i.e. initial upper case with no spaces such as customerLastName) should be used, and case (i.e. upper case, initial upper case, or lower case).

GENERAL TO ENTITIES, DATA ELEMENTS, AND RELATIONSHIPS

Use alphabetic characters only; avoid using special characters like "/?!@#$%^&*()+=',."

Category Overview

Validating naming standards

The Production Product table from our publishing ERP system

Syntax and Term look pretty good here, but what about Structure? Which of these data elements need valid primes and/or classwords?

Field Name	Data Type
ProductID	AutoNumber
ISBN	Text
SubTitle	Text
RetailPrice	Number
Weight	Number
Notes	Memo
InActive	Yes/No
PublicationDate	Date/Time
EditionNumber	Text
Description	Memo
ProductHeight	Number
ProductLength	Number
ProductWidth	Number
ProductsPerCarton	Number
CartonHeight	Number
CartonLength	Number
CartonWidth	Number
ImageID	Number
Subscription	Yes/No
NotIndividuallyForSale	Yes/No
ProductName	Text
TitleID	Number

BACKGROUND

I always find it amazing how frequently production systems have inconsistent or incomplete names. Put a check next to each name in this production table that has good structure, and an 'x' next to each that is lacking in structure.

Standards recommendations

Some thoughts on naming standards

Some thoughts on naming standards:

You can't tell me what to do!

A naming standards document should be easily accessible and include a one page summary.

In the pursuit of consistency and purity, don't lose sight of one of the fundamental objectives of modeling: communication. Sometimes we must sacrifice rigid adherence to standards for familiarity and better quality feedback from non-technical participants in the modeling process.

Graeme Simsion, Data Modeling Essentials

From the Table of Contents from a government agency standards document:

- Introduction
  - Purpose
  - Audience
  - Drivers
  - Exceptions from Use
- Standards
- Bibliography
- Appendix A: Quick Reference Guide
- Appendix B: Authorized Class Words
- Appendix C: Data Model Scorecard® Template
- Approval Signature

Standards recommendations

Some thoughts on naming standards

YOU CAN'T TELL ME WHAT TO DO!

In most organizations the person or group responsible for ensuring naming standards compliance has no organizational authority to make the project team comply. In many cases in comes down to influencing skills.

NOT OVERKILL

I really like Graeme Simsion's quote on the facing page. It reminds me to keep standards in context, and always make sure to give model communication and presentation the priority. I believe an ideal standards document should be short and sweet, and if it is long, there should be a "cheat sheet" provided.

STANDARDS DOCUMENT TABLE OF CONTENTS FROM A GOVERNMENT AGENCY

The facing page contains a subset of a table of contents from the standards document from a government agency. I like that in the introduction it talks about the purpose of standards yet also lists exceptions (such as not renaming data elements in packaged software). The appendices offer value too, especially the "cheat sheet" (aka "Quick Reference Guide"). The last page of this document contains the signature of a top government official, symbolizing that not following these standards means going against what he believes is right. Now that adds a large incentive to following the standard!

Standards resources

Naming standards resources

Data modeling tools can help check adherence to standards

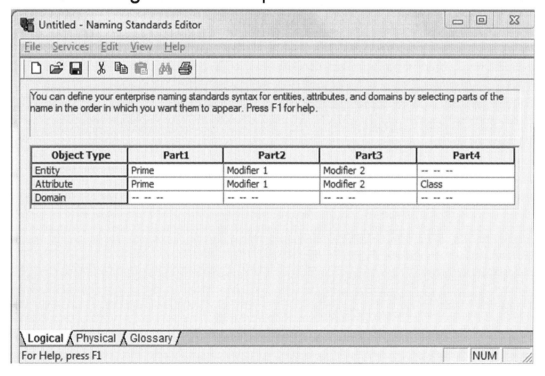

Standards resources

Naming standards resources

BACKGROUND

There are a number of useful naming standards resources available for free (or almost free) on the Web. ISO 11179 is the most well-known. Advantages to using someone else's standards (and preferably an industry standard) is that someone else has already done a lot of work on them and you don't have to reinvent the wheel. Also, someone else maintains them, so time and money are saved on an ongoing basis as well. In addition, when people first join a company, it can be a quicker learning curve if they are already familiar with the naming standards. Also, with mergers and acquisitions, using similar naming standards can facilitate integration.

ISO 11179

International Standard ISO 11179, *Information Technology Specification and Standardization of Data Elements* describes a set of rules for developing naming conventions together with standards for data classification, attribution, definition and registration. Here is a link to a good summary of this standard: http://www.gils.net/naming.html. And here is a link to a site which lists all of the ISO 11179 documents: http://metadata-standards.org/11179/.

DATA MODELING HANDBOOK

The Data Modeling Handbook, by Reingruber and Gregory, includes many pages on standards that are very useful.

ERP VENDORS

If you are using an ERP package, chances are that sooner or later you will need to expand it with additional data elements and tables. ERP vendors are very explicit about how to name these new objects, to distinguish them from those that come with the package. For example, SAP/R3 recommends adding a 'Z_' in front of customized tables.

DATA MODELING TOOLS CAN HELP

Data modeling tools can help check standards compliance, and some tools can even help you with coming up with new abbreviations. The screen print on the facing page is from ERwin Data Modeler and shows one of ERwin's naming standards features – this feature helps define logical name structure.

Applying the Data Model Scorecard®
Interaction Report for Product BB40 from May 2011

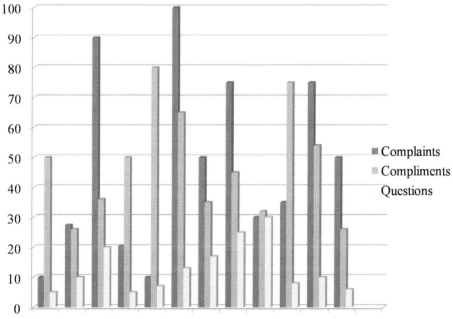

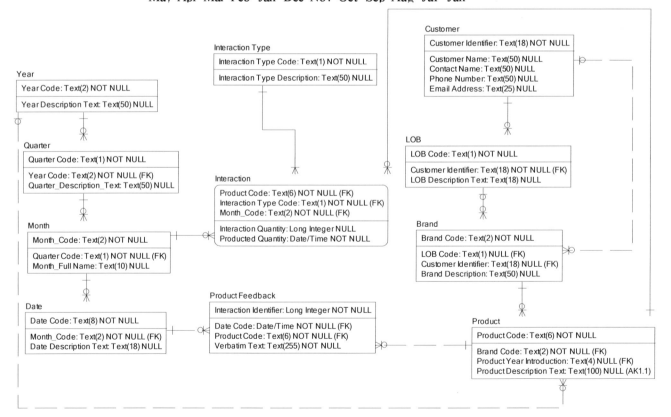

Applying the Data Model Scorecard®

6. How well does the model follow naming standards?

EXPLANATION

This category focuses on naming standard structure, abbreviations, and syntax.

ANYTHING YOU
WOULD CATCH IN
THE MODEL ON
THE FACING PAGE
FOR THIS
CATEGORY?

1.

2.

3.

4.

5.

6.

7.

8.

9.

10.

#	Category	Total score	Model score	%
1	How well does the model capture the requirements?	15		
2	How complete is the model?	15		
3	How well do the characteristics of the model support the type of model?	10		
4	How structurally sound is the model?	15		
5	How well does the model leverage generic structures?	10		
6	How well does the model follow naming standards?	5		
7	How well has the model been arranged for readability?	5		
8	How good are the definitions?	10		
9	How consistent is the model with the enterprise?	5		
10	How well does the metadata match the data?	10		
	TOTAL SCORE	100		

Module 7

Category Question: How well has the model been arranged for readability?

This module is your guide to: Arranging the model for maximum understanding

Category overview

How well has the model been arranged for readability?

readability

Confirms the model is visually easy to follow so that the other scorecard categories can be accurately measured

> *A diagram is a sentence in a graphical language.*
> *The purpose of any language is to communicate.*
> *A "good" diagram is therefore one which*
> *communicates effectively.*
> Daniel Moody

Category overview

How well has the model been arranged for readability?

EXPLANATION

A data model is a communication tool and therefore needs to be easy to read. Readability needs to be considered at a model, entity, data element, and relationship level. At a model level, I like to see a large model broken into smaller logical pieces. I also search for the "heart" of the model.

At an entity level, I like to see child entities below parent entities. Child entities being on the many side of the relationship, and parent entities on the one side of the relationship. So if an *order* contains many *order lines*, *order line* should appear below *order*.

At a data element level, I like to see some logic applied regarding the placement of data elements within an entity. For example, on reference entities such as *customer* and *employee*, it is more readable to have the data elements listed in an order that makes sense for someone starting at the beginning of the entity and working down sequentially. For example, *city name*, then *state name*, then *postal code*. For transaction entities such as *order* and *claim*, I have found it more readable to group the data elements into class words, such as all amount data elements grouped together.

At a relationship level, I try to minimize relationship line length, and the number of direction changes a relationship line makes. I also look for missing or incomplete relationship labels, if labels are appropriate on the model. The larger the model, the less useful it is to display labels as the extra verbiage can make the model harder to read.

PURPOSE

Ensures your model is easy to read so that the other scorecard categories can be accurately measured.

Readability tips

Characteristics of a beautiful model

Model in general

- Look for the heart
- Aim for a frame
- Treat white space like air
- Group subjects
- Background

Relationship

- Minimize relationship line length and direction turns
- Crows fly south
- Supertypes above subtypes
- Avoid lines passing through entities
- Minimize crossing lines

Entity

- Effective use of color
- Reasonable number of entities on page
- Avoid UPPERCASE
- Stretch important entities
- Align entities

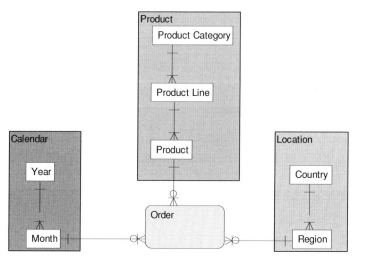

Data element

- Reference DEs by chronology
- Transaction DEs by class word
- Effective use of text style
- Avoid UPPERCASE
- Avoid alphabetical

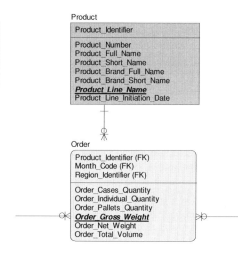

Readability tips

Characteristics of a beautiful model

DATA MODEL IN GENERAL

Make the most important entity (or entities) the heart of the model, and work your way out from there. So for example, on a dimensional model, starting with the meter in the center and working out is a good approach. The human brain likes to see pictures in squares or rectangles, so if possible, at least for the bottom, make it straight across. Daniel Moody says "Treat white space like air", meaning it is ok and desirable to have sections of the model where there are no modeling structures, as a way to separate groups of entities from each other. Group subjects that are meaningful together, and it can be much more readable to have the background for the model be a different color than the entities (such as a 10% gray background with white entities).

ENTITY

Color can be very useful to show many things, such as issues, subject areas, and phase complete. Try not to put too many entities on the page, as that detracts from readability, and avoid uppercase which can slow down reading by as much as 20% and sometimes portray emotion (CUSTOMER!). If an entity is more important than its surrounding entities you may want to stretch its box to indicate such (also good if there are lots of relationships connecting to this entity). Aligning entities is easy to do with most modeling tools and makes the model look much sharper.

RELATIONSHIP

Minimize line length and direction changes because it can be confusing to have long relationship lines that keep turning different directions. Keep the many side of the relationship pointing down as it can be easier to read the model top down rather than bottom up. Similar comment applies to supertype/subtypes (supertype above subtypes). Sometimes we have a relationship line that passes behind the entity. This gives the false appearance that this entity is somehow attached to and therefore participates in this relationship. Also minimize crossing lines, as long as it does not lead to lots of long relationships with many bends.

DATA ELEMENT

It is a good practice to sequence reference entities (such as Customer and Product) by chronology (meaning in the sequence that makes sense for business professionals to see them in), and transaction entities by class word (e.g. Date, ID, Name). Text style, such as bold or italic, can call attention to an element (e.g. if there is an issue). Uppercase as mentioned detracts from readability, and sorting the data elements alphabetically usually makes it hard to find a data element you are looking for.

Applying the Data Model Scorecard®

Interaction Report for Product BB40 from May 2011

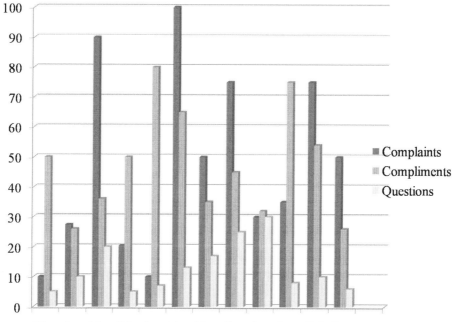

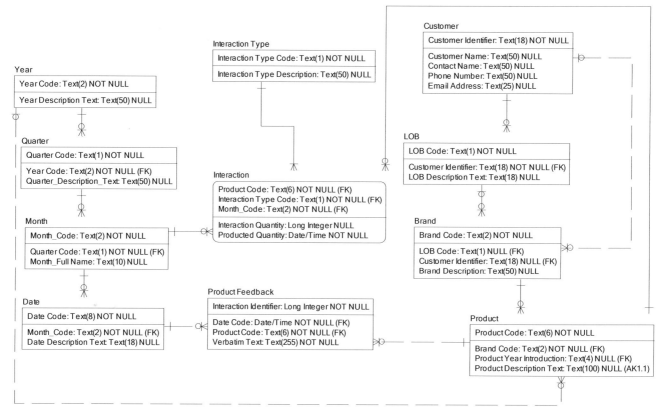

Applying the Data Model Scorecard®
7. How well has the model been arranged for readability?

EXPLANATION

A data model is a communication tool and this category ensures the data model is arranged to make it easy to understand and walk through.

ANYTHING YOU WOULD CATCH IN THE MODEL ON THE FACING PAGE FOR THIS CATEGORY?

1.

2.

3.

4.

5.

6.

7.

8.

9.

10.

#	Category	Total score	Model score	%
1	How well does the model capture the requirements?	15		
2	How complete is the model?	15		
3	How well do the characteristics of the model support the type of model?	10		
4	How structurally sound is the model?	15		
5	How well does the model leverage generic structures?	10		
6	How well does the model follow naming standards?	5		
7	How well has the model been arranged for readability?	5		
8	How good are the definitions?	10		
9	How consistent is the model with the enterprise?	5		
10	How well does the metadata match the data?	10		
	TOTAL SCORE	100		

Module 8

Data Model Scorecard® Category #8: Definitions

Category Question:	How good are the definitions?

| *This module is your guide to:* | Writing clear, complete, and correct definitions |

http://egrc/ → IT Standards
                    └ Meta Data & Modeling Std.

http://taxonomy/ → Meta Data Repository
                        ┌ Definitions
                        └ Domain Values

Category overview

How good are the definitions?

definitions

Confirms entity and data element definitions are clear, complete, and correct

| Product | —— Appear on —○<— | Order Line |

Does Product include Research Items not yet available for sale?

Why am I seeing negative quantities in Order Line Amount? Does Order Line include returns?

Is Product always a finished tangible product ready for sale, or can it include raw materials, packaging items, or even services?

Category overview

How good are the definitions?

EXPLANATION

This category confirms all definitions are clear, complete, and correct. Clarity means that a reader can understand the meaning of a term by reading the definition only once. Completeness ensures the definition is at the appropriate level of detail, and that it includes all the necessary components such as derivations and examples. Correctness focuses on having a definition that totally matches what the term means, and is consistent with the rest of the business.

PURPOSE

Minimizes doubt that may exist about the contents of data elements and the relationships between entities. Doubts and misinterpretations lead to model ambiguity.

CHALLENGE

You will need to find business people from outside your department or project to validate the definitions. As data governance catches on, this challenge will become easier and easier.

QUESTION TO ASK

For completeness in our question-driven modeling process, ask "How is this term defined?"

Evaluating definitions

Definitions need to be clear, complete, and correct

Put an 'X' in any cell where you are confident your organization has one clear, complete, and correct definition for this term. Can anybody yell Bingo?

B	I	N	G	O
Customer	Product	Account	Prospect	Calendar
Visit	Contract	Department	Credit	Citizen
Site	Order	★	Resource	Service
Employee	Agency	Consumer	Revenue	Case
Organization	Facility	Expense	Project	Event

A Customer is a person or organization who obtains our product for resale. The Customer normally obtains the product through purchase. An example of a customer who does not purchase our product is the Salvation Army, which receives the product for free as a charity organization. A person or organization must have obtained at least one product from us to be considered a Customer. That is, Prospects are not Customers. Also, once a Customer, always a Customer so even Customers that have not obtained anything in 50 years are still considered Customers. The Customer is different than the Consumer, who purchases the product for consumption as opposed to resale.

Examples:
Walmart
Bob's Grocery Store
Military Base 1332

Clear   Complete   Correct

Evaluating definitions

Definitions need to be clear, complete, and correct

BACKGROUND

Despite their importance, definitions tend to be omitted or written with minimal attention to their audience. Therefore, when writing definitions, we need to be aware of three characteristics that lead to a high-quality definition that the audience can understand. Those characteristics are clarity, completeness, and correctness.

CLEAR

Clarity means that a reader can understand the meaning of a term by reading the definition only once. A clear definition does not require the reader to decipher how each sentence should be interpreted. The definition contains what the entity represents, and not what the entity contains or when the entity is used. A good way to make sure your definition is clear is to think about what makes a definition unclear. We need to avoid restating the obvious and using obscure technical terminology and abbreviations in our definitions. Let's say, for example, that the definition of *associate identifier* is "associate identifier" or "the identifier for the associate."

COMPLETE

This category focuses on making sure the definition is at the appropriate level of detail and that it includes all the necessary components, such as derivations, aliases, exceptions, and examples. Having a definition at the appropriate level of detail means that it is not too generic as to provide very little additional value, yet not so specific that it provides value only to an application or department—or that it adds value only at a certain point in time.

CORRECT

This category focuses on having a definition that completely matches what the term means and is consistent with the rest of the business. *Correctness* means that an expert in the field would agree that the term matches the definition. One of the difficulties with this category is that as we define broader terms that cross departments, such as *product, customer,* and *employee,* we tend to get more than one accurate definition, depending on who is asked.

Writing good definitions

Useful techniques

See what's available externally

Web   Images   Video   News   Maps   more »

define: student   Search

Overly precise

Let's see. I'm not sure if Customer includes prospects. Let me add it to the definition and see what the business says.

Define before name

Is this Insurance Type Code or Line of Business Code? Defining first really helps!

Create a definition template

Order Scheduled Delivery Date

List of subject area definitions to choose from

List of classword or domain definitions to choose from

Provide your team with helpful pointers

- The definition of a data object should answer all "what?" questions
- The definition should be expressed in *simple complete* sentences
- Verbs used in the definition must be in their present tense
- Only approved abbreviations and acronyms may be used
- Do not define a thing in terms of itself

Writing good definitions

Useful techniques

SEE WHAT'S AVAILABLE EXTERNALLY

Search engines such as Bing can make coming up with a definition (or at least a starter definition) very easy. Type "Define:" and then what you would like to define, such as "Define: Student".

OVERLY PRECISE

I know a modeler who will write the initial definition and then have the business user review. In writing the initial definition, she is deliberately overly precise – so precise that she knows the definition is wrong. Then when a business person reviews the definition they correct the one or two sentences that are not accurate and the entire definition is approved. It is easier to correct a sentence than it is to think of it from scratch.

DEFINE BEFORE NAME

A good technique is to define the term before you even name it. If we define the term first, we can create a better name for it after understanding what it is. For example, instead of naming a data element Insurance Type Code, we might name it Insurance Line of Business after first defining and understanding what the data element really means.

CREATE A DEFINITION TEMPLATE

You can provide an easily accessible list of subject area definitions, as well as a list of class word or domain definitions and append these definitions to the definition of the entity or data element so that all the person defining the term needs to do is define the new terms.

PROVIDE YOUR TEAM WITH HELPFUL POINTERS

Here are examples of pointers provided by a large retail organization in their standards documentation:
- The definition of a data object should answer all "what?" questions.
- The definition should be expressed in *simple complete* sentences.
- Verbs used in the definition must be in their present tense.
- Only approved abbreviations acronyms and may be used in the text of definitions.
- Do not define a thing in terms of itself.

Writing good definitions

Defining Customer ID

Writing good definitions

Defining Customer ID

BACKGROUND

I was showing examples of both complete and incomplete definitions during a recent training class, when I shared the following incomplete definition for a Customer Identifier:

A Customer Identifier is the unique identifier for a Customer.

"What else can you say about Customer Identifier anyway?" a participant asked.

CHALLENGE

What else can you say about Customer Identifier (or any identifier) to add more meaning to its definition?

Writing good definitions

Now let's define some "simple" terms!

MY DEFINITION FOR "BOOK":

A published work of literature, science, or reference, or a work intended for publication.

MY DEFINITION FOR "TITLE":

Writing good definitions

Now let's define some "simple" terms!

BACKGROUND

Come up with clear, complete, and correct definitions for "book" and "title". Then compare your definitions with those of the people around you. Can you come up with one agreed-upon definition for each of these terms?

Reconciling definitions

Useful techniques

Iterative meeting technique

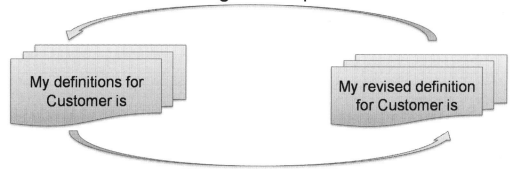

My definitions for Customer is

My revised definition for Customer is

Batman technique

Customer is an organization who opens a contract with our company. So any organization with a date in the Contract Open Date field is a customer.

Venn Diagram Technique

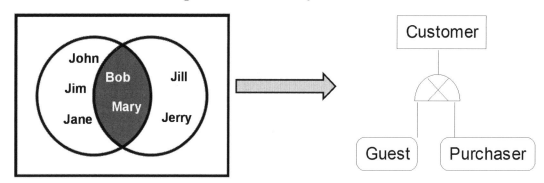

John
Jim
Jane
Bob
Mary
Jill
Jerry

Customer

Guest   Purchaser

Industry standard definitions

Let's see how our industry data model defines Customer…

Overly generic terms and definitions

What do you guys think of Party and Role for now…

Reconciling definitions
Useful techniques

OVERVIEW

Sometimes we may find that we have multiple clear, complete, and correct definitions for the same term. This usually happens when we are working on large cross-department projects such as a data warehouse. There are a number of techniques we can use to get to one definition.

ITERATIVE MEETING TECHNIQUE

Sometimes in a meeting situation, there is a win/lose mentality, where if two or more competing definitions are presented, one may be chosen and that person wins and everyone else loses. A useful technique to avoid this scenario, is to provide each attendee with everyone else's definitions and ask for a revised definition for the next meeting. In just a few meetings there may be one agreed-upon definition or several very close definitions.

BATMAN TECHNIQUE

Batman once said, "It's not who I am underneath, but what I do that defines me." We can apply this idea to writing definitions as well. We can define a term by what that term does instead of what that term "is", such as the Customer example on the facing page.

VENN DIAGRAM TECHNIQUE

We can sketch on a flipchart or whiteboard sample values from each of the participants, with the hope of getting a common set (the overlap). The overlap can become the supertype and what is unique can become subtypes.

INDUSTRY STANDARD DEFINITIONS

One way to diffuse emotion and come up with one agreed-upon definition is to find an industry standard definition, such as from an industry data model or other well-recognized source. Make sure it is not too abstract though, as then its value may be limited.

OVERLY GENERIC TERMS AND DEFINITIONS

As a last resort, you can use terms and definitions so generic that everyone agrees, and it is possible this may solve the problem, or the issue will get postponed.

Applying the Data Model Scorecard®
Interaction Report for Product BB40 from May 2011

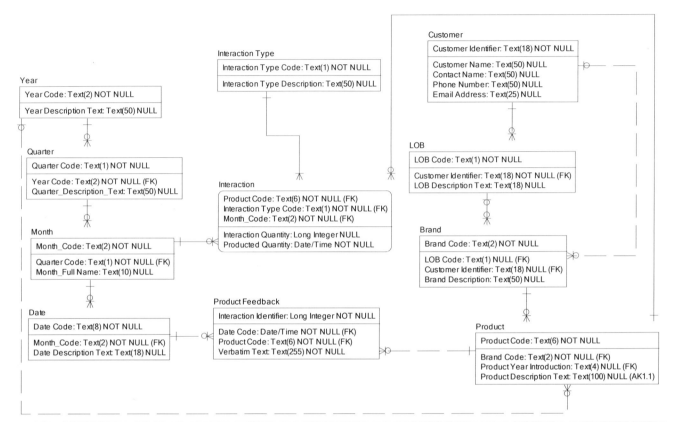

#	Category	Total score	Model score	%
1	How well do the characteristics of the model support the type of model?	10		
2	How well does the model capture the requirements?	15		
3	How complete is the model?	15		
4	How structurally sound is the model?	15		
5	How well does the model leverage generic structures?	10		
6	How well does the model follow naming standards?	5		
7	How well has the model been arranged for readability?	5		
8	How good are the definitions?	10		
9	How consistent is the model with the enterprise?	5		
10	How well does the metadata match the data?	10		
	TOTAL SCORE	100		

Applying the Data Model Scorecard®

8. How good are the definitions?

EXPLANATION   This category confirms all definitions are clear, complete, and correct. Clarity means that a reader can understand the meaning of a term by reading the definition only once. Completeness ensures the definition includes all the necessary components. Correctness focuses on having a definition that totally matches what the term means. The only definitions you were provided with are shown below and on the following pages. How good are these definitions? Review the definitions and give a point score.

Table Name	Column Name	Column Comment
Product Feedback	Interaction Identifier	
	Verbatim Text	The actual comment from the consumer who contacted us, such as "I found something in my product."
	Date Code	The full date in YYYYMMDD format.
	Product Code	The unique way of identifying the product. This is a business natural key.
Date	Date Code	The full date in YYYYMMDD format.
	Date Description Text	
	Month_Code	The code for the month, a number between 01 and 12.
Interaction Type	Interaction Type Code	The code corresponding to whether the interaction with the consumer is a complaint, compliment, or question. Examples: 01 = Complaint 02 = Compliment 03 = Question
	Interaction Type Description	The description corresponding to whether the interaction with the consumer is a complaint, compliment, or question. Examples: 01 = Complaint 02 = Compliment 03 = Question

Table Name	Column Name	Column Comment
Interaction	Interaction Quantity	The number of interactions.
	Producted Quantity	The amount of product produced.
	Product Code	The unique way of identifying the product. This is a business natural key.
	Interaction Type Code	The code corresponding to whether the interaction with the consumer is a complaint, compliment, or question. Examples: 01 = Complaint 02 = Compliment 03 = Question
Month	Month_Code	The code for the month, a number between 01 and 12.
	Month_Full Name	The name for the month.
	Quarter Code	The number 1, 2, 3, or 4 depending on which fourth of the year it is.
Year	Year Code	The four digit code (e.g. 2011) for the period of 365 days (or 366 days in leap years) starting from the first of January, used for reckoning time in ordinary affairs.
	Year Description Text	The text description for the period of 365 days (or 366 days in leap years) starting from the first of January, used for reckoning time in ordinary affairs.
Quarter	Quarter Code	The number 1, 2, 3, or 4 depending on which fourth of the year it is.
	Quarter_Description_Text	The full description for the quarter of year.
	Year Code	The four digit code (e.g. 2011) for the period of 365 days (or 366 days in leap years) starting from the first of January, used for reckoning time in ordinary affairs.
Customer	Customer Identifier	The identifier for the customer.
	Customer Name	Customer Name.
	Contact Name	The first and last name of the key person to reach at the Customer site. This is usually someone in Consumer Affairs.
	Phone Number	Contact phone number.
	Email Address	Contact email address.

Table Name	Column Name	Column Comment
LOB	LOB Code	The 2 character code corresponding to the line of business. Examples: 01 = Automobiles 02 = Motocycles 03 = Trucks
	LOB Description Text	The description corresponding to the line of business. Examples: 01 = Automobiles 02 = Motocycles 03 = Trucks
	Customer Identifier	The identifier for the customer.
Brand	Brand Code	The American Marketing Association defines a brand as a "name, term, design, symbol, or any other feature that identifies one seller's good or service as distinct from those of other sellers. The legal term for brand is trademark. A brand may identify one item, a family of items, or all items of that seller. If used for the firm as a whole, the preferred term is trade name."
	Brand Description	
	LOB Code	The 2 character code corresponding to the line of business. Examples: 01 = Automobiles 02 = Motocycles 03 = Trucks
	Customer Identifier	The identifier for the customer.
Product	Product Code	The unique way of identifying the product. This is a business natural key.
	Product Description Text	
	Brand Code	The American Marketing Association defines a brand as a "name, term, design, symbol, or any other feature that identifies one seller's good or service as distinct from those of other sellers. The legal term for brand is trademark. A brand may identify one item, a family of items, or all items of that seller. If used for the firm as a whole, the preferred term is trade name."
	Product Year Introduction	The four digit code (e.g. 2011) for the period of 365 days (or 366 days in leap years) starting from the first of January, used for reckoning time in ordinary affairs.

Who wants to be the Data Architect?

Module 9

Data Model Scorecard® Category #9: Consistency

Category Question: How consistent is the model with the enterprise?

This module is your guide to: Matching the model with the enterprise

Category overview

How consistent is the model with the enterprise?

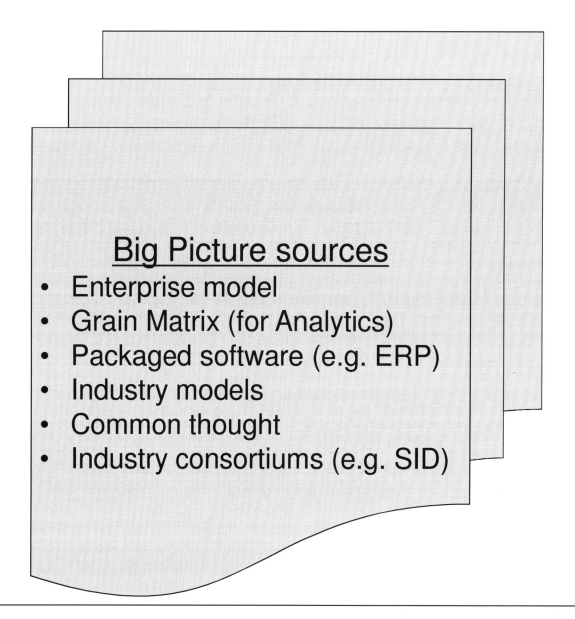

Confirms the model complements a "Big Picture"

Big Picture sources
- Enterprise model
- Grain Matrix (for Analytics)
- Packaged software (e.g. ERP)
- Industry models
- Common thought
- Industry consortiums (e.g. SID)

Category overview

How consistent is the model with the enterprise?

EXPLANATION

The structures that appear in the model being reviewed should be consistent in terminology and usage to structures that appear in related data models, and with the enterprise model if one exists. This way there will be consistency across projects.

PURPOSE

Ensures the information is represented in a broad and consistent context, so that one set of terminology and rules can be spoken in the organization.

CHALLENGE

Not all organizations have a "big picture" to compare the data model to for consistency.

Grain Matrix

Explanation

> The Grain Matrix captures the levels of reporting for each measure. It can be built from business questions or reports, top down or bottom up.

 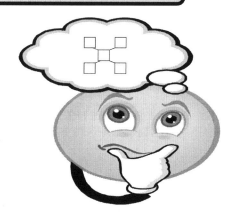

Example:

1. Show me the number of students receiving financial aid by department and semester for the last five years. [From Financial Aid Office]
2. Show me the number of students on full or partial scholarship by department and semester for the last four years. [From Accounting Department]
3. How many students graduated by department and semester over the last three years? [From Alumni Affairs]
4. How many students applied to the university over the last ten years? I want to compare applications from high school students vs other universities. [From Admissions Department]

	Student Count
Financial Aid Indicator	1
Semester	1, 2, 3
Year	1, 2, 3, 4
Department	1, 2, 3
Scholarship Indicator	2
Graduation Indicator	3
High School Application Indicator	4
University Application Indicator	4

Grain Matrix

Explanation

BACKGROUND

The Grain Matrix captures the levels of reporting for each measure – it is the translation of questions into a spreadsheet. The measures become columns, and the ways of looking at these measures become rows. It is used for precisely capturing requirements, and for scoping and prioritizing dimensional applications, as shown below.

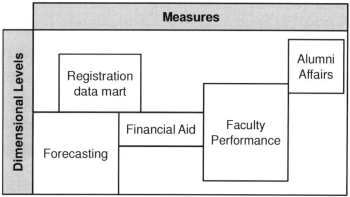

EXAMPLE

The example on the facing page illustrates that we can take business questions from different departments and plot them on the same spreadsheet, and possibly create a design such as the one below which satisfies multiple needs with the same structure.

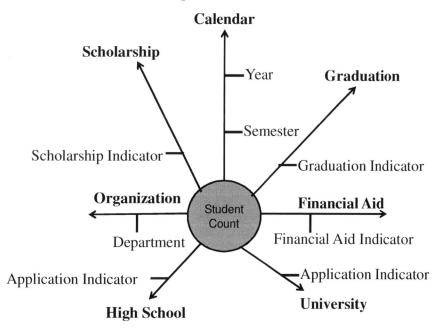

Grain Matrix

The need for precise and complete business questions

	Precise?	Complete?	Rewritten (include assumptions)
How is my company doing?			
What is our top sales channel?			
What is our average cost per book?			
How many copies of **Secrets of Analytical Leaders** should we print?			
Will ebook sales cannibalize print book sales?			

Grain Matrix
The need for precise and complete business questions

MANY WAYS TO ACHIEVE GOAL OF PRECISE AND COMPLETE BUSINESS QUESTIONS

The end result of the elicitation process for analytical applications is a set of precise and complete business questions. Precision means it is obvious and clear in the business question which measures the user needs to see. Completeness means it is obvious and clear what the user needs to see it by. There are many sources of valuable business questions, including, your own experience, organization drivers and goals, business processes, measures, key terms, and existing reporting. Beware that some of these questions though, can lead to privacy or security issues.

"The key is not getting the right answers; it's asking the right questions."
– Ken Rudin, Head of Analytics at Facebook, Secrets of Analytical Leaders

IMPORTANCE OF CLEAR AND COMPLETE DEFINITIONS

Also, clear and consistent definitions of key terms in business questions are essential for getting a refined set of questions (e.g. removing duplicates). For example, what does Net Sales Amount mean? What does a Customer mean? Clear definitions remove all ambiguity and confusion.

ON THE FACING PAGE

Would you consider the business questions on the facing page to be precise and complete? If yes, put a check mark in the appropriate Precise and/or Complete columns. If no, make assumptions and fix them!

USE BUSINESS QUESTION PRIORITY MATRIX TO...

categorize the business questions. Those questions in the upper left quadrant are the ones that normally should be delivered first. Those questions in the lower right quadrant hopefully will never get implemented!

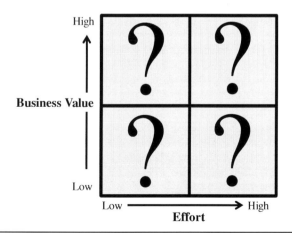

Grain Matrix
Book Sales Grain Matrix

1. How is my company doing? What is our percent change in gross revenue, net revenue, and books sold by title over the last three years?

2. What is our top sales channel for the last six months in terms of books sold?

3. What is our worst sales channel for the last six months in terms of books sold?

4. What season this past year did we experience the greatest percent increase in net revenue by title? Greatest percent decrease?

5. Compare net sales last quarter between Amazon and Barnes & Noble.

6. Which region did we sell more books last quarter, North America or Europe?

7. I want to see the total number of books we sold by title and sales channel.

8. I want our total net revenue by title and sales channel.

9. How many copies of **Secrets of Analytical Leaders** did we sell in the Asia/Pacific region last year?

10. Will ebook sales cannibalize print book sales? Compare ebook and print sales measured in gross revenue, net revenue, and books sold for two of our titles, **fruITion** and **recrEAtion**, over the last two years.

Assumptions:

Grain Matrix

Book Sales Grain Matrix

INSTRUCTIONS Fill in the grain matrix below based upon the business questions on the facing page. Write the measurements in columns, levels of detail in the rows, and reference the questions within each cell. Keep track of any assumptions you make.

	Gross Revenue Change Percent	Gross Revenue Amount	Net Revenue Change Percent	Net Revenue Amount	Books Sold Change Percent	Books Sold Quantity
Title	1	1	1,4	1,4	1	1
Year	1	1	1,4	1,4	1	1
Sales Channel						2,3
Month						2,3
Season			4	4		

Grain Matrix
Converting Grain Matrix to Logical Dimensional Data Model

	Gross Revenue Change Percent	Gross Revenue Amount	Net Revenue Change Percent	Net Revenue Amount	Books Sold Change Percent	Books Sold Quantity
Title	1	1,10	1,4	1,4,8,10	1	1,7,9,10
Year	1	1,10	1,4	1,4,10	1	1,9,10
Quarter				5		6
Season			4	4		
Month						2,3
Sales Channel				5,8		2,3,7
Region						6,9
Medium		10		10		10

One Business Solution

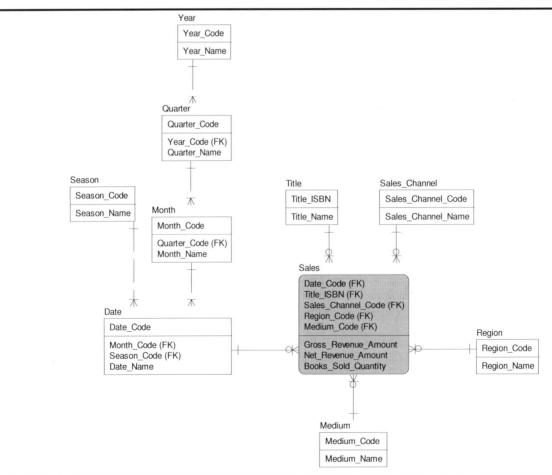

Grain Matrix
Converting Grain Matrix to Logical Dimensional Data Model

EXPLANATION　　The grain matrix can be scoped into one or many business applications. In this example, you see two logical dimensional models that can be built from the complete grain matrix for Book Sales.

Another Business Solution

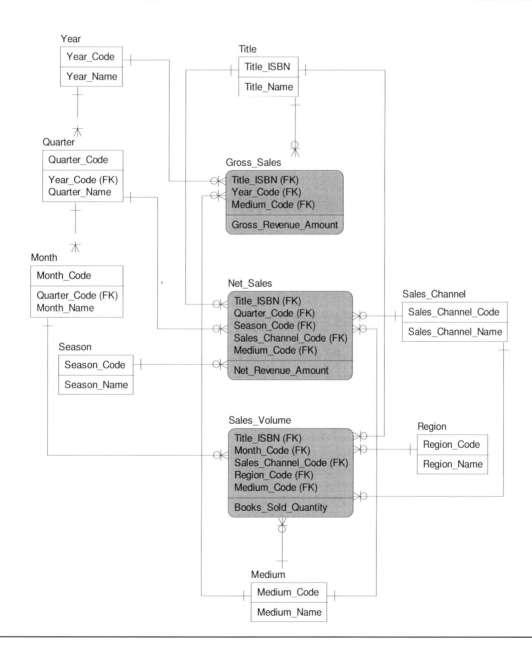

Data Vault

Explanation

Recall a subset of our publisher log file and the logical data model we previously built:

#	ISBN	Title	Subtitle	Author(s)	Library of Congress #	Format	Publication Date
1	9780977140022	Data Quality Assessment		Arkady Maydanchik	2007902970	Print	May 14th, 2007
3	9780977140077	Data Modeling for the Business	A Handbook for Aligning the Business with IT using High-Level Data Models	Steve Hoberman Donna Burbank Chris Bradley	2008912011	Print	April 2009
4	9780977140084	DAMA Guide to the Data Management Body of Knowledge		DAMA International		CD-ROM	April 2009
8	9781935504429	Data Quality Assessment		Arkady Maydanchik		Kindle	May 14th, 2007

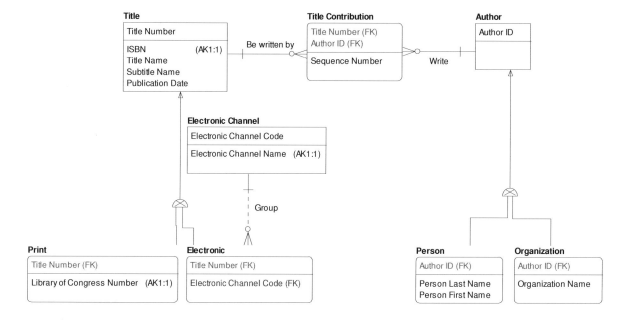

Data Vault

Explanation

CHARACTERISTICS

Data vault modeling, created by Dan Linstedt in 1990, is a physical data modeling technique for modeling enterprise data warehouses. What makes the data vault unique is the separation of "the thing" from how that thing changes over time. Data Vault separates the business keys (the "things") from the associations between those business keys from the descriptive attributes of those keys (which often change over time). For example, separating the customer business key from the customer descriptive information such as their contact information from the customer's relationship with products. This can create a flexible integrated data warehouse data model that accommodates SCD Type II history. Another characteristic that makes the data vault unique is that there is no distinction between good and bad data, enabling storing of all data. So if Bob the Customer has different keys in different systems, these would be stored as separate records and not cleansed (until it gets to the data mart, if needed). Data Vault's philosophy is that all data is relevant data, even if it is not in line with established definitions and business rules. Read the five series of articles on www.tdan.com and visit http://danlinstedt.com/ to learn more.

HUBS, LINKS, SATELLITES, AND REFERENCE TABLES

There are four types of tables in a data vault:
- **Hubs**. The hub represents the "thing" and contains a surrogate key (used for connections with other tables), a business key (which could be composite), source information, and optionally system fields such as when the table was last updated. If there is more than one business key for a "thing", it is simply stored as another row.
- **Links**. Links are the equivalent of associative entities, resolving the many-to-many relationships between hubs (sometimes more than two entities can be resolved through a hub). Hubs only relate to other hubs through links, so there are no one-to-many relationships between hubs. Links are identified by the surrogate keys from the hubs. They also contain a load date and record source.
- **Satellites**. Satellites contain the descriptive information for a hub and sometimes for a link. Often this descriptive information changes over time so satellites are designed to be temporal and can have varying levels of complexity in how they change over time, with sometimes containing just a simple effective and expiration date. Attributes are grouped into satellites by type of information (such as size, cost, speed, amount or color) or rate of change.
- **Reference tables**. Reference tables are code tables, such as Gender, Country, Customer Type, etc. They have one-to-many relationships with satellites which is often not enforced for performance reasons.

Data Vault

Example

Here is a data vault model created based upon this logical, with sample data shown:

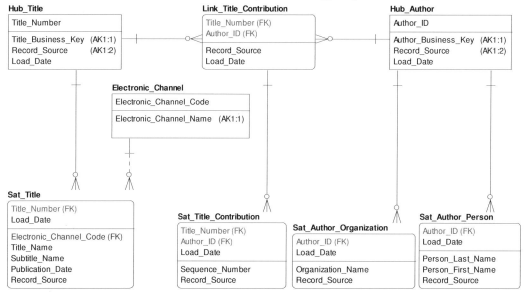

Hub_Title

Title_Number	Title_Business_Key	Record_Source	Load_Date
1	9780977140022	Bowker	5-Apr-2013
3	9780977140077	Bowker	11-Nov-2013
4	9780977140084	Bowker	25-Aug-2012
8	9781935504429	Bowker	10-Jan-2013

Sat_Title

Title _Number	Load_ Date	Electronic _Channel _Code	Title_Name	Subtitle_Name	Publication _Date	Record _Source
1	5-Apr-2013	01	Data Quality Assessment		May 14th, 2007	Bowker
3	11-Nov-2013	01	Data Modeling for the Business	A Handbook for Aligning the Business with IT using High-Level Data Models	April 2009	Bowker
4	25-Aug-2012	02	DAMA Guide to the Data Management Body of Knowledge		April 2009	Bowker
8	10-Jan-2013	03	Data Quality Assessment		May 14th, 2007	Bowker

Data Vault

Example

Electronic_Channel

Electronic_Channel_Code	Electronic_Channel_Name
01	Print
02	CD-Rom
03	Kindle
04	ePub

Hub Author

Author_ID	Author_Business_Key	Record_Source	Load_Date
53	555-55-5555	Dashbooks	15-Apr-2013
58	454-55-3233	Dashbooks	12-Nov-2013
59	343-23-2222	Dashbooks	23-Aug-2012
60	33-343444-33	Dashbooks	1-Jan-2013
143	111-11-1111	Dashbooks	2-Aug-2013

Sat_Author_Organization

Author_ID	Load_Date	Organization_Name	Record_Source
60	1-Jan-2013	DAMA International	Dashbooks

Sat_Author_Person

Author_ID	Load_Date	Person_Last_Name	Person_First_Name	Record_Source
53	15-Apr-2013	Arkady	Maydanchik	Dashbooks
58	12-Nov-2013	Steve	Hoberman	Dashbooks
59	23-Aug-2012	Donna	Burbank	Dashbooks
143	2-Aug-2013	Chris	Bradley	Dashbooks

Link_Title_Contribution

Title _Number	Author_ID	Record_Source	Load_Date
1	53	Dashbooks	15-Apr-2013
3	58	Dashbooks	12-Nov-2013
3	59	Dashbooks	11-Nov-2013
3	143	Dashbooks	11-Nov-2013
4	60	Dashbooks	1-Jan-2013
8	53	Dashbooks	15-Apr-2013

Sat_Title_Contribution

Title _Number	Author_ID	Load_Date	Sequence_Number	Record_Source
1	53	15-Apr-2013	1	Dashbooks
3	58	12-Nov-2013	1	Dashbooks
3	59	11-Nov-2013	2	Dashbooks
3	143	11-Nov-2013	3	Dashbooks
4	60	1-Jan-2013	1	Dashbooks
8	53	15-Apr-2013	1	Dashbooks

Enterprise Data Models

Explanation

> An enterprise data model (EDM) is a **<u>subject-oriented</u>** and **<u>integrated</u>** data model representing all of the data produced and consumed across an entire organization.
>
> **<u>Subject-oriented</u>: through the eyes of the CEO**
> **<u>Integrated</u>: Single version of the truth, yet maps back to the chaotic real world.**

Top 5 EDM Tips

1. Stakeholders need common agreement on the EDM purpose
2. Mapping equally (if not more) important than model
3. IT is primary EDM consumer
4. Maintenance and use incorporated into project plans so accessibility critical
5. If EDM failed in the past, bring back with new name (i.e. Data Trust)

EDM Example

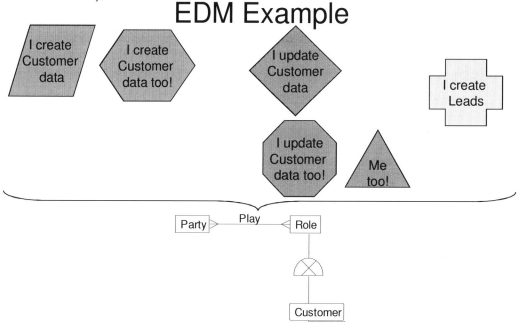

Enterprise Data Models

Explanation

DEFINITION

An enterprise data model (EDM) is a subject-oriented and integrated data model representing all of the data produced and consumed across an entire organization. Subject-oriented means that the concepts on a data model fit together as the CEO sees the company, as opposed to how individual functional or department heads see their view of the company. Integration means that all of the data and rules in an organization are depicted once and fit together seamlessly.

TOP 5 TIPS

1. **Stakeholders need common agreement on the EDM purpose.** Make sure there is agreement from all parties on why the EDM is being built.
2. **Mapping equally (if not more) important than model.** Knowing where all of the data lives today is equally if not more important than having a data model of an aspirational view.
3. **IT is primary EDM consumer.** With the exception of the enterprise conceptual data model, the EDM is used by IT to design applications quicker and with greater consistency.
4. **Maintenance and use incorporated into project plans so accessibility critical.** Every project should have a two-way arrow back to the EDM – when the project starts, we can jumpstart a project data model using the EDM, and at the conclusion of the project we can contribute learnings back to the EDM. This keeps the EDM fresh.
5. **If the EDM failed in the past, bring back with new name (i.e. Data Trust).** Several projects I have worked on have rebranded their EDM initiative to avoid being associated with a prior EDM failure.

EDM BRINGS ORDER

"Data is one of an organization's most valuable assets. All current and future business decisions hinge on data. An EDM is essential for the management of an organization's data resource. The core principle of data management is order; applying order to the vast universe of data. To manage data is to apply order. According to the second law of thermodynamics; the universe and everything in it, continually heads toward chaos; it takes energy to bring order. The same holds true for data, left alone, it continually deteriorates to a state of disorder. It takes concerted effort to keep data in order. An EDM brings order."

Noreen Kendle, Enterprise Data Architect, Delta Airlines

Enterprise Data Models

Mapping example

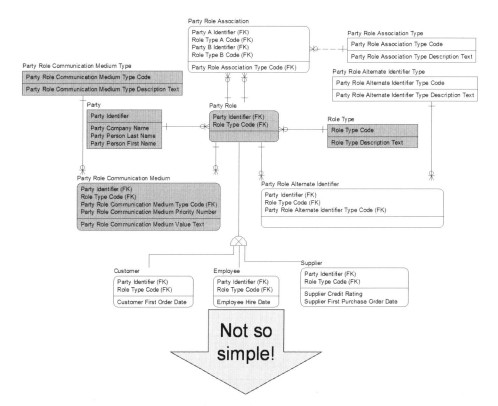

Source field	Source table	Source system	Mapping logic	EDM field	EDM table
email	Employee	HR Payroll	Role Type.Role Type Code = "01" (for Employee)… Party.Party Person Last Name = "Employee.LN", and Party.Party Person First Name = "Employee.FN"… Party Role Communication Type Code = "04" (for email)…	Party Role Communication Medium Value Text	Party Role Communication Medium
e_mail_addr	Supplier	Supplier Contact	Role Type.Role Type Code = "02" (for Supplier)… Party.Company Name = Supplier.Contact…		
company	Customer	Customer Contact	Role Type.Role Type Code = "03" (for Customer)… 90% of time this is the email address and 10% it contains the company name. Search for @ to ensure you have the email address…		

Enterprise Data Models

Mapping example

EDM IS INTEGRATED

An EDM provides organizations with a single integrated view of their business information. Integration means connecting disparate information pieces into a single united whole. Integration can lead to information consistency.

CHALLENGE

Integration is very difficult for many organizations to achieve, yet it is a prerequisite for most organization-wide initiatives. If an organization can integrate their data, the rewards are great.

EXAMPLE

The more abstract our enterprise data model, the more challenging our mapping will be, as can be seen in the example on the facing page with the "simple" data element Email Address.

QUICK ASIDE

A cowbird is a data element that is used for a purpose for which it was not originally designed. From Wikipedia: "cowbirds feed on insects, including the large numbers that may be stirred up by cattle. In order for the birds to remain mobile and stay with the herd, they have adapted by laying their eggs in other birds' nests. The cowbird will watch for when its host lays eggs, and when the nest is left unattended, the female will come in and lay its own eggs."

Enterprise Data Models
Benefiting from the EDM

<u>Data Warehousing and ERP example</u>

How can I better calculate royalties?

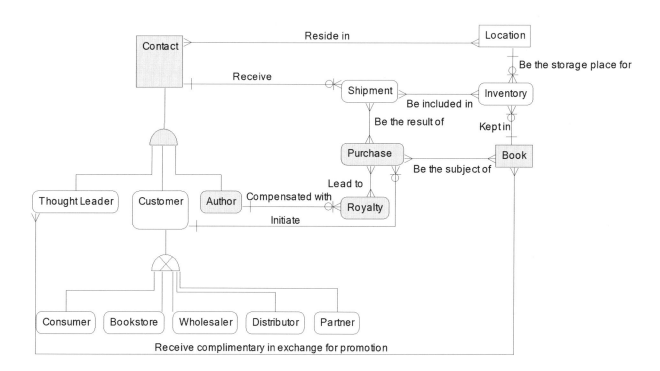

Enterprise Data Models

Benefiting from the EDM

AREAS THAT BENEFIT

The EDM along with a mapping back to existing systems offer the greatest benefits for organization-wide initiatives such as enterprise resource planning, master data management, and data warehousing.

ERP

An EDM is a great tool for determining whether a particular ERP package would be a good fit for your organization. ERP vendors should provide some type of model of their system along with definitions, and an analyst can map the ERP system to your EDM to identify any potential data issues prior to investing time and money in the package. Impact analysis is also a frequent use of the EDM for ERP. I participated in a SAP rollout for a global manufacturing company. There were several hundred business and IT employees working very hard to ensure the rollout was a success. However, despite the enormous amount of testing that was done within each of the SAP rollout departments, several unanticipated issues occurred. I built a high level model of part of SAP/R3 for this company to help identify touch points and overlaps within SAP rollouts. It also became a very good communication tool for describing how SAP interacts with other systems and functional areas.

MASTER DATA MANAGEMENT

Master data is all of the data that is shared outside of a single application. Most of the time master data refers to reference data such as Customer and Product, but it can also include event data such as Orders and Credits. An EDM forces a single set of metadata for each data element. This metadata includes a single name, definition, format, domain, and set of business rules. Defining all of this data at an organization level makes master data management possible.

DATA WAREHOUSING

The Data Warehousing Institute defines business intelligence as "The processes, technologies, and tools needed to turn data into information, information into knowledge, and knowledge into plans that drive profitable business actions. Business intelligence encompasses data warehousing, business analytic tools and content knowledge management." The data warehouse is responsible for this first part of the definition: turning data into information. To turn data into information requires both a subject-oriented and integrated view. These are also the two main ingredients of the EDM and therefore the reason the data warehouse needs the EDM.

Applying the Data Model Scorecard®

Interaction Report for Product BB40 from May 2011

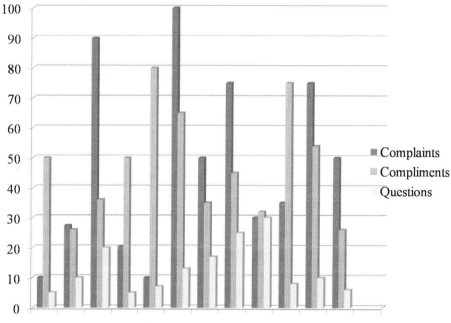

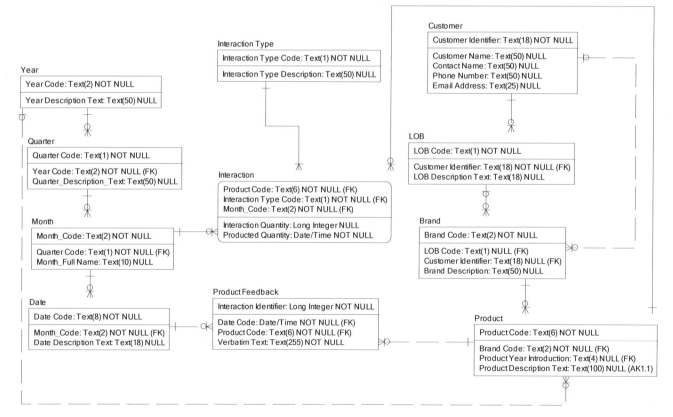

Applying the Data Model Scorecard®

9. How consistent is the model with the enterprise?

EXPLANATION   Confirms the model complements the "big picture". The data model being reviewed should be consistent with the enterprise view.

ANYTHING YOU
WOULD CATCH IN
THE MODEL ON
THE FACING PAGE
FOR THIS
CATEGORY?

1.

2.

3.

4.

5.

6.

7.

8.

9.

10.

#	Category	Total score	Model score	%
1	How well does the model capture the requirements?	15		
2	How complete is the model?	15		
3	How well do the characteristics of the model support the type of model?	10		
4	How structurally sound is the model?	15		
5	How well does the model leverage generic structures?	10		
6	How well does the model follow naming standards?	5		
7	How well has the model been arranged for readability?	5		
8	How good are the definitions?	10		
9	How consistent is the model with the enterprise?	5		
10	How well does the metadata match the data?	10		
	TOTAL SCORE	100		

Module 10

Data Model Scorecard® Category #10: Data

Category Question: How well does the metadata match the data?

This module is your guide to: Comparing the metadata with the data

Category overview

How well does the metadata match the data?

Confirms how well the data elements and their rules match reality

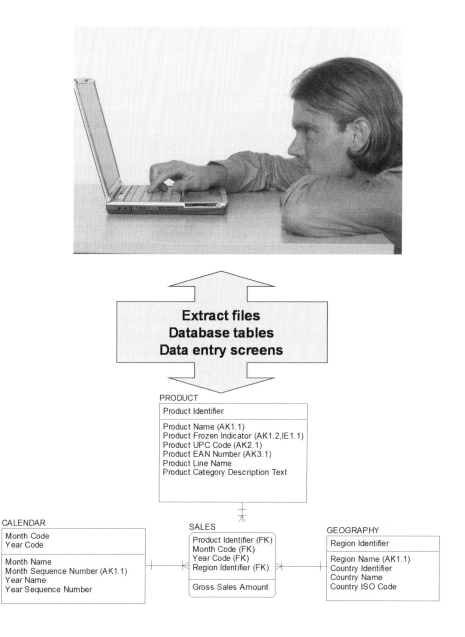

Category overview

How well does the metadata match the data?

EXPLANATION

Confirms how well the data elements and their rules match reality. Does the data element Customer Last Name really contain the customer's last name, for example?

PURPOSE

Ensures the model and the actual data that will be stored within the resulting tables are consistent with each other, so to reduce surprises later on in software development.

CHALLENGE

This might be very difficult to do early in a project's life cycle because data can be difficult to access from the source system before development has begun. However, the earlier the better so you can avoid future surprises which can be much more costly.

WHAT YEAR DO YOU THINK G.H. MEALY SAID THIS?

"We do not, it seems, have a very clear and commonly agreed upon set of notions about data—either what they are, how they should be fed and cared for, or their relation to the design of programming languages and operating systems."

Domain

Explanation

> A domain is the complete set of all possible values that a data element contains. It could be a format, range or list.

Order Status Code: Char(1)

Order Status Code: {O,S,R,C}

Today's Date <= **Order Delivery Date** <= (Today's Date + 3 months)

Corporate Unit Code: {01, 02, 03, 04, 05, 99}

Order Comments Text: Varchar(250)

Book cover: {*.jpg, *.pdf, *.tiff}

150 < **Image quality dots per inch** <= 300

Domain

Explanation

BACKGROUND

The complete set of all possible values that a data element contains is called a domain. A data element never can contain values outside of its assigned domain, which is defined by specifying the actual list of values or a set of rules. *Employee gender code*, for example, can be limited to the domain of (*female, male*).

PURPOSE

Domains are very useful for a number of reasons including:
- Greater consistency within and across applications
- Improves data quality by checking against a domain before inserting data
- Greater efficiency in building new models and maintaining existing models

QUESTIONS TO ASK

Ask these two questions to capture domain information:
- What is the length and format of this data element?
- What are the valid values this data element can contain?

Family Tree

Explanation

A Simple Example

Source		Data element in our data model		
Data element	Table	Transformation	Data element	Table
LIST_PRICE	PRICE	Price * Qty	TOTAL_AMOUNT	SALES_FACT
ORDER_ QUANTITY	ORD			

You can use the Family Tree to

- ❑ Document lineage for each data element
- ❑ Get reality check
- ❑ Capture how to calculate derived measures
- ❑ Capture data requirements when working in complex project teams

Family Tree

Explanation

BACKGROUND

The Family Tree contains the complete list of data elements (including derived data elements) for the application, and the sources and transformations for each, along with several other key pieces of data element metadata, including definition and format.

YOU CAN USE THIS TOOL TO...

document the lineage for each data element in the data model, including derived measures for business usage in a reporting application. It serves as a great reality check against the requirements identified in the Grain Matrix. It also is helpful when working on complex project teams as it lets you "divide and conquer".

EXAMPLE

The example on the facing page illustrates a simple mapping from the source to a data element in our model. TOTAL_AMOUNT is derived by multiplying LIST_PRICE by ORDER_QUANTITY.

TOOLS

The most common tool for creating and maintaining a mapping document is Excel. The advantage is its widespread use and everyone understands a spreadsheet. The disadvantage is they are difficult to centralize and control. More recently, organizations are storing this mapping in Extract, Transform, and Load (ETL) tools and therefore the mapping can be centralized and automatically ported over to the reporting tool for use by the business (e.g. reading definitions).

Data Quality Validation Template

Explanation

A document containing how well the metadata matches the data

Is the metadata correct?

Documents the accuracy of the metadata

Assigns ownership and responsibility to determining if there is a quality issue

Contains results of data quality checking and validation

Product Identifier (PRO_ITEM_REF_DB_ID)

First 10-25 distinct values	Business review (✓ or ✗)	% null	Business review (✓ or ✗)	Max length	Business review (✓ or ✗)	Min length	Business review (✓ or ✗)
12452 33855 85958 37580 38447 38936 33490 48476 38111	✓	0	✓	5	✓	5	✓

Data Quality Validation Template

Explanation

EXPLANATION

The spreadsheet on the facing page shows one way of validating data quality early. The Data Quality Validation Template, documents how well the metadata and some of the actual data compares for each data element. This tool contains an expert's opinion of how good or bad the data within each data element actually is.

PURPOSE

- **Documents the accuracy of the metadata**. To make sure that the metadata and data captured side by side is of acceptable quality.
- **Assigns ownership and responsibility to determining if there is a quality issue**. Having the expert's opinions documented, adds more evidence as to whether there is a problem or not.
- **Highlights problem areas**. One of the benefits of any spreadsheet is how easy it can be to highlight information. Cells in a spreadsheet are much easier to find than paragraphs in a long document.
- Uncovering complex business logic early.

Applying the Data Model Scorecard®

Interaction Report for Product BB40 from May 2011

Brand

Brand Code: Text(2) NOT NULL
LOB Code: Text(1) NULL Customer Identifier: Text(18) NULL Brand Description: Text(50) NULL

Product

Product Code: Text(6) NOT NULL
Brand Code: Text(2) NOT NULL (FK) Product Year Introduction: Text(4) NULL Product Description Text: Text(100) NULL (AK1.1)

1.

2.

3.

4.

5.

6.

7.

8.

9.

10.

Applying the Data Model Scorecard®

10. How well does the metadata match the data?

EXPLANATION On the facing page is part of the interaction data model we are reviewing and below are a representative set of data for each of the entities on this model. Anything you would catch on the model in this category? Write the score for this category and from all of the previous categories in the Scorecard below.

Brand

Brand Code	LOB Code	Cust Id	Brand Desc
W1	Q4	391238198	Widgets
	Q4	321912999	
W9		2919128920	Wizards
99			
B3	B2	392191	Warlords

Product

Product Code	Brand Code	Year Introduction	Product Desc
M43431	WI	11	Widget Light
B45328	W1		Widget Heavy
NA		99999	Not Applicable
C21392	B3	2010	Evil Warlords
47	W99	1999	Good Wizards

#	Category	Total score	Model score	%
1	How well does the model capture the requirements?	15		
2	How complete is the model?	15		
3	How well do the characteristics of the model support the type of model?	10		
4	How structurally sound is the model?	15		
5	How well does the model leverage generic structures?	10		
6	How well does the model follow naming standards?	5		
7	How well has the model been arranged for readability?	5		
8	How good are the definitions?	10		
9	How consistent is the model with the enterprise?	5		
10	How well does the metadata match the data?	10		
	TOTAL SCORE	100		

Agile Data Warehouse Design, Corr, L. and Stagnitto, J.
DecisionOne Press, 2012

Another Look at Data, G.H. Mealy, Proc. AFIPS 1967 Fall Joint Computer Conf., Vol. 31

Building the Agile Database, Burns, L.
Technics Publications, LLC, 2011

Building the Unstructured Data Warehouse, Inmon, W.H., and Krishnan, K.
Technics Publications, LLC, 2007

DAMA Dictionary of Data Management 2nd Edition, DAMA International.
Technics Publications, LLC, 2011

DAMA Guide to the Data Management Body of Knowledge (DAMA-DMBOK), DAMA International.
Technics Publications, LLC, 2009

Database Design & Relational Theory, Date, C.
O'Reilly Media, 2012

Data and Reality, Kent, W.
Technics Publications, LLC, 2012

The Data Modeler's Workbench, Hoberman, S.
John Wiley & Sons, Inc., 2001

Data Modeling Essentials, Third Edition, Simsion G., Witt G.
Morgan Kaufmann Publishers, 2005

Data Modeling for the Business, Hoberman, S., Burbank, D.
Technics Publications, LLC, 2009

Data Modeling Made Simple, 2nd Edition, Hoberman, S.
Technics Publications, LLC, 2009

Data Modeling Theory and Practice, Simsion, G.
Technics Publications, LLC, 2007

Data Quality Assessment, Maydanchik, A.
Technics Publications, LLC, 2007

Data Resource Simplexity: How Organizations Choose Data Resource Success or Failure,
Brackett, M. Technics Publications, LLC, 2011

Design Challenge: What is the Enterprise Data Model ROI, Steve Hoberman.
DM Review, May 2006

The Enterprise Data Model, Noreen Kendle.
The Data Administration Newsletter (www.tdan.com)

Enterprise Model Patterns, Hay, David.
Technics Publications, LLC, 2011

A Guide to the Business Analysis Body of Knowledge® (BABOK® Guide) Version 2.0,
IIBA, International Institute of Business Analysis, 2009

How Work Gets Done: Business Process Management, Basics and Beyond, Mahal, A.
Technics Publications, LLC, 2010

Leveraging the Industry Logical Data Model as your Enterprise Data Model, Hoberman,
S. Teradata whitepaper, 2006. (Can be downloaded from www.teradata.com)

*The Nimble Elephant: Agile Delivery of Data Models using a Pattern-based
Approach,* Giles, J.
Technics Publications, LLC, 2012

For more on the data vault, read the series of five articles on www.tdan.com.

For more on the HL7 Reference Information Model (RIM): hl7.org

For more on the SID (Shared Information Data Model): www.tmforum.org

For more on the Global Justice XML Data Model: www.it.ojp.gov/jxdm

For more on the ACORD life, annuity and other insurance model: www.acord.org

For more on the National Retail Federation (NRF's) Association of Retail Technology
Standards (ARTS): www.nrf-arts.org

Hotel Chain Case Study

Putting the pieces together

Case Study – MySeat[1]

The airline industry is extremely competitive and it is common knowledge that the most loyal and frequent flyers make up the majority of airfare revenue. In most airlines for example, the top 20% frequent flyers make up over 80% of the airline's revenue. Therefore the airlines are constantly looking for differentiators to lure frequent flyers to their airlines, while retaining their existing frequent flyers.

United Air operates over 6,000 flights a day to more than 400 airports across the globe. Last year over two million flights carried over 150 million passengers to their destinations. United Air currently has 25 million frequent flyers: 15 million Silver status, 5 million Gold status, 3 million Platinum, and 2 million 1K status. To retain and grow their frequent flyer base, United Air is initiating a new program called *MySeat*, which will make seat recommendations to frequent flyers. The goal of *MySeat* is to make the best seat recommendation to frequent flyers to ensure they have a pleasant flying experience, and also save them time during the booking process.

Traditionally, the most an airline can do is suggest an aisle or window seat. With *MySeat* however, a seat can be recommended to a frequent flyer, based upon three sources of information:
1. This frequent flyer's past seat choices on this type of aircraft
2. Feedback from this frequent flyer's completed survey forms from past flights
3. Seat choices made by similar frequent flyers

So for example, when frequent flyer Steve Hoberman books a flight on an Embraer RJ145, this would be his recommended seat (marked with a "1" in a circle):

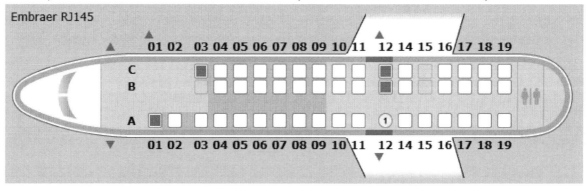

---

[1] This case study is fictitious and not based on any real organization, person, or project.

And this would be his recommended seat on the Airbus A319:

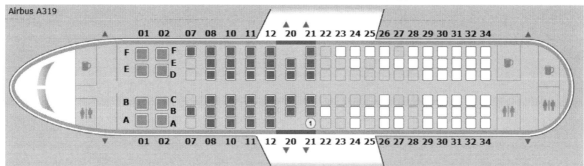

And this would be his recommended seat on the Bombardier Q400:

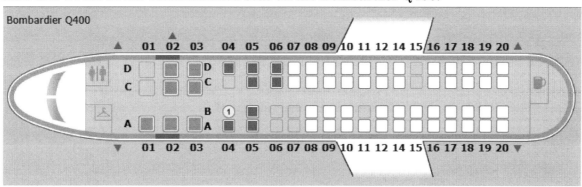

Due to the number of passengers and flights, coupled with the rapid response time required to make seat recommendations, this project has been classified as a "big data" project. The developers have already been working on this project for two months, and although producing results, the data management of the project is not going as well as the project sponsor, John Jones, Vice President of Sales, would like.

John Jones would like you to leverage your survey knowledge on this project to build the relational conceptual data model for *MySeat*, including definitions. In addition, John Jones would like to routinely run analytics on the number of passengers within each frequently flyer status level, to see if this program is working. Therefore a dimensional conceptual data model is also needed. These two models will be built based on provided documentation, your own knowledge and research, and a brief interview with John.

Each group will present their relational and conceptual data models, and we will use the following Data Model Scorecard spreadsheet to identify the strengths (by putting a ✓ next to the appropriate category) and areas for improvement (by writing comments) for each *relational* CDM.

Recall the ten categories of the Scorecard, referenced only by number in the spreadsheet that follows:

#	Category
1	How well does the model capture the requirements?
2	How complete is the model?
3	How well do the characteristics of the model support the type of model?
4	How structurally sound is the model?
5	How well does the model leverage generic structures?
6	How well does the model follow naming standards?
7	How well has the model been arranged for readability?
8	How good are the definitions?
9	How consistent is the model with the enterprise?
10	How well does the metadata match the data?

Category	Group 1	Group 2	Group 3	Group 4	Group 5
1					
2					
3					
4					
5					
6					
7					
8					
9					
10					

As input to the data modeling, you are provided with:

- Aircraft information
- Sample flight itinerary
- Existing snippet of MongoDB code

Aircraft Information

United Air owns 800 aircraft which include:

- 100 Widebody Jets
- 200 Narrowbody Jets
- 400 Regional Jets
- 100 Turboprops

There are over 50 types of aircrafts, each with their own unique seat configuration, spanning these four aircraft categories. For example, here are the aircraft types within the Widebody Jet category:

Widebody Jets				
Aircraft with seat map	Economy	Premium Economy	Business	First
Boeing 747-400 (744)	✓		✓	✓
Boeing 767-300 (763) Three Class	✓		✓	✓
Boeing 767-300 (763) Two Class	✓		✓	
Boeing 767-400ER (764) Intl	✓		✓	
Boeing 777-200 (772) V1 Three Class Intl	✓		✓	✓
Boeing 777-200 (772) V2 Three Class Intl	✓		✓	✓
Boeing 777-200 (772) V3 Three Class Intl	✓		✓	✓
Boeing 777-200 (772) V4 Domestic	✓			✓
Boeing 777-200 (772) V5 Two Class Intl	✓		✓	
Boeing 787-8 (788)	✓		✓	

Sample Flight Itinerary

Traveler	eTicket Number	Frequent Flyer	Seats
HOBERMAN/STEVEMR	0162373873910	UA-UC92XXXX Premier 1K / *G	20A/20C

FLIGHT INFORMATION

Day, Date	Flight	Class	Departure City and Time	Arrival City and Time	Aircraft	Meal
Sun, 08SEP13	UA17	U	NEWARK, NJ (EWR - LIBERTY) 9:15 PM	LONDON, ENGLAND (LHR - HEATHROW) 9:25 AM (09SEP)	757-200	Dinner
Fri, 13SEP13	UA115	U	LONDON, ENGLAND (LHR - HEATHROW) 6:00 PM	NEWARK, NJ (EWR - LIBERTY) 9:25 PM	757-200	Dinner

Existing Snipit of MongoDB code

```
db.airport.insert(

{

"Airport_Code" : "EWR",
"Airport_Name" : "Newark Liberty International Airport",
"Airport_City" : "New Jersey",
"Airport_Region" : "New York Area",
"Airport_Country" : "United States"})
```

Interview: Vice President of Sales

John Jones is the Vice President of sales at United Air. He is our key business user for *MySeat*. You can record your questions and responses in this spreadsheet.

Interview Question	Response

MySeat Relational Conceptual Data Model

Create a relational CDM for *MySeat* based upon the interview results and provided documentation. Identify the camera settings below.

MySeat Relational CDM Camera Settings

Scope	Abstraction	Time	Function
__Project	__Bus Clouds	__Today	__Bus
__Program	__DB Clouds	__Tomorrow	__App
__Industry	__Ground		

MySeat Dimensional Conceptual Data Model

Create a dimensional CDM for MySeat based upon the interview results and provided documentation. Identify the camera settings below.

MySeat Dimensional CDM Camera Settings

Scope	Abstraction	Time	Function
__Project	__Bus Clouds	__Today	__Bus
__Program	__DB Clouds	__Tomorrow	__App
__Industry	__Ground		

Answers

Responses to select exercises

Modeling a Publisher Log File

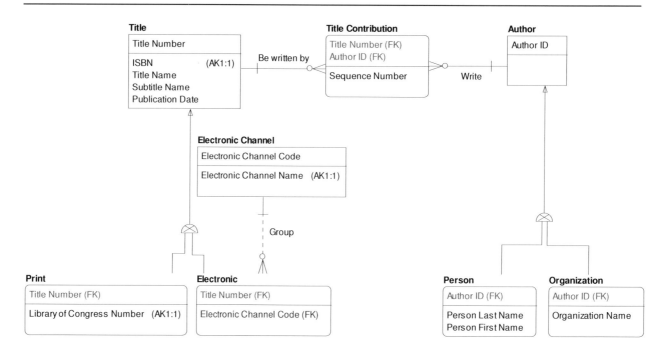

Hierarchy and Network Exercises

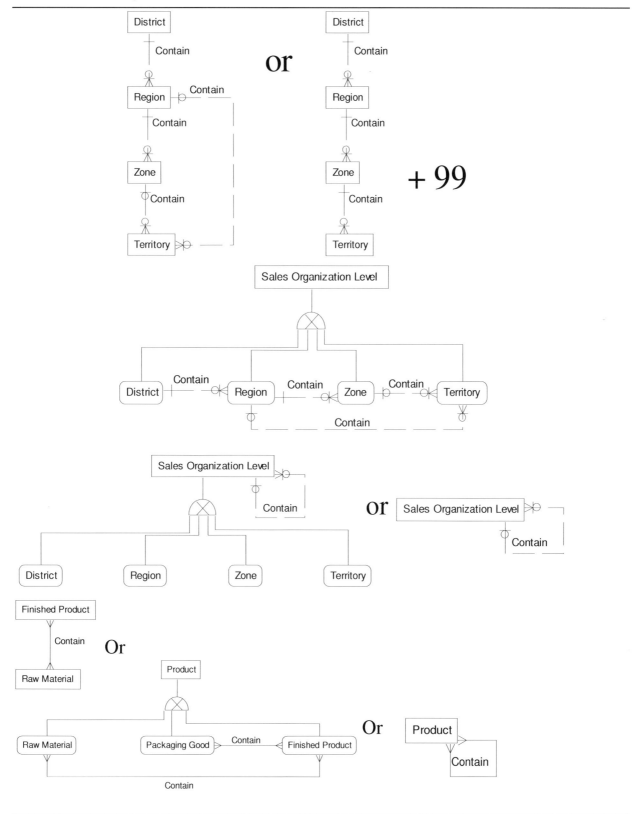

The Corner Office

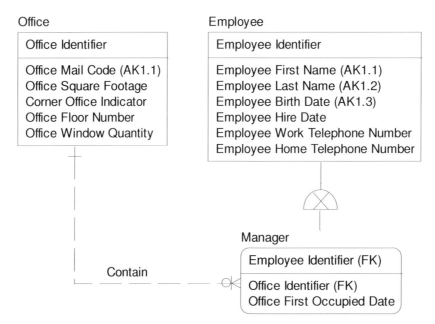

Office

Office Identifier
Office Mail Code (AK1.1)
Office Square Footage
Corner Office Indicator
Office Floor Number
Office Window Quantity

Employee

Employee Identifier
Employee First Name (AK1.1)
Employee Last Name (AK1.2)
Employee Birth Date (AK1.3)
Employee Hire Date
Employee Work Telephone Number
Employee Home Telephone Number

Manager

Employee Identifier (FK)
Office Identifier (FK)
Office First Occupied Date

Contain

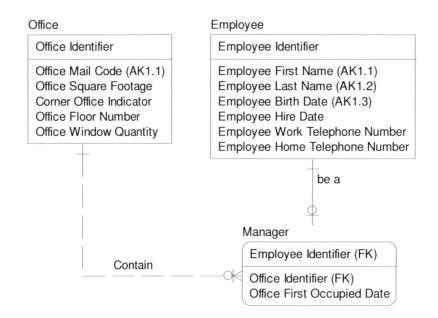

Office

Office Identifier
Office Mail Code (AK1.1)
Office Square Footage
Corner Office Indicator
Office Floor Number
Office Window Quantity

Employee

Employee Identifier
Employee First Name (AK1.1)
Employee Last Name (AK1.2)
Employee Birth Date (AK1.3)
Employee Hire Date
Employee Work Telephone Number
Employee Home Telephone Number

be a

Manager

Employee Identifier (FK)
Office Identifier (FK)
Office First Occupied Date

Contain

Option 3:

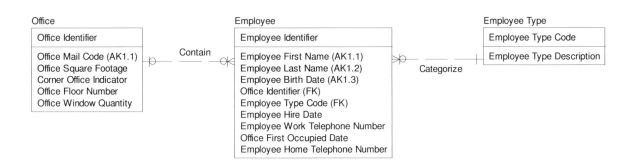

Option 4:

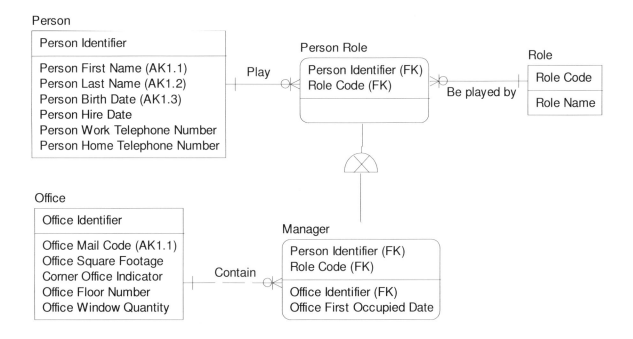

Technics Publications CDM

Technics Publications Offerings Camera Settings

Scope	Abstraction	Time	Function
__Project	__Bus Clouds	X Today	X Bus
X Program	__DB Clouds	__Tomorrow	__App
__Industry	X Ground		

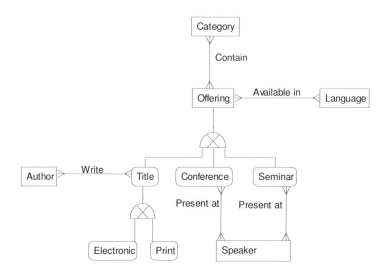

Technics Publications Dimensional LDM

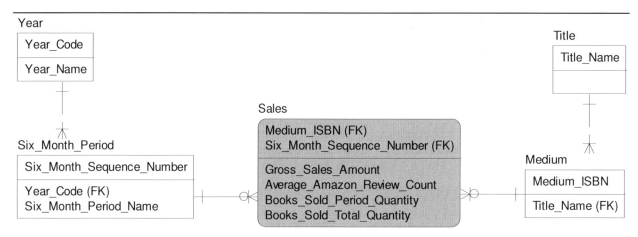

Survey Relational LDM

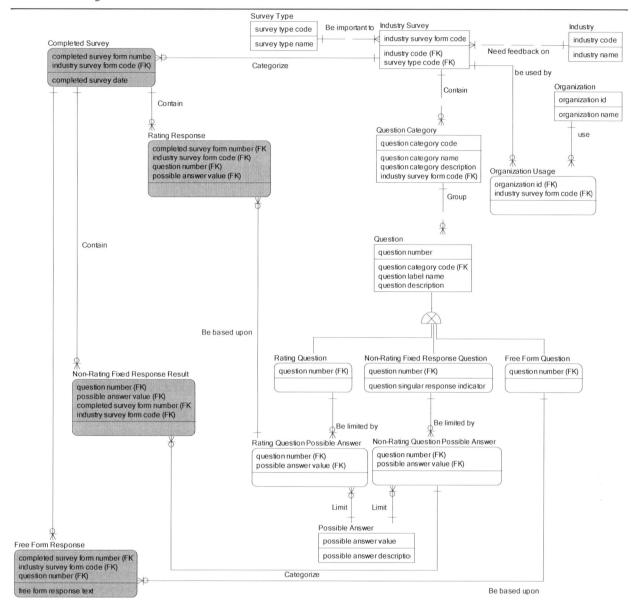

Fun with Aggregation

Rolling down

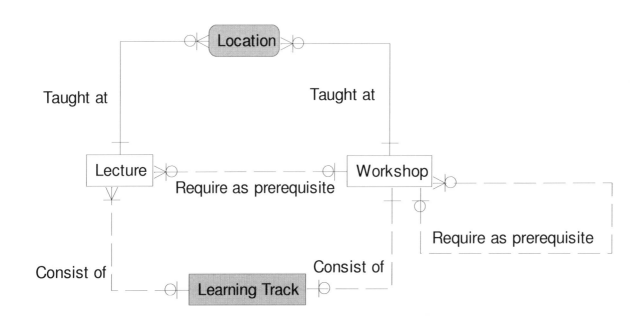

Rolling up

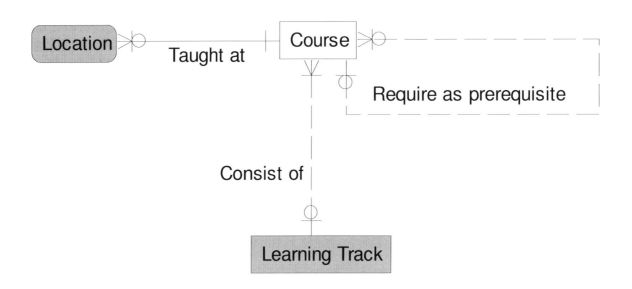

Identity

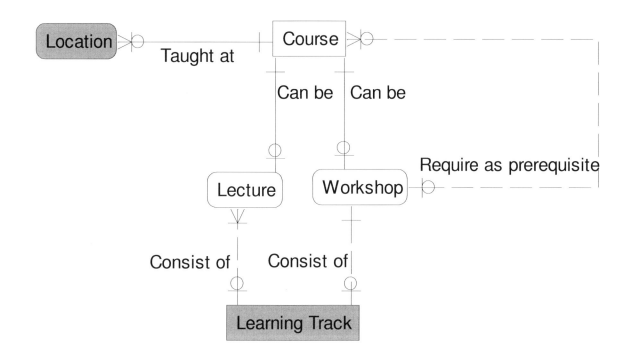

MySeat Case Study

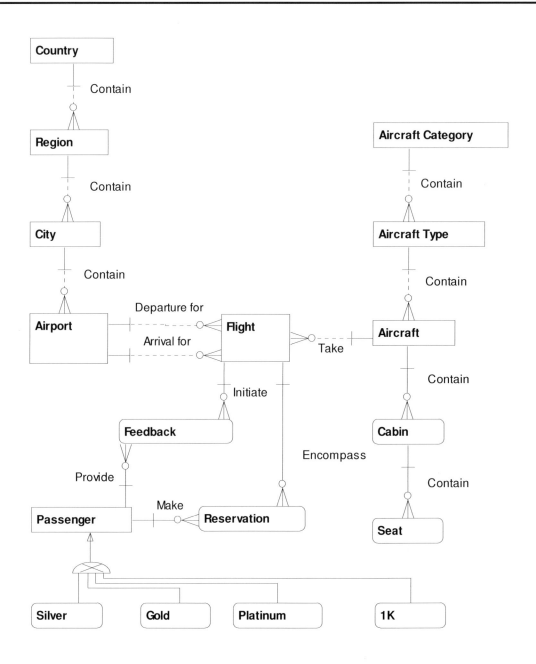

Dimensional CDM

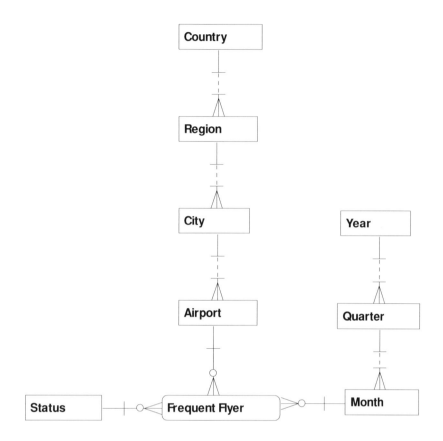